Tattvasiddhi & Madhyamakalankara

TATTVASIDDHI
the attainment of suchness

&

MADHYAMAKALANKARA
the ornament of the middle way

SHANTARAKSHITA

with commentaries by

KHENCHEN PALDEN SHERAB RINPOCHE

AND

KHENPO TSEWANG DONGYAL RINPOCHE

with an Introduction by

Marie-Louise Friquegnon

EDITED BY

MARIE-LOUISE FRIQUEGNON AND ARTHUR MANDELBAUM

THE TRANSLATION COMMITTEE:

Khenchen Palden Sherab Rinpoche
Khenpo Tsewang Dongyal Rinpoche
Marie-Louise Friquegnon & Arthur Mandelbaum
in collaboration with Geshe Lozang Jamspal

TRANSLATION OF THE *MADHYAMAKALANKARA*
INTO SANSKRIT BY GESHE LOZANG JAMSPAL

coolgrovepress – a zangdokpalri edition

First published in the United States by
Cool Grove Press, an imprint of Cool Grove Publishing, Inc. New York.
512 Argyle Road, Brooklyn, NY 11218

www.coolgrove.com

For permissions and other inquiries write to info@coolgrove.com

ISBN 13: 978-1-887276-77-1

ISBN-10: 1-887276-77-7

First Edition

with commentaries by

Khenchen Palden Sherab Rinpoche
and Khenpo Tsewang Dongyal Rinpoche
On *Tattvasiddhi & Madhyamakalankara*
with the original texts in Sanskrit and Tibetan

edited by
Marie-Louise Friquegnon and Arthur Mandelbaum

The image of Nagurjuna on page xii from BuddhaNet
after John P. Bollenbacher (JB) - Angelfire

coolgrovepress – a zangdokpalri edition

This book is dedicated
to all the great Buddhist philosophers of the past

Praise for Shantarakshita

Shiwaitso, Shantarakshita, Abbot of Samye
At the lotus feet of the hero Manjushri you composed yourself as his supreme disciple and assimilated the depth and breath of the dharma. Homage to the great abbot Shantarakshita.

I venerate the great abbot Shantarakshita,
whose skill opened the way of using logical reasoning,
to explain to his disciples in accordance with their
dispositions, the Middle Way path of emptiness, devoid
of duality. He spread the conqueror's teachings in the
Land of the Snows."*

—His Holiness the Dalai Lama
Translated by Geshe Lozang Jamspal

Glorious Shantarakshita, the sacred holder of
the vows, Padmasambhava, the master of both
yoga and accomplishment, Losel Wangpo Kamalasila:
these are second Buddhas in this age of decadence.*

—Sakya Pandita

He was accepted by Manjushri as disciple
And reached the shore of ours and others' tenets.
He is the sovereign of teachings so profound.
To glorious Shantarakshita I bow.

When he first brought the Buddha's doctrine
To this Snowy Land, so well did this protector lay conditions
That Nagarjuna's teaching should be spread among us
That even now there is a constant stream of those
Aspiring for profound Madhyamaka.
To spread therefore without impairment
The teaching of this mighty scholar-
Than this there is no better way to thank him for his kindness.
Brought forth by reasoning unbounded as the sky itself
And through the strength of love beyond all reference,
This text that ornaments the Middle Way is great indeed.
By tasting of the feast of reasoning contained therein,
One will become a crown and summit of the many learned ones
Who on the path of reasoning for many lives,
Through many hardships came to mastery in proof and refutation,
Uprooting every falsehood.
Even in the noble land this master's like was rarely found.
Ah, such was the great fortune of the people of Tibet
He was invited by their king and sovereign!
And as I think of it my mind
Is helplessly transported with a wondrous joy.*

—Je Tsongkhapa

Great scholar of the Madhyamaka and Mind Only
schools, Great siddha who lived for nine hundred years,
Great compassion's lamp of stainless teachings,
Great bodhisattva Shiwatso, I pay homage to you.

—Khenpo Tsewang Dongyal Rinpoche

---

* Padmakara translation. *The Adornment of the Middle Way: Shantarakshita's Madhyamakalankara with commentary* by Jamgon Mipham, Padmakara Translation Group. Boston: Shambhala, 2005. p. 379

Drawing of Shantarakshita from Nyingma Icons of Gomchen Oleshe.

The wondrous way of dependent origination
Is expressed by a supreme and unequaled voice
That liberates from the bondage of existence.
Homage to the protector, the Lion of the Sakyas!

By merely recalling his name, the beginningless darkness of
existence,
That enemy that has slumbered so long in the heart, is overcome–
Such is the Youthful Sun of Speech.
Kind guru, you who are inseparable from him, please nurture me!

"In the dark lands of inferior views, the tongues of those who speak wrongly are moved like lightning, persisting through many deceits.
Cut them up and chop them up, with the sharpness of a reasoning more powerful than the weapon of Brahma and Lord [Indra]!" Thus he was empowered by the sword of Manjushri.

In the Noble Land, the Cool Abode, and elsewhere, the Bonpos and the extremists, deer who live in the mountain ranges of belief in self,
Are thus brought to panic in a thousand different ways, merely by the sound of his name. Let that fearless Lion of Speech be victorious!
His excellent statement, the profound *Ornament of the Middle Way*,
Is the ocean in which hundreds of thousands of rivers of reason merge.

Here the supremely learned lords of the nagas frolic in the millions–
And I, the lowly one, have also entered with joy.
Masters of unequaled, supreme intellect
Have striven and endeavored to realize this.
The uncorrupted, excellent scriptural traditions of these experts
Will here, by the kindness of my guru, be briefly explained.
The power of this reasoning of this supreme chariot way
Has remained dormant within the realm of time.
But when kindled here, like fire in a dense forest,
All wanton talkers, do be careful!*

—by Ju Mipham

*Speech of Delight: Mipham's *Commentary on Shantarakshita's Ornament of the Middle Way* by Ju Mipham. Trans Thomas Doctor. Boston: Shambhala, 2004. p. 7

Om Aa Ra Pa Cha Na Dhi

Arya Nagurjuna

Contents

Acknowledgements

The authors, editors and translators would like to thank the following scholars for reading and commenting on this and earlier versions of the manuscript:

Khenpo Tsewang Gyatso Rinpoche, James Blumenthal, Edward Burns, Thomas Doctor, Lama Dragpa, Brad Gooch, James Halper, Ann Helm, Hyun Hochsmann, Mardee Kravit, Alan Pope, David Shapiro, Laura Shapiro, Toy Tung and Philippe Turenne. We thank Raziel Abelson, Karma Gonde, Toy Tung, Noe Dinnerstein, Pema Thinley and Cynthia Friend for their invaluable assistance in copyediting. We are very grateful to Tibetan Buddhist Resource Center Asian Classics Input Project (ACIP) for allowing us to use their Tibetan text of *The Tattvasiddhi* and Professor Ngawang Samten, Vice Chancellor of the Central University of Tibetan Studies, Sarnath, and Professor K. N. Mishra for providing us with the Sanskirt text of the Tattvasiddhi. Most of all, we thank Geshe Lozang Jamspal for making the translation a part of his Sanskrit/Tibetan seminar attended by Marie-Louise Friquegnon and Arthur Mandelbaum, and for reconstructing the Sanskrit version of the *Madhyamakalankara* text. To Lama Lorraine O'Rourke, Mary Ann Doychak, Claudia Geers and Norman Guberman, our gratitude for their support and aid through the process of production.

The editor would also like to thank William Paterson University for years of support during this project through its Academic Released Time program, Columbia University for its visiting scholar program through the South Asian Institute in 1996, as well as through the Department of Religious Studies visiting scholar's program in 2004. Special thanks to Douglas Duckworth and Johnathan Gold, for agreeing to read the manuscript; Dione Madric and R.J. Coat for proofing and layout, and our publisher P. Tej Hazarika for his indispensable help, sensitivity and wisdom in publishing this book.

—The Translation Committee

EDITOR'S INTRODUCTION

In 8th Century India, within and outside its Buddhist traditions, Shantarakshita's works were the pinnacle of philosophy. He was the most thorough synthesizer of what went before and no one gave a clearer indication of the direction Indian philosophy would take in the future.

For Western philosophers, pushed to the limits of skepticism, Shantarakshita offers an alternative approach. By his refusal to make any metaphysical assertions—while at the same time offering a path of non-conceptual meditation—he promises access to liberation.

Shantarakshita argues that the knowledge gleaned from perception is 'like a mirage, or instantly changing bubbles of water'. Nevertheless, we can still rely on it as a springboard to reality. Sensation, properly understood (non-dualistically and free from conceptions) is the condition required for bliss to arise. He affirms that this kind of blissful experience bears some similarity to 'suchness', or true nature. It is the only way to penetrate reality, beyond sensation and thought, and in so doing, attain supreme and irreversible enlightenment, for one's own sake and for the sake of others.This book is attempt to chart that noble path. More than a thousand years later, Buddhist scholars Khenchen Palden Sherab Rinpoche and Khenpo Tsewang Dongyal Rinpoche, offer us clear and accessible discussions on Shantarakshita's two related treatises, the *Tattvasiddhi* and the *Madhyamakalankara*. We sincerely hope, that for scholars and students, this book will open the door to Shantarakshita's insights.

*Historical background and Shantarakshita's life**

King Trisong Detsen [Khri–srong–lde–btsan], the powerful ruler of Tibet, deeply attracted to Buddhism even having written a book on logic, dispatched his ministers to India to find an qualified teacher who could open a window of opportunity for monastic and academic study in Tibet. After an extensive search, they settled on Shantarakshita, then abbot of the legendary monastic university of Nalanda. It was the triumvirate of Khenpo Shantarakshita, the legendary Vajra master Guru Padmasambhava and King Trisong Detsen that brought the light of the Buddhism to Tibet by establishing it as a philosophical as well as a spiritual tradition into the Tibetan culture.

Nalanda had long been associated with the Buddhist tradition from the time of King Ashoka (2nd century BCE). Along with the other earlier traditions of India, all schools of Buddhism were also studied there, including the Sarvastivadin, lineage associated with the Buddha's son Rahula. It was from the Sarvastivadins that Shantarakshita would receive

*Historical background and Shantarakshita's life was contributed by P. Tej Hazarika

his monastic or Vinaya vows. India at the time of Shantarakshita was home to many philosophical traditions apart from those of Buddhist origin, including those stemming from 'Hinduism' and Jainism, as well as those of the skeptical and materialist Carvaka tradition. 'Hinduism', a much later and broad term adopted to refer to 'other than Islam', had six orthodox philosophical schools, two of which were nontheistic. Buddhist traditions included the eighteen early schools popularly known as Early School, and the idealist and emptiness schools that comprised the Mahayana. Lively debates were requirements, generally in a spirit of tolerance. However, by convention, losers in a debate would convert to the other side. Occasionally a loser, rather than convert, would commit suicide.

By the 8th Century, Nalanda was a world renowned university city supporting major Buddhist viharas and attracting students and scholars from China, Indo-China and South East Asia to study diverse subjects. Through centuries of Pala patronage Nalanda had also become a repository of old and new texts as they emerged from a living culture further south. It became an important incubator of Mahayana based Vajryana systems of meditative skills and means to liberation that were practiced, verified and exported to countries overseas from sea ports on the Bay of Bengal. Mahayana's attraction was that it dignified every individual for his/her inherant potential providing a pathway to enlightenment without abandoning one livelihood or family. It offered open pathways to fit the diversity of perceptions with clear parameters defining a code of behavior requiring cultivation of disciplines necessary for harmonious civil societies. For lay and for monastic communities, cruelty as punishment for breaking rules was strictly prohibited. The buddhist world had numerous documented models of previous successful cases of organized polities based on Mahayana principles. Buddhist literature abounds in nuances of interaction between people, between lay and monastic communities displaying wide array of human responses in social settings also itemized in great detail in the Abhidhrama texts. In keeping with historical precedents and standards, kings were judged by their enlightened and just rules while kingdoms were ranked by their size and prosperity, the level of their educational institutions, their arts and architecture, the vibrancy of their traditional customs and above all the quality of life enjoyed by it's citizens. The growth of merchant classes with their economic independence and exposure to such mature societies found in Mahayana buddhism access to elaborate, practical and time tested guidelines governing rules of human conduct in societies dedicated to producing the maximum happiness. Rulers and merchants fully understood the advantage of living in civic and rural societies comprised of fulfilled citizens aware of ethics and honoring the parameters of conduct. Such ideal societies were not only heard or read about but seen and experienced by travellers of that period. Much can be gleaned from the level of the arts, literature, dance and theater that were revered, cultivated and survive to this day in these regions. Oral traditions of story telling were accompanied by music, dance and theater becoming the popular folk medium for delivering moral and ethical education to all ages. This was accomplished by recitation or dramatization of the stories from the Jatakas, Sutras and hagiographies and the life of Buddha. In parallel, also active was spread of Vedic lore and ritual promoted by their mercantile followers and their priests. Shiva worship seems to have been in Southeast Asia long before any of the other Indian traditions.

The Pala kingdom, conveniently located on the trade route connecting oceanic traffic to Tibet, it also became the primary source of buddhist culture as it radiated out of its various centers including Nalanda. Indonesian destinations were common along the merchant ships of the Srivijayan mariners long associated with the Indianized [by the 4th cen-

tury] Funanese states located on the Indo Chinese peninsula covering present day coastal lands of Thailand, Cambodia and Vietnam. After the 5th century, Funan had became a dynamic center of Mahayana culture contemporary with that of the Palas. Following the historical pattern in the spread of Mahayana, it also began with the introduction of scripture. The central text, Prajnaparamita, was translated into Chinese by the Funanese monks Mandrasena and Sanghapala in the 5th century. An older Chinese translation was in existence as early as the 2nd century AD. After Imperial China's liquidation of Funan the patronage and spread of Mahayana culture continued unabated along a vast network of river and oceanic trade routes connecting Southeast Asia to India and China. A succession of buddhist kings of the Shrivijan Empire became active patrons of the Mahayana-Vajrayana systems integrating them creatively into native culture with significant social and economic benefit. The monumental Borobodur Stupa and other centers in Java-Sumatra, Malasia, Angkor Wat and others were modeled after classical Indian forms but bear the distinct stamp of native aesthetics. Sizable buddhist university-monastaries flourished in the weathy Shrivijayan cities attracting scholars and pilgrims from afar to learn from teachers or to acquire yet unread texts to translate. Dharmakirti [6th-7th century] a famous scholar at Nalanda, whose works and positions were defended by Shantarakshita, is said to been a Shrivijayan educated in one of it's monasteries. In India, even as buddhism enjoyed favorable conditions, pre-Vedic traditions [ancient Shaivism and Goddess cults with their tantrik manifestations, Jainism, the materialists, the 'manichean' Sun-Moon traditions and primordial animists] as well as Vedic traditions [Brahmanism, the incipient populist Advaita based Vaishnavist cults], existed alongside with patronage of their royal or lay followers. Shaivism and brahmanism made inroads into Southeast Asia along the same routes with their merchant followers. A similar top down assimilation of Indian buddhist culture occured in Tibet beginning as early as the 7th century when it was patronized by the first Buddhist king Songtsen Gampo supported by his two buddhist queens. He was followed by Trisong Detsen, the second Dharma king, under whose rule Vajrayana Buddhism became so woven into the the fabric of life that it remains vital inside Tibet and in it's diaspora to this day surviving its annexation and supression by China in the mid 20th century. In general, Southeast Asia, Tibet, Japan, Korea, Mongolia and China, represent the countires that became influenced by some form Buddhist culture and it was usually due to a desire of the elite to adopt it for their people and it provided time honored props and guidelines for better kings and state craft.

Mahayana teachers, while committed to the three baskets [Sutra, Vinaya and Abidharma] of the Early school, closely followed and practiced the Prajnaparamita, which, in a marked distinction from the Early schools, argued that true compassion bound one to the will to be reborn over and over into samasara—simply because the goal of liberation is not attained until all sentient beings are saved. The one who vows to liberate all sentient beings is a bodhisattva.

Nagarjuna's presentation of Prajnaparamita in the context of earlier traditions made him the central column of the Madhyamaka teachings which held the view that nirvana—the cessation of suffering—is not a separate realm but rather, an enlightened view of samsara and that enlightenment, is essentially a shift of perspective. The enlightened perspective is the unobscured view of reality, whereas samsara is a vision obscured by the veil of maya. There are two kinds of truth, one representing an absolute level, termed emptiness, or that which is beyond conception, and the other, a relative level of awareness. As one sadhana expresses this ultimate point of view, "Nirvana and samsara are the same. One's perspective is the difference."[1]

In the fourth century AD, two brothers, Vasubandhu and Asanga expanded the vast lineage of Buddha's teachings and emphasized those on the nature of mind. Their views influenced the Chittamatra [Mind Only] school of Buddhism which held that reality was mental in nature. Unlike the Early schools, they rejected the notion of a material universe existing independently of consciousness.

These various Buddhist philosophical schools, as well as others, Buddhist and non-Buddhist ones, engaged the good scholars at Nalanda in unending spirited debates for the purpose of discovering the truth. So, when Khenpo Shantarakshita arrived in the eighth century, the stage was set for a unification of some of these ideas into a single system. He is famous for uniting the Madhyamaka view with the Chittamatra.

Very little is known of Shantarakshita's early life. Accounts indicate that he was born a prince in Rewalsar in the modern day state of Himachal Pradesh and that from an early age he showed no interest in the trappings of royalty. His association with Bengal is not unreasonable, it could be plausibly conjectured that he moved there to study in one of the many famous Buddhist university-monasteries that flourished from farther east in Assam (Kamarup) the ancient cities of Guwahati and Goalpara on banks of the Brahmaputra and scattered across the Ganges delta down to Chittagong a major buddhist center and seaport, among others, to lands overseas. Significant segments of people of these north-eastern lands had been followers of a syncretic and non–casteist buddhism for many centuries by now. Shantarakshita became a fully ordained monk to evolve into a professor of philosophy and subsequently, abbot of Nalanda University. He is said to have travelled to China in which case he could easily have reached there in less than four weeks by ship. He would most likely be interested in visiting centers in Indonesia and Indo-china, having heard of the oppulence and interest in those lands for Dharma. After all, it was his own culture and tradition. Already reknowned as a important philosopher, and at a relatively advanced age, he accepted the request from King Trisong Detsen (khri srong–lde–brtsan) to introduce philosophical education into his country. In Tibet, he was able to initiate the transmission of Dharma teachings and the training of the brightest Tibetans of both sexes, but when confronted with the task of establishing a monastery as a physical center for the proliferation of Buddhism, Shantarakshita encountered stiff opposition from Tibet's indigenous Bon heirarchy—traditional advisors and oracles to the kings—who were threatened by buddhism—they would lose their influence in the kingdom. Shantarakshita left for Nepal saying his métier was philosophy, not magic. He recommended that the king invite a certain Guru Padmasambhava who would be up to the task. As described in numerous chronicles of his life Guru Padmasambhava accepted the king's request and successfully subdued the disturbing factions thus allowing Shantarakshita to return to establish Samye Monastery with a rigorous educational tradition based on the university–monastery model. Simultaneously he presided over one the greatest and fastest feats of translating incredibly huge numbers of Buddhist texts from Sanskrit (or prakrit) and Pali into Tibetan, using a newly created Tibetan script based on the Bengali. He was also at the heart of Padmasambhava's training program for his closest disciples who quickly became realized and motivated to become teachers and translators themselves. Even as they attained heights of realization, from the Tibetan Plateau, in plain view was the disturbing move eastwards of an intolerant Islamic invader leaving behind a trail of destroyed buddhist communities, monasteries, iconography and looted stupas which were later mined for bricks. Wherever found, buddhist texts were burned as being ungodly. This stark reality added a great urgency to the translation project which, protected and sponsored by the king, proceeded with a hyper earnestness and elevated performance seen only in an urgent war effort to defend one's country against a harsh and barbaric invader. With the assistance of Padmasambhava's extraordinary attributes and unusual skills, precious texts, many of which never travelled to other countries, rare even in India, were subsequently preserved and saved from obliteration. By the 12th century most of those texts or even knowledge of them was absent in India until they were brought back by Tibetans refugees escaping from the Chinese in the late 20th century. Fortuitously, untouched by the socio political ravages on the Gangetic plains below, in less than a lifetime Tibetans had embraced the Three Jewels as their abiding refuge and began reaping the benefits of an unprecedented cultural renaissance involving a conscious integration of a complex practice-based Buddhism (with Indian roots) into Tibetan language and culture. Not only was the transmission successful, the endeavor spawned a powerful and highly durable system for transmitting the essence of Buddha's teaching through the ages. Unbroken lineages of practicing knowledge holders trained to teach the special skills and means survive to this day. Generally, then as now, teachings, practice and guidance were given to men and women, regardless of their social standing, by request. Serious lay followers and householders could now practice the highest and most secret teachings, with guidance from teachers. A culture of monks and nuns in their services to the public further engendered a peaceful and compassionate society. While there were some extraordinary realized women practitioners like Yeshe Tsogyal, among others, in general, Tibetan women's distinguished themselves with their legendary devotion to the three jewels expressed by their generous support of monastic communities. Shantarakshita was also known to have a kind disposition; in his writings, he displays a refreshing attentiveness to the needs of women and families. Affectionately known as 'Bodhisattva Khenpo', in imagery he usually potrayed with a smile.

Major Philosophical Works

1. Commentary on Dharmakirti: Shantarakshita's commentary on Dharmakirti, The Nyaya/Hetu-bindu Shastra, is a defense and clarification of Dharmakirti's views on negation, universals and inference. His explanation of universals is particularly interesting. He defends Dharmakirti's nominalism by arguing that the supposed similarity between two trees, for example, is really a similarity between one's experiences of two trees. The "similarity" is then superimposed on the trees, but is a mere convention2.

1. *Two Commentaries on Jnanagarbha* have also been attributed to Shantarakshita in which he comments on his teacher's views on the relation between the subject and object of experience.[3]

2. *The Investigation into the Ultimate* has been lost, existing neither in Sanskrit nor Tibetan.

3. The *Tattvasamgraha*, a compendium of Indian philosophy, translated by

Ganganatha Jha in 1937, is a critical analysis of philosophical positions extant during Khenpo Shantarakshita's lifetime. Shantarakshita criticizes many of them using the arguments of Chittamatra thinkers, particularly in his criticism of atomism. In this work, he does not discuss his own Madhyamaka view at length. In the *Tattvasamgraha*, he defends the validity of inferences on the relative level.[4]

Consider an analogy with modern mathematics. Euclidean geometry is not considered to be applicable to astronomical conceptions of space. It is, however, useful on earth for practical purposes, like construction. And conclusions drawn from its assumptions are perfectly correct relative to the Euclidean system, even though they may be useless relative to another system; for example, Riemannian geometry that is useful in astrophysics. Similarly, Shantarakshita defends the validity of a conclusion that is drawn from premises representative of the relation between generally accepted ideas.

This argument played an important role in debates between Tibetan philosophers, some of whom were concerned that accepting the validity of inferences deduced from experiences might commit one to the assertion that things had real existence. Take, for example, in the (autonomous) syllogism:

> *Where there is smoke, there is burning.*
> *As in a kitchen.*
> *There is smoke.*
> *Therefore, there is burning.*

Accepting the conclusion, some were concerned, commits one to the existence of burning. Shantarakshita did not accept this entailment, because the premises were only considered to be conventionally (relatively) true.

The *Tattvasiddhi* presents the logical deduction of the feasibility of the tantra. Although very much of a philosophical treatise, it is also a practice text. It offers an explanation of the effectiveness of tantric practice, grounded on solid logic. It presents a rationally acceptable and powerful path to liberation through happiness. Although it is primarily a tantric text, in which the meditational method for achieving enlightenment is clearly taught, the philosophical sections are impressive. For example, in folio 73, Shantarakshita seems to be introducing the notion of a category mistake. [A category is a class of entities that collect certain predicates. A category mistake is to assert or deny predicates of a subject that belongs to another category or group.]

For example, a lotus that is composed of space would be impossible, since space is unreal. Shantarakshita considers space to be merely the relation imposed by the mind on objects. He then applies the four-fold negation to the notion of a sky [space] lotus. It is, he asserts, incorrect to say the space lotus exists, does not exist, does exist and not exist, and neither exists nor fails to exist. I believe he means that a space lotus is not the sort of entity of which one can predicate either existence or nonexistence. An example of the Western case of a category mistake would be to ask if the Pythagorean theorem is blue or not blue. Shantarakshita's example of whether the space lotus exists or not seems similar to this.[5]

In the *Tattvasiddhi*, Shantarakshita addresses a central concern of the tantra as expressed in texts such the *Guhyasamaja Tantra*, which is to offer a technique to propel the mind beyond habitual patterns. David Snellgrove has carefully studied this text, and in his interpretations, wonders if encouragements to commit what are almost universally considered immoral acts are merely hyperbole or a secret language with another meaning.[6] For example, as Khenchen Palden Sherab has mentioned, the admonition to kill your mother and father has to be understood in terms of this language. 'Father' refers to negative activities in this context, and 'mother' refers to attachment.[7]

Shantarakshita's arguments are designed to lead us to the understanding that that on the ultimate level there are no natural negatives. No thing or activity is evil in and of itself. If this were the case, the bodhisattva could not gain merit by killing someone who was about to kill many people (folio 69). Further, enlightened beings, through the gaining of great wisdom and compassion, have certainty about the consequences of actions, and can make wise decisions about when to set aside moral rules.

The essential point, however, is that bodhicitta, the synthesis of wisdom and compassion, is necessary and sufficient to justify any action whatever. Because of this, Shantarakshita is leading the bodhisattva through logic, to the understanding that, because on the absolute level all is emptiness, morality is also empty in nature. For a bodhisattva, the attachment to rules and regulations might be hard to relinquish. But someone who has internalized bodhicitta is able to act spontaneously without following these rules and regulations. In actuality, the bodhisattva's actions may also conform to custom and generally accepted morality, but this is not always necessary. No one, however, who has not mastered bodhicitta, that is, both wisdom and compassion, is in a position to set aside conventional rules of conduct.

One might ask whether bodhicitta itself is absolute or relative. It is both. There are two types. "Relative bodhicitta is the actual manifestation of loving kindness and compassion for all beings. Absolute bodhicitta is the realization of emptiness as the profound, true nature of reality."* But if emptiness is beyond conception, what right do we have to call it *bodhicitta*? And if bodhicitta is beyond conception, what are we to make of its meaning?

Shantarakshita understands the key to absolute bodhicitta to be non-duality. Anything one says about the absolute level would be dualistic, because in asserting it is "x", one must assert it is not other than "x". Shantarakshita says in *Madhyamakalankara* that we cannot fault him because [on the absolute level] he does not assert anything to be true. In *Tattvasiddhi*, he often speaks about the way one views reality. His answer seems to be that bodhicitta is a perspective that is generated by non-dual awareness. The starving child from the absolute view neither exists nor fails to exist. On the relative level, the Buddha does not perceive the star-ving child, but because non-dual awareness generates bodhicitta, wisdom and compassion, the Buddha is totally aware of the starving child. It is similar to what Kamalashila says about the Buddha's knowledge of the future. The future does not exist, so the Buddha does not perceive it. Nevertheless, the knowledge of the

*Teaching notes from a lecture at Padmasambava Buddhist Center

future arises in the Buddha's mind as in a dream.

The Reins of the Two Chariots

The overcoming of duality is the unifying concept of *Tattvasiddhi* and *Madhymakalankara*. In the former, one is led to this through logic, the abandonment of concepts, and tantric practice. In the latter, one is led to this through logic and the abandonment of concepts.

As Shantarakshita says, there is no proof that this practice will lead to enlightenment. But there is no reason that it will not.

If ultimate reality is beyond conception, how can awareness of it ever be attained though the relative level? Shantarakshita argues that very special causal conditions can bring about a very special result, e.g., the removing of the obscurations that hide our enlightened nature. For example, a certain sort of seed when planted will produce a plant with a bitter fruit. But if the seed is first soaked in milk, the fruit will be sweet. Similarly, certain activities, such as touch, can produce problems such as excessive attachment when performed in the ordinary way. But when performed in accordance with non-conceptual wisdom and compassion, they can lead to enlightenment. This is because the bliss produced by touch is not completely dissimilar to the bliss of enlightenment. Bliss leads to a higher bliss, when it has become a special kind of cause. And enlightenment is reachable, because it is already present. One only needs to provide the correct causal conditions that will remove the obscurations blocking realization. And since the enlightened state is unobscured reality, attainment of it is irreversible, since there is no further cause for confusion.

But why should we accept that this special cause of non-dual bliss would produce enlightenment? Natural reasoning shows that a special cause can bring about a special effect, so nothing precludes the attainment of suchness through the special causes of the tantra. Shantarakshita appeals to scripture (folio 73), but in order to have certainty, the student must also enter into the practice (folio 75). Here, seeing is believing.

Finally, before leaving the *Tattvasiddhi*, it is important to consider for whom this text is intended. Shantarakshita says quite clearly that the special practices mentioned are not intended for ordinary people but for yogis and yoginis who are willing to engage in them in accordance with the tantric obligations. That is, they must be done with the guidance of a teacher, with a mind set on non-duality, and with boundless wisdom and compassion. Otherwise, it is worse than "entering into the fire."

Shantarakshita, following Dharmakirti, says that the logical analysis that leads to an understanding of the emptiness of the self and the world provides an occasion of non-dual meditation that will not impede one's progress towards enlightenment (folio 74). So logic, far from being an obstacle, if properly used along with the tantra, can be a guide on the path. But one needs more than logic.

In the *Madhyamakalankara*, Shantarakshita integrates the Chittamatra school of Asanga and the Madhyamaka school of Nagarjuna. His aim, as he states it, is to show the correctness of the Chittamatra claim that non-mental objects do not exist, even on the relative level, and the correctness of the Madhyamaka view that, on the absolute level, mind itself is empty of concepts (sloka 92). When dealing with the absolute level, he employs only *reductio ad absurdum* arguments.

In the *Madhyamakalankara*, or *Jewel Ornament of the Middle Way*, the Chittamatra is defended, not as true in itself, but as true in a relative way. This position correctly represents the way the world is understood by sentient beings. And it is through this relative level that sentient beings learn to transcend their conceptual schemes and to gain enlightenment. Logic leads us to the point where it self-destructs. And only then can we pass beyond it.

What is the point of this difficult text, which I liken to Kant's *Critique of Pure Reason* were it to be condensed into ninety-seven four-line slokas? As Buddha said to his disciple Malunkyaputta, idle metaphysical speculation takes time away from the search for enlightenment. Buddha elsewhere warned of quarrels arising due to disparate views. There is no point in arguing as an intellectual exercise.[8] But Shantarakshita, rather than engaging in debate for its own sake, uses philosophical analysis as a tool to achieve nonattachment. To be attached to the nonexistent would be, in his view, like a magician falling in love with an illusory woman he had created.

The *Madhyamakalankara* begins with a critique of the monism of the Samkhyas, who held that all that exists has a single nature, the Advaita Vedantins who held that all that exists is the self nature of Brahman, the skepticism of the Charvakas, and the unchanging mind of each sentient being postulated by the Mimamsas and Jainas. Then Shantarakshita turns his attention to the refutation of atomism, for which he relies on the arguments of Vasubandhu. Atomism was the view of the Vaibhashika and Sautrantika Buddhist schools. Entities can be said to be composed of atoms that are the indivisibly small components of all objects. This atom is not the same as the empirically understood atom of modern physics, which is divisible. It is an a priori notion. And upon analysis, one discovers its paradoxical nature. If it is really indivisible, it must have an extension of zero, because zero is the only number that cannot be divided. And since zero plus zero is zero, atoms could not combine to add up to anything. Also, they could not combine, because they could have no sides. If they contacted another atom, therefore, they would take up the same space.

When criticizing the atomistic materialism of the combined Vaibhashika and Sautrantika schools, Shantarakshita is attempting to convince us that we must renounce the security of clinging to the reality of an external (non-mental) object. Obviously, his arguments, following the great fourth century philosopher Vasubandhu, are directed against the ancient materialist view of atoms as the smallest possible indivisible particles. Today, we know that atoms are divisible, and may be made up of vibrating strings, which are far smaller.

If Shantarakshita's whole theory were to rest on the refutation of ancient atomism, modern views on fundamental particles might pose a problem, though it is fun to imagine what sort of holes he might poke in string theory were he alive today. But his critique rests rather on the impossibility of viewing reality in terms of the categories of one or many, and since they are exclusive and exhaustive, it seems as if we are not to be allowed to make sense of anything, ultimately speaking. It is interesting to note that at least one contemporary physicist has asserted that fundamental particles may not lend themselves to being viewed as either simple or compound.[9]

And Michel Bitbol's private commentary on the aptness of Shantarakshita's critique to Shantarakshita's argument is of this type*:

(1) How are these problems overcome in modern atomism? Few people usually raise this question. But I think interesting answers are available. The answers are quite simple to state:

(a) The "properties" of elementary particles, including their spatial properties such as position or size, are not intrinsic but contextual (or relational);

(b) The very "existence" of these elementary particles is not intrinsic but contextual (or relational).

Point (a) was made clear by Bohr and Heisenberg. Heisenberg thus said that in modern physics a Lockean distinction between nonspatial "secondary" qualities and spatial "primary" qualities had become pointless. In fact, all the "qualities" of microphysics are "secondary," where secondary means relational. Point (b) arises from a straightforward reflection about Quantum Field Theory Indeed, in QFT, the number of particles is an "observable," namely a value which arises with probability P when an interactive relation between the environment and an apparatus occurs. The number of particles is thus not inherently defined. Paul Teller says that this means particles are not the sort of things that either exist or do not exist in the absolute.

It is then very clear that the modern answer to the conundrums of classical atomism is exactly what Shantarakshita had in mind in Karikas (slokas 14&15): partless atoms are ascribed no intrinsic nature, no intrinsic existence. They are only correlates of a certain activity of investigations, whose by-product is ordered by quantum theories. No intrinsic partlessness but rather partlessness relative to a certain range of method of partitioning; no intrinsic directions, or geometrical properties, but rather spatial properties relative to certain modes of geometrical measurements; no intrinsic existence but rather existence relative to one another and to certain methods of detection.

The difference between the two cases is that Shantarakshita formulated this idea as part of the Madhyamaka systematic deconstruction of any "essence," or assertion of inherent being, showing that it provided a rational dissolution to the problem of classical Indian atomism. Whereas modern physics was, so to speak, forced to this solution by the very limits of operativity of the old schemes of classical physics in the microscopic domain. But there is still reluctance against this solution nowadays: "Many physicists think this is a renouncement of the ideal of their science, and desperately look for 'realist' interpretations of quantum theories (where they mean interpretation that ascribes inherent properties and inherent existence to their entities).

Some thoughts on self-awareness [*rang rig*]:

For Shantaraksita there is no *rang rig* on the ultimate level. There is *rang rig* on the relative level. *Rang rig* is not to be thought of in terms of the usual threefold relation of subject, object and activity. *Rang rig* in no way refers to even a relative

* Quoted with permission from private correspondence from Michel Bitbol.

object as when one refers to a chair or one's body. *Rang rig* is a way of knowing. One is always implicitly aware that it is oneself that is eating, thinking, etc., ratherthan someone else. One is always [Raziel Abelson's point] capable of reflecting that one knows, eats, etc.

Shantarakshita then turns his attention to the relationship between the mind and the perceived object. He considers the problem both from the Sautrantika point of view [which asserts the reality of objects apart from the mind] and from the Chittamatra view [which holds that the perceived object is mental in nature]. A brief outline of this complex argument is given in the Appendix for the convenience of the reader.

The Vaibhasikas feared to acknowledge the subject of experience, because in their eyes this was tantamount to asserting the existence of a substantial self. Shantarakshita argues that this is not the case, and that these philosophers are fooled by the general view that almost all activities of sentient beings can be analyzed in terms of subject, object, and activity. So self-knowledge, it would seem, must have an object and, they concluded that, if this is true, the subject would have substantial existence. So they felt bound to deny the subject altogether. Shantarakshita points out that they are misled by a false model. Self-awareness is unique in that it cannot be analyzed in this way. One must renounce this simple model.

As previously noted, in the *Madhyamakalankara*, the Chittamatra is defended, not as true in itself, but as true in a relative way. The Chittamatra correctly represents the way the world is understood by sentient beings. And it is through this relative level that sentient beings learn to transcend their conceptual schemes and to gain enlightenment.

Yet, the Chittamatra are correct in asserting the reality of awareness. One knows there is awareness, for awareness is a precondition for even the denying of awareness. But when one tries to analyze precisely what this awareness is, problems arise. Many of these problems are the same as those that cognitive scientists are wrestling with today (e.g. Daniel Dennett). Among other questions which concern Shantarakshita is how we can manage to perceive anything whatever in an instantaneous present moment.

The movie "The Matrix"[10] presents a vision of the world in which the mind is driven by habitual patterns analogous to the operating systems of computers. These result in a misleading vision of the nature of reality. How then to escape from "the matrix"? The answer given in *Tattvasiddhi* is the achieving of enlightenment. One achieves the ability to take the view that transcends duality—transcends subject and object.

George Dreyfus has pointed out that Shantarakshita's view is closer to the Great Perfection [*Dzogchen*] than any of the other Indian Madhyamaka views. "This view emphasizes the centrality of the mind, presenting phenomena as its display, but only on the conventional level. The mind itself is presented as empty, thereby avoiding its reification. In this way, reality is described as focusing on the mind and its emptiness. Such a description is well suited as a propaedeutic (preliminary instruction) for the Great Perfection view of reality as empty and luminous."[11]

This congruence between Shantarakshita's view and Dzogchen is not surprising. The philosophical views of the great Dzogchen master Guru Padmasambhava were very similar, as is evidenced by the following passages [among others] from *The Light of Wisdom*:

> *In particular, external objects are grasped by fixation.*
> *All are unreal and appear like an illusion.*
> *Not permanent, yet in their transience able to function.*
> *They are not singular, since a variety emerges and changes.*
> *They are not independent, but follow the karmic deeds.*
> *They are not particles, since partless atoms do not exist.*
> *If they did exist, gross things could not be assembled.*
> *If they had parts, this would contradict the assertion of partlessness.*
> *They are nothing but a non-existent and false appearance,*
> *an interdependence*
> *Like dreams, magical illusion and the reflection of the moon in water.*
> *Regard them as a city of gandharvas and as a rainbow.*[12]

The Dzogchen aspect appears most clearly in folio 76 of *Tattvasiddhi*, when Shantarakshita refers to the *Collection of All Realization Tantra*, that states that whatever is perceived by the senses [realized non-conceptually] is the Buddha, and through sensation, one is united with all the buddhas.

NOTES ON TRANSLATION

One of the most extraordinary aspects of Shantarakshita's achievements is his amazing ability to put philosophy into a melodious poetic form. From what we can gather from its sole surviving Sanskrit verse, the *Madhyamakalankara* was written in magnificent poetry, replete with internal rhythm, which eludes adequate expression in English. For example, in English (*sloka* 1):

> *Whatever my schools and others assert,*
> *All things are completely free of*
> *The characteristics of one and many.*
> *Therefore, they lack existence, like reflections.*

Here is how it reads in Sanskrit:

> *Nihsvabhavam bhavas tattvata svaparodita*
> *Ekanekasvabhavena viyogat pratibimbavat.*

When chanted, the melody is exquisite.

Finally, it is important to point out that some terms have been translated in special ways to preserve the meaning. For example, *dewa* has been translated differently in different contexts. In some contexts we have translated dewa as "blessing" rather than "bliss" or "happiness" which is its more ordinarily understood meaning. In tantric contexts, dewa may also mean "bodily blessing" or "bliss" whereas "yid dewa" means "mental bliss." Chittamatra is used synonymously with Yogachara.

The philosophical interpretation of the *Madhyamakalankara* was a challenge. Fortunately, we had access to Shantarakshita's auto-commentary, as well as the commentaries of Kamalashila, Je Tsong Khapa, and Mipham Rinpoche. We have profited from the translation of Masamichi Ichigo, the unpublished translation of Peter della Santina, the recently published translations of Thomas Doctor and James Blumenthal, and the Padmakara translation group. For assistance with both texts, we relied on the generous help of Khenchen Palden Sherab Rinpoche, Khenpo Tsewang Dongyal Rinpoche and Dr. Lozang Jamspal, who gave us his reconstructed Sanskrit version of the *Madhyamalalankara* as well as invaluable advice on the translations.

The editors apologize for any errors in reflecting the thought of Khenpo Shantarakshita, Khenchen Palden Sherab Rinpoche and Khenpo Tsewang Dongyal Rinpoche. So we offer these root texts and commentaries, paying homage to Khenpo Shantarakshita, and hoping that whatever problems remain may challenge future scholars to improve on our work.

— Marie Friquegnon
William Paterson University

COMMENTARY ON

TATTVASIDDHI

the attainment of suchness

Khenchen Palden Sherab Rinpoche
and
Khenpo Tsewang Dongyal Rinpoche

This commentary was transcribed from oral transmissions given by the authors to Marie Louise Friquegnon over a ten years period in the 80's, at various locations in India and the United States of America.

Please note: Because of the extremely concise phrasing of Shantarakshita's works, it may be useful to read the commentaries in conjunction with the root texts.

Shiwaitso, 'Khenpo Bodhisattva', Shantarakshita, Abbot of Samye

The Sanskrit word, *Tattvasiddhi,* may be translated in the following way: tattva means the true nature, which is sometimes referred to as "suchness" in Buddhist literature. In *Tattvasiddhi,* Shantarakshita presents arguments designed to demonstrate how to reach the accomplishment of siddhi or suchness. These arguments are based on an understanding of *tattva* or the true nature.

Tattva has two meanings, depending on whether one is speaking in the context of the relative or absolute. The relative can be divided into the pure and impure relative. The absolute can also be divided in the following way: the *tattva* of the absolute which is still contained within the limits of imagination or thought [proximate absolute], and the *tattva* of the absolute which is beyond those limits.

Shantarakshita begins with an analysis of the relative, and then continues with an examination of the meaning of the absolute. It is impossible to understand the absolute without an understanding of pure relative truth. It is through pure relative truth that one attains the realization of the absolute. This is the subject discussed and analyzed in these sections [*prakranas*].

Siddhi is completion, since in its nature there is neither exaggeration nor denial in the study, contemplation, and understanding of reality. Thus, briefly, *Tattvasiddhi* means all phenomena, completely studied, contemplated and understood without exaggeration and deprecation.

The work (as translated from Sanskrit into Tibetan) begins with homage to Manjushri Rinchen Zangpo (*rinchen bzangpo*). This follows the ancient tradition of rules of the Dharma kings of Tibet, such as Trisong Detsen [*khri srong ldet btsan*] and his grandson Triralpachen [*khri ral pa can*]. Their rules decree that translators must place their texts into one of the following categories: *abhidharma, vinaya,* or *sutra,* that is, into one of the three baskets [*pitakas*].[13]

All Buddha's teachings are summarized in these three baskets. The *Vinaya* teachings are mostly directed towards helping people become calm and clear, and to act morally in terms of body, speech, and mind. The *Sutra* teachings are intended to help keep the mind from being scattered, as well as focused and concentrated. The *Abhidharma* teachings enable one to know the nature of all phenomena. This is the level of wisdom, free from duality, calm and clear—the aspect of great emptiness.

Then the translator had to include a specific homage for that type of text. This rule must be followed whether or not the text was a translation from one of the originals or a commentary by a great master. For example, if they were translating *vinaya* or a commentary belonging to the *vinaya*, the translator would pay homage in the following manner: "I pay homage to the Omniscient One [*Sarvajra*], who has knowledge of all phenomena past, present and future." As soon as one reads this, even when one does not know what the text is about, one immediately knows it belongs to the *vinaya*. Or, when the text begins: "I pay homage to the Buddhas and the Bodhisattvas," then those teachings or commentaries belong to sutra, irrespective of whether their origins are Early School, Mahayana or Vajrayana. Or, if it begins with "I pay homage to Arya Manjushri," one will immediately know that it is from Buddha Sakyamuni's *abhidharma*, or is a commentary on *abhidharma* by a great master, no matter what *yana* it comes from.

What is *abhidharma*? *Abhidharma* is a description of Sakyamuni's wisdom aspect of Dharma. It is less about rules of conduct and more about logical analysis, investigation, and inner wisdom. This is Shantarakshita's concern in the *Tattvasiddhi*.

Not only is Manjushri the wisdom aspect of all Buddhas but, as a great temporal bodhisattva, he is the manifestation of this wisdom aspect. He is the embodiment of Buddha's wisdom. For this reason, he is the object of homage of the translators of the works included in the category of abhidharma. After paying homage, they offer prayers to Manjushri that they will fulfill their commitment to translating a particular abhidharma text.

There are three ways to pay homage: 1. through one's realization of the absolute nature, which is wisdom; 2. through one's meditation experiences, that is, focusing the mind through concentration; and 3. through one's body, speech and mind's good behavior, calmness, good ethics — understanding that in so paying respect, one is honoring the special quality of that enlightened being or person. The homage paid by translators is called *gyur chag* (*hgyur chag*). Having paid such homage, they commit themselves to the task of completing the translation of the text.

At this point, the main section begins. Although, on the ultimate level all distinctions are transcended, relatively the great bliss of the true nature can be understood in terms of ground, path and result. The ground or basis of the ultimate nature is, of course, always present. But, as sentient beings, we must achieve realization of this true nature by following the right path. So, in this text, Shantarakshita is concentrating on the path, rather than on the ground or result. It is to this path that he is paying homage.

This true nature, this great blissfulness, which is called *dewa chenpo* in Tibetan, (*mahasukha* in Sanskrit) is totally free of any complexity. Within this true nature, all distinctions are transcended. Suffering itself is great blissfulness. Everything is the movement of great blissfulness. This is true independently of our realization of it. When you realize that, then that's it! This is the great blissfulness—this is the true nature. When one achieves realization of the primordial nature, then no suffering exists at all, not even the name of suffering. All is entirely, totally, the state of great happiness.

So, this is the great realization. But how do we know it? How do we come to attain it? This can only be done through the Vajrayana, the *mahasukha* of the *vajra*, which is the source of the true nature. This path invokes the great blissfulness. The *vajra* [in Sanskrit] is the *dorje* [in Tibetan], meaning the indestructible. This means that in spite of dualistic thinking, the primordial nature endures. The primordial nature includes the path that is symbolized by the vajra. So, the "*dorje thegpa*" [*rdo rje theg pa*], or Vajrayana, is the teaching that reveals the primordial nature, that teaching to which Shantarakshita is paying homage, and to which we who are devoted to those teachings also pay homage.

On the last page of the text, it says that Shantakrakshita did not supervise the translation. This is hard to understand because Guru Padmasambhava's students were also students of Shantarakshita, such as the learned translator Kawa Paltzek (*skawa dpal btsek*), and they would have wanted to read this in a Tibetan translation. Perhaps Rinchen Zampo (*rinchen bzangpo*) retranslated this text later, in the tenth century, under the direction of Atisha. It was a common practice for translators to retranslate texts and put their own names on as translators.

The commitment section of the text states as its purpose the dispelling of ignorance about the Vajrayana teachings of the primordial nature, the great blissfulness. The method is logical analysis designed to demonstrate the nature of suchness [the true or primordial nature] and the manner in which realization of this nature may be achieved. This analysis will dispel any doubts, ignorance, or hesitation people may have about Vajrayana teachings, which are the perfect highest teachings leading to enlightenment.

Some people, however, do not have a real [karmic] connection with the Vajrayana, nor do they have the habits of virtue needed for its practice. These people are victims of exaggerated imaginative thought construction. Words, for example, are merely produced through natural laws of cause and effect. But, many people imagine that someone created language. This cannot be justified by reasoning. Another example is consciousness. It is just one of the aggregates, but people imagine that, in addition to this, we have a soul or ego that is indestructible and completely unchanging. They conclude that the self endures eternally changeless. All of these exaggerated thought constructions are analyzed and refuted by Shantarakshita in the *Tattvasamgraha*.

Such people cling to phenomena that do not exist apart from their imagination, their mental habits. In Tibetan these mental exaggerations are called *drotagpa* [*sgro 'dogs pa*]. Shantarakshita states that these people are not qualified to study or practice Vajrayana. They are prevented from doing so by ten different obstacles:

1. They have no deeply rooted habits of virtue;
2. They habitually conceive of phenomena in terms of exaggerated mental constructions;
3. Their numerous thoughts are like a powerful, destructive wind, which attack whatever wisdom or understanding they possess;
4. They are deeply sunk into the mire of the ways of thought of our degenerate age;
5. They lack the perfect method or skill required for crossing the ocean of samsara;
6. Their imagination stains and distorts their thoughts about the world;
7. They have fallen into a valley of misery, poverty and weakness in which they are attacked by their own obscurations—obscurations which are like cobras, rattlesnakes, thorns, stones;
8. These demons or rivers of wickedness make it very difficult for them to realize their true nature. Because of this, they become restless, disturbed, crazed;
9. They are not in contact with a qualified teacher; and

10. They have not received the pith instructions on how to meditate on the absolute.

In this way, people are deceived by these obstacles and prevented from recognizing the truth of the Vajrayana teachings.

One can describe those people qualified to practice the Vajrayana in the following way. They are first of all, those qualified to recognize the special qualities of the Vajrayana. In them, the Vajrayana takes effect quickly due to meditative sharing of the blissfulness of Buddha Vajrasattva. Through his great blissfulness, enlightenment is achieved with great speed. Another ingredient is the blissfulness which comes from our primordial nature– its ground. This blissfulness, then, ensures another quality of the Vajrayana. Through it there is no suffering. Suffering itself is transformed into great bliss. Samsara as a whole is transformed into a pure land and emotion is transformed into wisdom. Wisdom and emptiness, wisdom and skillful means, are united in the union that is Vajrasattva himself. Through Vajrasattva, we are able to describe and focus on the vajra nature or primordial nature that is pure from the beginning [Tib. *kadak*] and indestructible. Through the courage of Vajrasattva, we generate the quality of compassion, that is, skillful means and thoughts of loving kindness for the benefit of all sentient beings. That is the true meaning of the great blissfulness, the union of Vajrasattva. People who cannot recognize this must practice dharma for many aeons to gain enlightenment. But, those who recognize this teaching achieve enlightenment very quickly.

Also, people who possess the techniques of the Vajrayana can achieve enlightenment without any problem in this very lifetime. This is because sentient beings in spite of their confused state, possess some *rigpa*, awareness of true reality. Thus, the true or intrinsic state of all sentient beings is bliss without beginning or end. This true nature pervades all of existence. It pervades all conscious and unconscious beings equally. Although this is true on the absolute level, on the relative level, sentient beings exist in a state totally dominated by confusion and illusion. This confusion has no source– it doesn't arise from anything– it has no basis in reality.

Because of this awareness that all beings possess of their intrinsic nature (although almost always dominated by confusion), they have available to them a source of great merit. Because of this awareness, wonderful things exist unendingly within them, even though they are not capable of recognizing this inner reality. The Vajrayana teaching shows how to recognize this true nature, the reality that is hidden within. *Rigpa* makes such recognition possible.

Shantarakshita is not just giving a partial view of the Vajrayana– the indestructible holy of holies– but is giving a complete summary of all of its aspects Using the words of Buddha Sakyamun in the sutras and tantras, his intention is to remove the cataracts of ignorance from the eyes of those who fail to see the point of these teachings. He also makes use of techniques of logic as well as his own inner wisdom. For one is not supposed to accept what the Buddha says as true without careful examination.

The basis of reasoning in Buddhism is the teachings of Sakyamuni Buddha combined with logic and one's own intuitive wisdom. From Buddha until the present day, Buddhist teachers have always insisted that no one should accept the truth of

Buddhism through blind faith. Conviction should come as a result of careful analysis. One needs reasoning as well as the words of enlightened persons.

Buddhists developed this method of careful examination in contrast to the procedure common among Hindus of accepting the truth of the Vedas through faith without the need of proof. But, in Buddhism, if one finds that a scripture conflicts with reason or is self-contradictory, one must not believe in it. The scriptures are unique and important, but they need to be combined with logical analysis. Sometimes, when one finds an apparent contradiction, upon further reflection the paradox will dissolve, for there are many possible interpretations of scripture, many different ways to understand it.

In general, the words of the Buddha are true. One cannot find anything definitively false on every interpretation. One has to search for the proper meaning. This is why Buddhists are famous for their debate tradition. They do not debate through anger or jealousy, or to create doubts, or hurt people in any way. But each person must find his or her own path that will satisfy the mind and lead to the recognition of reality on the absolute level. Even the tradition of Buddhism is not important. All that matters is to see the true nature of reality. Buddha's teaching is a support, but it cannot take the place of our own personal search, our knowledge, and our wisdom.

Buddha taught, for example, that all things are impermanent. It is not just enough to accept this through blind faith, for if one does, one will not gain an adequate understanding of what this means. One must at least reflect on our own experience, noticing that everything one sees comes and goes. When one reasons in this way, Buddha's words and one's own insight have come together. Without this, one cannot see the truth.

This type of reflection can also be helpful in seeing the essential unity between Early School and Vajrayana teachings. Under analysis their apparent contradictions dissolve, and one sees them flowing together as one great river. Buddha taught that the wise man should examine his words the way a goldsmith examines whether or not a piece of metal is pure gold. The goldsmith uses many means, such as rubbing, cutting, and burning. In the same way, one should not accept Buddha's teaching out of devotion, but as the result of careful reasoning.

There are three methods that will allow us to examine statements in order to determine their truth or falsity. They are hearing, contemplation (analytical), and meditation. Acceptance of the truth of any part of the teaching should, ideally, result from a combination of all three.

All forms are potential objects of knowledge. When we know them and use them through wisdom and skillful means, there will be a very great result. Of course, this does not happen right away. Even with very talented and intelligent people, it takes experience and practice to turn knowledge into wisdom and skillful means.

How is it the case that all knowledge can be used in this positive way? This is because causal conditions are complex. Even if a cause usually produces a bad result, if the causal conditions are carefully modified, a good result can occur. The *churura* (*skyu ru ra*) fruit, for example, is usually very sour. But if one soaks the seed in milk or molasses, its fruit will become sweet. Once one learns how to transform the plant in this way, one can do it again and again. One may first learn this by accident, through chance perception, but then after repeated experience one may infer that it will always happen.

By analogy, this is the heart of the teaching of the *Tattvasiddhi.* No matter what the objects of experience are, when they are combined with skillful means and wisdom, they will always bring about a good result. One knows through experience that this is true. Smart children, for example, when placed in a good school with good teachers, if they develop good habits and good character (and there are no negative influences from bad companions, and so forth), will become well-educated people. How could the result be otherwise?

It is similar when yogis meditate on *mahamudra.* This meditation is the continuous application of the Vajrayana teaching to all objects external and internal — the continual application of a single perspective. This technique of visualization combined with the blessings of mantra and special mudra is a system of causes in combination that produce a very special result.

In the mahamudra meditation, everything is visualized as the body of the Buddha Vajrasattva– as his *mandala.* All sounds are heard as the mantra of Vajrasattva and all thoughts are understood as Vajrasattva's wisdom. Combining this perspective with objects of body, speech, and thought will bring realization.

This will happen because of the interconnectedness of all things. One single causal factor in isolation never brings about an effect. The nature of phenomenal reality is such that all of reality at one moment acts together to bring about all that exists at the next moment of time. This is known as the system of interdependent co-origination. Because of this system, an infinite number of causes can be specially combined to bring about the extraordinary result of enlightenment. Of course, we cannot begin to enumerate the infinite number of special factors that lead to enlightenment. But, through the special technique of *mahamudra,* we can use them.

In summary, reason demonstrates that whatever is, comes to be by a special combination of causal conditions which bring about a special result. As I mentioned before, when one soaks the seed of the churura fruit in milk, the fruit becomes sweet. Because the causal conditions are special, the result is special. So, if you have special experiences, this will produce a special result. So, when Vajrayana techniques are applied to forms, sounds, and thoughts, that application will also produce a special result. This is not imagination, but rather occurs because of a natural process, the way things are.

This conclusion concerning the special result, attained when one's sensory perceptions are transformed through skillful means and wisdom, is arrived at through a process termed "natural reasoning." This type of reasoning is based on experience. All phenomena go through processes of change. This is the basis for the assertion that they are not permanent. A second type of reasoning, also based on experience, is used in analysis of causal relations. The famous example:

Where there is smoke,
there must be burning.
As in a kitchen.
There is smoke.

Therefore, there is burning.

This is a type of reasoning called "result reasoning." Finally, Buddhist logic recognizes a third type of reasoning called "non-perceived reasoning" or "invisible reasoning." This allows us to infer what is not the case. An elephant, for example, is the sort of thing that is perceivable. If one doesn't see an elephant on a table, then one may infer there is no elephant there.

To return to the discussion of natural reasoning, one knows that when certain powders are combined into potions, even snake poison will lose its ill effects. Similarly, the objects of the senses are usually the cause of much suffering and many obstacles to enlightenment. But, when one has the potion of transformed awareness through skillful means and wisdom, then there is nothing such a practitioner may not safely do. There are no limitations. Fearlessly and without any doubts or hesitations, such a person may enjoy all the sense objects of desire. This is stated in the *Secret Moon Tantra* and in all supreme inner tantras without exception.

The difference in the way yogis enjoy objects and the ordinary way lies mainly in the factor of clinging. Ordinary people are never satisfied when they desire objects. They cling to them, want their enjoyment to be permanent. When, for example, they are enjoying music, they can never get enough. But, when objects are enjoyed without clinging, because one's perception of them is combined with skillful means and wisdom, then these objects become the very means to enlightenment rather than obstacles. One is able to do this because one's bodhicitta is very stable, and for this reason one's liberation is assured.

In the same tantra, instructions to yogis about how to the practice the Vajrayana system are given. First, one should carefully study and analyze this system as a whole. Then, one should receive the initiation and transmission as well as the general and pith instructions. A practitioner who does this will understand what he or she is doing and will be able to practice successfully. To try to practice Vajrayana without doing this will be sixteen times worse than falling into fire.

In summary, a practitioner who knows what he or she is doing will achieve a great result very quickly by contacting a consort and practicing Vajrayana. Someone, on the other hand, who has no understanding and no skills, who is poorly prepared and yet claims to be a Vajrayana practitioner, will in contacting a consort produce a hellish result.

The reason why the enjoyment of objects does not produce a bad result in the Vajrayana is because objects in themselves are not the cause of falling into the lower realms, even though they are a condition of unstable emotional development. This is because the form this emotional development takes is dependent on mind. For emotions are internal, not external. They depend on the mental attitude of the person experiencing them. Negative emotions are developed by clinging to one's ego, property, body, and so forth. It is this clinging that causes negative emotions to arise– objects themselves are not the cause of this. External objects are innocent.

It is the clinging to ego that simultaneously produces the thought of the other. As soon as one distinguishes between self and other, one begins to love oneself and what belongs to oneself, and to alienate oneself from others. Soon hatred, jealousy, and anger are felt towards other people. One becomes afraid of them as well. So, all the mental poisons can be said to originate from this metaphysically baseless distinction between another and oneself. If, however, through careful meditation, one has been able to develop an attitude that is egoless, then those poisons will not arise. Since one is not aware of a distinction between self and other, one will spontaneously act towards others as if they were [no different than] oneself. Since poisons have not arisen, one's actions spontaneously exhibit compassion and loving kindness.

Concepts of dirty and clean, pure and impure also arise from subjective distinctions. Apart from mental attitudes, objects are neither clean nor dirty — pure or impure. They just are (i.e., in their natural state). To overcome one's experience of reality in terms of subjective distinctions such as pure and impure [which are just mental constructions, or exaggerations], the Vajrayana method substitutes pure and beautiful visualizations for common perceptions and evaluations of objects. These also are in a certain sense mental exaggerations, for in the beginning the practitioner does not really see reality this way. It is a kind of make-believe. But, in a deeper sense, this visualization is the truth. Accustoming oneself to see reality this way, one discovers that it is really the way things are. So, this activity of visualization is a special causal condition that brings about the transformation of consciousness.

Early School practitioners, however, would not agree that all objects of the senses can be transformed. Rather, one must run away from them or ignore them. Shantarakshita argues against them in the following way: Hinayanists would agree, for example, that the body of a young woman could be seen in three different ways– as by a fully ordained monk, a lustful person, and a lion. The monk will just see a useless body, the lustful man will see a desirable sexual object, and the lion will see it as some kind of food. Therefore, three different attitudes can arise from the same object.

It follows that if one's perception of an object can be controlled through visualization, one can control as well the quality of one's perception. All of one's field of perception can become a pure *mandala*. In this way, the conditions of samsara are not continued. Everything, even the virtues, will be transformed. Giving, for example, will not be seen as the bestowal of benefit to another by oneself. Since one is visualizing reality as free of the subject-object distinction, generosity will arise spontaneously, as if giving to oneself, with no thought of benefit or gain– with no clinging. Virtues are thus mingled with emptiness [*sunyata*] — subject, object, and activities [the three spheres] are all mingled with emptiness.

These three spheres are actually eternally pure. Because of the special blessings of visualization and mantra, when one deliberately views these three circles as pure, then eventually one comes to know them as they really are, in their essential purity. This method of visualization takes the form of seeing one's three doors (of body, speech, and mind) as identical to the body, speech, and mind of the Buddha. Thus, every perception and thought is purified and transformed into the ultimate state. This is because one's own mind has been purified. If this has not happened, external things cannot be perceived as pure. For example, a dangerous potion when skillfully combined with mantra can actually benefit the health. Taken in an ordinary way it will cause death. Similarly, through mingling with the Vajrayana techniques of meditation, visualization, and mantra, and other secret Vajrayana techniques, ordinary external objects when enjoyed, will not cause harm. Rather they will be of great benefit. It is said in the *First Glorious Tantra,"Palchog Dangpo"* [*dpal mchog dang po*] that even ignorance, attachment, and anger in this special way do not cause rebirth in the lower realms. Rather, used with equanimity, they become the nectar of immortality, life, and energy. Buddha also mentioned this in the Mahayana sutras, such as the *Heap of Jewels Sutra "Kon Chog Tzog Pa Theg Pa Chen Poi Do Ley"* [*dkon mchog btsogs pa theg pa chen poi mdo la*] where Buddha proclaims to Kasyapa, "O! Kasyapa, in this way the waste, or excrement, of big cities can help the sugar cane and grapes."[14]

Excrement used as fertilizer becomes of special benefit to those fields. Buddha also said that because of their skillful means and wisdom the emotions of the bodhisattvas, like manure, become a cause of development of the crop of enlightenment in the same way as mantra and potion are be used to save someone bitten by snakes. This is true even when the activities of these bodhisattvas appear bad or emotionally obscured. Because they are mingled with skillful means and wisdom, those activities will not lead them from the path of enlightenment into the lower realms. In other Mahayana sutras Buddha also taught this special desire and attachment is a very special and powerful method of attaining enlightenment.

Nagarjuna also said, "O! Great protector, Lord Buddha, you totally subdued or removed all negativities and obscurations, even habitual stains. Yet, through understanding the essence of emotion, you attained from emotion itself supreme potion of *amrita* (true nectar). You never gave up those emotions, but rather used them to gain the realization that leads to enlightenment."

How is it possible for emotion and attachment to result in enlightenment? Because, those [properly transformed and motivated] emotions arouse the compassion of bodhisattvas, creating a bridge between them and all sentient beings. In addition, this pure experience of emotion leads to the realization of the insubstantiality of all phenomena, and thus to the realization of emptiness. This very set of causal conditions is precisely those that are sufficient for bringing about the state of enlightenment. It is not necessary to do anything else, such as ascetic practices of fasting or abstaining from other forms of enjoyment. Rather, mingling one's ordinary activities with skillful means and wisdom will bring about enlightenment.

For this reason, it says in the great Buddha Union tantra [*sangs rgyas nyam sbyor*]: "I myself am the embodiment of all Buddhas, as well as heroes [*dakas*] and heroines [*dakinis*] and other highly realized beings that spring from those Buddhas." When one visualizes oneself in this way, one is able to open the door of realization and accomplish great deeds.

Thus, when the yogi or yogin does this practice with skillful means and wisdom, with bodhicitta and with joy, then he or she can achieve the state of buddhahood. Ascetic practice is just the opposite. If a yogi were to turn to ascetic practice, he or she would be abandoning skillful means, bodhicitta and compassion, and instead be torturing the body of Buddha himself. Instead, therefore, the yogi should seek as much enjoyment as possible, comfortably and conveniently mingling enjoyment with skillful means and wisdom. Whoever does this is the Buddha of the future. His or her next step is enlightenment.

So, the yogi does not have to engage in the activities prescribed in the Kriya Tantra, for example, of taking ritual showers or baths, etc., or adhering to [conventional] moral codes or vows. Nor does one have to undergo hardships involving food restrictions or dressing poorly. This was said in the *Buddha Union Tantra*. For Buddha said that it is the nature of objects of the senses to give us joy, and the joy arising from these objects produces enlightenment. Because enlightenment depends on regular activities, there is no enlightenment without the relative level.

This is because of the three factors involved in every perception, the subject, the organ of perception, and the object. We tend to think of these three as essentially separate, and to concentrate on the object. But, in reality they are inseparable, while the object to which one clings is not a unity, but rather a composite. As one continues to analyze the object into its composite factors, one realizes that the object itself is illusory. This is equally true when we analyze each of its components. Thus, the nature of things is emptiness.

How a Buddhist reacts to these external objects depends on the yana to which he or she belongs. Hinayanists consider objects of the senses to be very bad, and distance themselves and their sense organs from them — push themselves far away. Mahayana sutra agrees that these objects may be obstacles, but can be used to advantage in certain ways. If one uses these objects with skillful means and wisdom, they can actually be helpful. These Buddhists do not totally reject objects, but use them as a path in the development of wisdom.

The Vajrayana view is completely opposite to that of the Early School. Objects are seen as already existing in a perfect enlightened state. One does not have to reject anything whatever. Nothing is an obstacle or a poison — there is nothing that is not beneficial. All things have always been this way, but those without realization, through ignorance, have failed to understand this. Not only is the actual sensation of the object pure, the conceptualization of sense data as object is also completely pure. This is because their nature is emptiness. When one grasps at these objects while failing to recognize their true nature, then problems arise. Seen correctly, there is no exception to this purity.

This understanding of how things are on the absolute level is symbolically depicted in thangkas. The deities, for example, are shown standing on delicate flowers surrounded by fire. On the conventional level this is impossible. So, meditation on these thankas is a technique designed to break down one's ordinary conceptions. Thus, all blissful sensations arising from touch and the joys arising from the six senses are similar to this. This in no way contradicts Buddha's teachings. For Buddha said by a special contact with objects you get a special result. Loving kindness and compassion are the way to enlightenment. But loving kindness and compassion are not only for oneself but for others. So, enlightenment depends on our external relationship to others.

Even though Buddha said that it is not good to be in contact with luxuries or pleasurable objects, he only meant this to be taken literally by certain people living in a particular time and place. As he said, even the interpretation of the two hundred and fifty vows of the Vinaya system depends on one's own motivation. If one's motivation is pure, one will not fall into error if one goes a bit beyond these rules.

But there are those who do not have wisdom or skillful means, lack compassion and the wisdom of perfect equanimity, and fail to understand that external objects are manifestations of their own mind, and think that subject and object are really distinct. If, in addition, such a person clings to objects using them in the ordinary way, failing to recognize their ultimate nature as emptiness, then, for such a person, external objects will be the cause of the continuation of existence in samsara, and a rebirth in lower states of existence. Thus, Buddha Sakyamuni said, "Both monks and nuns as well as ordinary people who cling to objects and to the distinction between subject and object, who understand things only in a conventional way, even if they are well renowned, have no understanding of the true nature. Their understanding is completely blocked." So, when he was in the presence of this kind of person, Buddha Sakyamuni thought it better to teach that they should not have contact with external objects. But, this was a temporary teaching. To protect a small child or baby from a dangerous place, the parent says, "Don't go there– there are tigers and snakes," even if it isn't true, because there is risk for the child. In the same way, Buddha warned these people away from external objects that could be risky for them.

This dualism between what is harmful and what is not harmful is all right for beginning students. Later, however, it should be transcended because it involves discrimination. And the absolute nature has one taste. As is said in the *Guhyasamadra Tantra*, people who reject the ten negative activities and accept the ten virtuous activities are practicing techniques that involve the abandoning of wisdom, since all dualism is contrary to the absolute state.

The early teachings of Buddha, according to the Vairocana tantra, were designed primarily to develop the wisdom [egoless] aspect of the teaching, rather than the skillful means aspect. This was intended to fit the capabilities of the Early School follower student.

More advanced students, who have the realization of ultimate truth, can enjoy objects of the senses night and day without obscuration arising. Because they have the highest realization, they will achieve the highest result. They understand that whether something is virtuous or non-virtuous is not dependent on a characteristic of the external object. It is only a function of one's intention. Actions done because of motivations of attachment or anger are non-virtuous. [Conversely] if one beats someone to save them from doing something that one believes will kill them, one acts virtuously. And someone who gives food or clothing in a friendly way, but really intends to kill the recipient would be acting non-virtuously.

Of course, if one were to perform a very harmful action with a good intention, it would still not be a completely good action. Buddha taught that for an action to be completely good, the intention, the action, and the result must all be good. So, a good intention is a necessary but not sufficient condition for the complete goodness of the action.

Nonetheless, a good intention is sufficient for an action to be virtuous. Nagarjuna taught that virtue depends on the mind. Actions motivated by wisdom, loving-kindness, and nonattachment are always virtuous. Virtuous and non-virtuous are, thus, mental aspects and do not exist in the external world.

The action of a buddha, however, would always be completely virtuous as well as completely good. This is because the perfect wisdom and skillful means inseparably combined in the motivation of a buddha will guarantee that the action and result will also be good.

If the yogi or yogini has the realization of the true nature, has discovered inner wisdom, then all appearances are reflected from the mirror of his or her wisdom. Everything that appears to these yogis or yoginis is a manifestation of this wisdom. All appearances that arise during their post-meditation state, as well as what they do during that time, are blended with their merit and wisdom. When their activities are performed with this wisdom and with mindfulness, then they are able to act without making judgments. Every appearance is seen as a reflection in water. But to see in this way, one needs a clear understanding of relative truth; one should not try to grasp at things or view them in dualistic terms (e.g., subject and object or good and bad). That is termed in certain Vajrayana texts as the "understanding of beings of high realization" of buddhas and high bodhisattvas. For, as the great yogis and yoginis know, objects are always changing. These compounded objects are like lightning in the sky or a magic city. As is said in the *Assembly of All Gods Tantra*, ordinary people do not realize this and allow themselves to be dominated by the appearance of external objects.

But yogis and yoginis do not hold onto even the tiniest atom. For they realize that on the absolute level the nature of everything is emptiness. Because they have joined together wisdom and skillful means, all things are seen as a magical display. When reality is understood in this way, without clinging or attachment, then bliss and happiness arising from the use of objects should be accepted and enjoyed. Since there is no clinging or attachment, there is no reason not to use these objects. For this bliss and happiness actually arise through the results of meditation achieved by means of familiarity with the true nature and through skillful means and wisdom. And wonderful qualities of mind and body result from the enjoyment of this bliss.

The ultimate result of this state is enlightenment. When one's mind and body are transformed, then the illusory level and the absolute level are no longer seen as contradictory. They are both equally in the true nature.

In this state, as is said in the *Supreme Glorious Tantra* [*dpalchog dangpo*] one's own self is known to be an embodiment of the buddhas. One also will realize that one encompasses all the heroes and heroines, thus, one will have no fears about or attachments to samsara. And, because the deities are one with the great blissfulness, one is also one with them. And, all change, all motion, is experienced as dance.

Further, a mind transformed by bliss will be very stable. Because of this, bliss attained through meditation will endure. That is not only because of mental stability, but because this bliss is a result of an understanding of the true nature of reality.

Because of that it is clear that torturing the body cannot lead to enlightenment, as is said in the *Supreme Glorious*, the vajra tantra beyond both samsara and nirvana. Those who perform terrible feats of fasting, jump into fires, or stand before the flames only create troubles for themselves and obstacles to enlightenment. In addition to weakening their bodies, these people of low capabilities, lacking skillful means and wisdom, find that they also become depressed and confused. As is said in the *Guhyasamadra Tantra*, one will never achieve enlightenment in this way. Nor does it help to go about saying mantras while begging and eating bad food. This will lead to a kind of hell. Rather one should maintain one's body and mind in comfort and blissfulness, and enlightenment will be at hand. For, not only is the enjoyment of objects not an obstacle in obtaining enlightenment, it is the very means of attaining it.

Why is this? Because attaining enlightenment is analogous to the learning process in general. At first, one knows little, but knowledge grows through experience. Similarly, at first when we use our five aggregates, we know little about them. But as we learn to use them skillfully and wisely, their true nature becomes apparent. Through contemplation and meditation both internal and external aggregates will be correctly understood. And it will become apparent that their true nature is blissful buddhahood.

According to the Buddhist view, buddha nature is realized through meditation. When objects are enjoyed in the ordinary way, without the view obtained through meditation, this will result in suffering, fear, etc. For this clinging produces disturbed mental states. This suffering and unpleasantness are followed by more unpleasantness. Unpleasant causes bring about unpleasant effects — pleasant causes bring about pleasant effects. One who has developed pure perception will perceive all things as pleasant and will not cling to them. Then, contact with objects will bring about more and more peace and happiness. So, all suffering, unpleasantness and anger will be transformed, leaving only a great blissfulness.

It is clear why there can be no more suffering when this method is followed. Heat and cold, for example, cannot stay together in the same place because they are contradictory. Suffering and happiness are similarly contradictory. They cannot stay together in the same mind. Thus, when the yogi or yogini has perceived the true nature and is always experiencing blissfulness as a result of this view, suffering can never reappear. There is no room for it. This is logically irrefutable.

In the same way, the great blissfulness of the absolute level, which is emptiness, and the relative level cannot be absolutely contradictory. Both these levels must support each other. Just as one achieves results in art and gymnastics through practice, so, by practicing the view [that is, by training oneself to perceive reality purely], we grow in wisdom, in realization.

It is true that in the early stages the absolute and relative levels seem to be contradictory. But as one develops, the apparent contradictions dissolve. For example, when meditators concentrate on perceiving all things as the earth element [there are ten different practices relating to the elements], and get to the point where they really perceive all things as earth, earth radiating in all directions, they are able to maintain that perception as long as they want. And this is an ordinary state. So, those yogis and yoginis who understand the nature of mind and have great clarity and bliss, mingling their minds with emptiness, can certainly maintain their minds permanently like this. For this state, unlike the perception of all things as earth, is a perception of absolute reality.[15]

One cannot return to samsara because the causal conditions for such a return are not present. There are many such processes in life which are irreversible. For example, one will never go back to babyhood. When you learn the alphabet, you will never have to go back and relearn it again. And when you reach the true nature, you will not return to samsara. Ignorance is replaced by wisdom, the habitual tendencies are removed, there is no ego clinging — hence, no causes of samsara. There is a state of complete equanimity, the absolutely open state free from illusions.

One might think that those beings who have achieved great realization still have the causes required to be reborn into samsara because buddhas and bodhisattvas are reborn. But this would be a mistake. They are reborn not because of any causal conditions, but because of their loving kindness and compassion for all. These are emanations rather than ordinary beings. They do not experience illusions, as do those who lack realization. For this reason, as Arya Maitreya explained, they will never experience the suffering of birth, sickness or death. They may appear from the ordinary point of view to be born, to get ill or old, but their experience of these things is totally pleasurable and joyful.

By analogy, one comes to realize that reflected lights of many colors come from a precious quartz crystal that is completely light and clear. Once one realizes this, one can never mistake the reflected color for the reality of the crystal.

Similarly, we have experience of many different things in this world, but when one understands their true nature, one will never mistake the appearance for the reality again. Dharmakirti says that if people are interested in things, they will follow after them in accordance with their nature and desires. This is part of the karmic system, the law of cause and effect. If it were not for cause and effect, one would not know what to expect. Anything could follow from anything else. But this is not the case. Whatever activities one performs in this or previous lifetimes, one will reap that effect. And when the effect is accomplished, then one does not have to go back to a previous state. It is similar to a farmer planting a seed. At first, the farmer plants but only sees empty fields. If he or she did not have faith in the law of cause and effect, he or she would never sow seed. But knowing the system of causal conditions, farmers plant and reap the results. Similarly, this system was explained by Buddha Sakyamuni in the *Prajnaparamita Sutra*. He told Subhuti:

Oh, Subhuti, the great courage of the Bodhisattvas when making offerings to the Buddha, the stupa of Buddha or objects of veneration of the Tathagatas, offering beautiful incense of the goddess, as they offer this incense, they are thinking, praying, dedicating, "Due to the power of this incense that I am offering to the Buddha, the Tathagatas, or the Stupa of the Tathagatas, and by this merit, whenever I get enlightenment, may my pure Buddha land be filled with the comforts and sensations of the god-realm to be experienced by all sentient beings."

They dedicated the merit in this way.

And, moreover, Buddha said to Subhuti,

By merely thinking, by my intention, may I offer all the luxurious objects of the five senses to the Tathagatas and the sanghas of the arhats, Sravakas, and all sentient beings. By understanding the power of this merit, may I obtain supreme enlightenment. And in my pure Buddha land, may all the arhats, may all the sanghas of students and all sentient beings, as a result of that merit, always achieve spontaneously their desires for all the items of luxury, merely by thinking about them.

Again, Buddha told Subhuti,

If you are merely thinking that the five types of luxuries are being offered to all the sentient beings, and Buddhas, and sanghas of arhats, this is also meditation power. If one has this bodhisattva thought when doing one's practice, and one dedicates the merit strongly for all sentient beings, then when one reaches the pure land, all these luxuries will actually exist because of this dedication, merit and thought.

Again, in the *Prajnaparamita Sutra* and other Mahayana teachings, there are other special cases of cause and effect described such as the thirty-two major marks and eighty minor marks of Buddha. Each of them has a special cause that developed when these buddhas were bodhisattvas. For our inner habitual tendencies, our powers of mind can also have special effects, transforming the external world.

For example, if you plant the seed of the *ja chik* (*rgya sgyeg*) tree that has been mixed with the seed of the matulunga, later on the plant will have the color of matulunga and its fruit will be sweet. Similarly if the mind mixes its ordinary experiences with positive, neutral or negative attitudes, it will become more and more uniform in its point of view. If its attitude is always positive, it will become happy in a stable way and vice versa. Again, if the cottonseed etc. is mixed with special ingredients, then the results will be a bit different. Our minds are like this. For when a mind that has experienced the bodily comfort and mental pleasure of the great blissfulness is in contact with objects, the result will be special, a higher, different result than usual. One will get more and more comfort and pleasure because this special way of experiencing objects rules out anything else. There will be no clinging or attachment, so, no suffering. No suffering will be present in this meditation. As Buddha said, if suffering arises, one should stop it immediately with the great bliss or happiness arising from meditation. One should, thus, maintain one's mind in that blissful state. Because the nature of suffering has been understood, one will be able to transform it in such a way that it will never be experienced again as an ordinary state of suffering.[16] For it is said in the *Assembly of All Gods Tantra* that godesses, asuras, and demons have no real existence– they are just thoughts. Suffering, too, is like this. In this way, sentient beings through the blissful experience of external objects will permanently remain in the state of enlightenment. For the fire of nirvana burns all one's habitual obscurations, not leaving even their dust or ashes. This is the result of the realization of the true nature.

What is the nature of this realization? It has no organs or aggregate — no definite form whatever. There are no six internal or six external dhatus– none of the six consciousnesses, eight principal minds or fifty–two minor minds. The seven types of pride or arrogance are not present — no sentient beings, no wisdom, no perfect view, nothing that has to do with the nature of mind. This state is similar to that of deep sleep. There is nothing in it at all, for there is no duality and no conceptions. So, there is no idea of "I" or "mine"– no dualistic conception of good or evil, no virtuous or non virtuous actions. There are no qualities of anything at all. This great nature which is like the open sky is nirvana — existing purely and selflessly from time without beginning. Liberation depends on understanding this clearly. This correct understanding is that samsara is nirvana for in the true nature they are one and the same. They do not contradict each other but exist equally in one state.

To understand nirvana, it is also necessary to neither desire nirvana nor fear samsara. For one is really in nirvana. It is like being asleep and having a nightmare. When you wake up, the nightmares disappear and you are in a safe situation. Similarly when you wake up from the nightmare of samsara, you find you have always been in nirvana perfectly free from all troubles.

The essential point is the realization that all things are insubstantial. To realize that, is to realize the true nature. While one is in samsara, one must use joyful effort in order to wake up in nirvana. But once one reaches the highest state, no further force or effort is needed. All one's thoughts and activities will flow spontaneously in the direction of nirvana. Making an effort involves making a distinction between what is the case and what one wants to be the case. And one clings to what one wants to be the case. So, when one has reached the highest state, there will be no distinctions and no effort. Yet in the beginning, yogis and yoginis must expect to make an effort. If they do not, and instead expect an immediate result, this will create obscurations in their practice. Yet just before enlightenment their efforts should cease. Nor should they be attached to their own bodies. Just as samsara and nirvana are equal, so one's physical body is also the body of the Buddha — one's mind, the mind of the Buddha. So, in achieving enlightenment, one must not think one is getting something new, something that does not already exist in our nature. No new buddha is created by the realization of great blissfulness, emptiness. This is why long ascetic practice is unnecessary.

It is essential, however, to prevent hope and fear from entering one's meditation. This clinging and grasping creates an obscured view, not the perfect view that is a fresh and open state, like the sky.

All yogis and yoginis that have achieved realization of the true nature are permitted to enjoy anything whatever — all the pleasures associated with the five types of luxuries and the five sense organs. These will never be obstacles to their realization because they are free from clinging and grasping. This is, of course, only true for these people of high capabilities who have, through an unbroken transmission, received teachings from Buddha Samantabhadra. These have been passed from master to master like nectar.

There is, however, a warning contained in *The Tantra Which Destroys All Thought* (*rtog pa 'dul wa*). Those who do not have the proper techniques needed for the practice of Vajrayana and whose minds are obscured by ignorant habits, who try to practice Vajrayana just to get something they want, will never reach enlightenment. Their false views will destroy them. They are just out for selfish purposes and to satisfy their vanity. So, they are wasting their time.

For according to the Vajrayana point of view, everything one perceives is the *mandala* of the male and female buddhas — of pure perception. This perception dissolves grasping and clinging and makes it possible to reach bliss — emptiness — enlightenment through one's own body, speech and mind. This is made possible by the favorable karmic connections of the yogi and yoginis and their perfect view. Through this, luxuries become the path of enlightenment.

When, for example, mercury is touched with fire, it does not burn and there is no smoke. It will, however, immediately return to its previous state. Similarly, the yogi or yogini, even if they are enjoying the luxuries of the external world, will always remain in the wisdom of the *mahamudra*, applying this wisdom to all of the external world. Through this understanding, even if the activities of the yogi and yogini may seem a little strange, they are never straying from the perfect view and the path of enlightenment.

All these quotations from the tantras are used by Shantarakshita to show that if one has skillful means and wisdom, one can perform any activity that brings pleasure and bliss. Not only will this not disturb one's realization, but it will bring about the ultimate blissfulness of emptiness and the transcendental blissfulness of the wisdom body.

The logic of this process leads to the conclusion that the result, enlightenment, is irreversible. Why is this? Because it is the nature of enlightenment to bring perfect pleasure to mind and body. As this comfort and blissfulness develop, the mind is totally satisfied. When ultimate bliss is reached, the mind stays in that state and will never depart from it. One's mind is totally mingled with the true nature and will never go back to a state of illusion. This process of attaining ultimate blissfulness is described in the tantra *The Basic Ground of Great Blissfulness of Mahamudra* [where it is called the Madhyamaka view of the path].

There are, for example, two types of natural processes. Some are reversible. For example, if one puts gold in the fire, it will melt, but if cooled, will return to its former state. But if wood is burned to ashes, it will never be wood again. The difference is in the nature of the objects involved in these processes. Mind is the type of thing that is subject to habit and desire. When mind becomes used to experiencing the great bliss, and when it finds total comfort and satisfaction in that, it will stay in that state and not change. This bliss has become part of the nature of one's mind. Brahmins, for example, are constantly concerned with matters of purity. But if a Brahmin trains his mind not to see the difference between purity and impurity, clean and unclean, such differences will cease to exist for him. Other Brahmins can become arrogant and uncompassionate if they habitually think of themselves as great practitioners and models of good conduct and think that other people are low and useless. If they persist in these attitudes, after awhile, they will not change. Similarly, those yogis and yoginis that have a perfect view will know the true nature indubitably by direct perception of one's own awareness, through self-knowledge. Their minds will always stay in perfect bliss and comfort. For suffering is illusory. It is not the true nature.

So in order to be free of suffering, one must remove its cause or root. One must cling to the seed of enlightenment and avoid the seed of suffering as one would avoid thorns or poisonous snakes. This avoidance of suffering, as has been shown, is achieved through meditation. This produces the great bliss, the perfect method for transforming suffering. This reasoning is perfectly clear. It is neither incomplete, nor uncertain, nor misleading.

Buddha Sakyamuni said when one meditates on what is disgusting as an antidote for attachment, or on loving kindness as an antidote for anger, on the system of interdependent co-origination as an antidote for ignorance, obscurations will be completely cleared away. Attachments similarly will be removed by detachment. But this method of removing obscurations was only for people of low capabilities, for beginning practitioners. By contrast, Buddha said in the *Guhyasamadra Tantra* that practitioners of high capabilities can remove desire through the use of desire itself. Desire is said in this tantra to be the purest wisdom of all the buddhas. Here it is also said that the great yogis who know both attachment and detachment will develop the great blissfulness that is totally free from both attachment and detachment, because from the absolute point of view, desires, attachments, etc., are not natural obscurations. If they were obscurations by nature, then the first stage of realization of the Sravaka, as well as the other realizations of the early schools, could not be attained, because one still has desire before attaining them. The early stage of realization cannot be achieved without desire. So, desire and attachment cannot be by nature obscurations, for if they were, they would prevent these realizations from being attained.

Another example of the relativity of desire as a virtue or obscuration is the teaching of Buddha Sakyamuni in a chapter on discipline. There, he states that the great bodhisattvas cannot be harmed by violating the ten virtuous actions. If a bodhisattva sleeps with a woman to prevent her from taking her life, since his motivation is to protect her, he will not be harmed by this action. This is true for both men and women. Further, if a bodhisattva takes the life of someone he or she knows will hurt millions of people, no obscurations will be created. The bodhisattva will not sink into the lower realms but will rather earn merit, because his or her action resulted in great peace and harmony for these millions of people. This could not happen if the performance of these activities, contrary to the ten virtuous actions, was negative in their very nature. Of course, the bodhisattvas, in order to be able to do these things must have the realization of emptiness and the true nature.

For different people, engaging in the same activities will produce different results. The ketak flower, for example, if eaten by the incense elephant *pokyi langpo (sposkyi glangpo)*, when it is digested will become like musk. But if eaten by an ordinary elephant, it will become dirty — ordinary excrement. The difference is not due to the flower, but to the difference in elephants. Similarly, when milk is drunk by a poisonous snake, the snake's poison increases, but the same milk will make a person healthy. Likewise, when people with an understanding of the true nature act in accordance with their desires, there will be a special result, for in the case of beings of high realization, desire is mingled with their realization. And when emotions are experienced by these beings, these too will bring a special result. If causal conditions are not combined with anything special, they produce the same effect. White lotuses will produce white lotuses. But if they are combined with special conditions, the results will be special, as when a doctor gives an aging patient a special substance to produce youthfulness. Copper, for example, combined with mercury, will produce new forms. Otherwise, the mercury will never change.

Acharya Shantideva taught that the method of using *ser gyur tsi* (*gser gyur tsi*) a special kind of mercury said to transform other substances into gold, is like the way an obscured body can be transformed into a priceless victorious body. The virtuous actions relax the body and the realization of the true nature relaxes the mind. This brings wisdom unobscured by the three poisons, that will destroy attachment and detachment and bring the ultimate great blissfulness. One's wishes will then be fulfilled until the end of samsara. And the activities that benefit all sentient beings will flow spontaneously, as part of the activities of Buddha. This is called "extracting the essence of bodhicitta because you are simultaneously benefiting yourself and others." This bodhicitta, it is easy to see, can transform all activities into the path of enlightenment.

So, one can neither achieve enlightenment by rejecting the emotions nor by using them in the ordinary way. Buddha transformed emotions "as a piece of cotton," for his emotions have the nature of enlightenment. Although through natural reasoning, it has been clearly demonstrated that a cause combined with special conditions will bring about a special effect, it has not been shown how such a process could bring about the state of enlightenment. There is a special problem here. Is the enlightenment that is gained a result of mingling meditation with a dualistic or non-dualistic state? How would a non-dualistic state arise? Even to want or think about such a thing involves dualistic thinking. The result cannot be completely different from the cause, so if all the causal conditions are dualistic, how can the result be non-dualistic?

Further, how could one show that the removal of habitual tendencies and emotions is sufficient to bring about enlightenment? How could the removal of these result in a state that is completely unrelated to any natural process? And how could such a thing be proved? For there are only two methods of proof — direct perception and inference. And it is clear upon analysis of both methods that neither can be used as a proof that enlightenment will result.

Direct perception can be divided into four types: Sense perception, mental perception, self perception and yogic perception. The first is perception through sense organs, the second, mental perception of a moment of sense perception, the third is reflexive perception that accompanies all perceptions, and the fourth, yogic perception, is the supra-mundane perception of a realized yogi through meditative concentration. None of these four types of perception are capable of realizing the omniscient state of enlightenment.

Nor can the existence of the omniscient state of enlightenment be demonstrated through logical inference.

1. Result reasoning: Every event has a cause, and every cause has an effect. When we see an oak tree, we can infer that an acorn must have germinated in that spot. Similarly, when we see smoke on a mountain, we can infer that a burning is there, or was there in the recent past. If the state of enlightenment were an event, it would necessarily have a cause. But what could such a cause be? There is no duality in enlightenment, so, how could it come about from one cause or several causes

as distinct from other causes? Further, from the absolute point of view, all causal processes are empty. All thoughts are insubstantial — they are not the true nature. So, how could insubstantial states permeated by thoughts bring about enlightenment, which is the true nature? How can the omniscient state come from dualistic thinking based on illusion? Since the cause of enlightenment must be emotional and conceptual processes, how could you prove the result, the omniscient state, is different from these? Yet one knows it must be.

Something cannot come from nothing. Yet there is nothing in samsara that has the necessary components to produce enlightenment. Further, the causal process is characterized by constant change. If there were no change, then the process would be blocked. This is true even if it were to happen for a moment. No result can occur if a cause becomes permanent, because the causal process is one of constant transformation. If a cause did not change, it would be like a sky flower that brings no real result. As the great masters have said, if the seed does not change, it cannot produce a result.

Yet the causal process itself when analyzed can be shown to be insubstantial. It is just like a magical display or an illusion. This is the nature of dependent co-origination — a nature first clearly described and understood by Buddha. So, it is not the case that this world came from nothing. Nor is it the case that it came from a permanently existing creator. Because all causality only exists relatively, the teachings based on causality are only skillful means designed for the liberation of sentient beings. Causality does not exist in the absolute state. This is the perfect knowledge of cause and effect, which only Buddha understood and taught to those of high capabilities. For these reasons, one cannot show that enlightenment derives from cause and effect.

2. Invisible reasoning: This is reasoning of the following type. The object in question is the sort of thing that would be perceived if it were present. Invisible or unobservable [or negative] reasoning: An example of invisible reasoning is as follows: If there were a golden vase on a table right in front of a person [the lights being on, etc.], he or she would be able to see it, for it is the kind of thing that can be seen. The vase cannot be seen. Therefore, one may conclude that it is not there. But enlightenment, the omniscient state, is not the kind of thing that can be seen. So, its absence cannot be proved by invisible reasoning. Since the non-conceptual is not perceptible, it can neither be proved nor disproved by invisible reasoning.

3. Natural reasoning (from the nature of a thing): An example of natural reasoning would be as follows: The nature of fire is opposed to water. So, if one observes fire, one can conclude that there is no water contained in the fire. But we cannot conceive of the nature of enlightenment. Thus, we cannot conclude that it is either contradictory in nature to thought process or not contradictory in nature. So, we cannot conclude either that it comes about with thought or without thought. So, we cannot argue from the nature of thought processes or their absence that enlightenment must follow. So, natural reasoning will not work either.

In summary, the analysis of the relation between the relative and the absolute has been analyzed by Nagarjuna and others in the following way. (a) Objects cannot cause themselves. If this were the case, the effect would be contained in the cause, and then one could not account for change. But if the effect does not exist in the cause, where could it come from? Something cannot come into existence from what is not there. Everything would be blocked. (b) Nor can an effect come from something distinct from itself, because then any effect could come from any cause and everything would be completely mixed up. (c) Nor can an effect develop from a combination of what exists and what does not exist, for these two things are totally contradictory and cannot be combined. By summary, since one cannot show, in general, how an effect comes from a cause, one cannot show that enlightenment can come from either a conceptual state or a thoughtless state.

Is there any way, then, to verify that the omniscient state is possible? There is, because the true nature of causality, the system of interdependent co-origination, is emptiness. Everything in the causal system depends on everything else. But none of the parts have intrinsic existence. This is why causality and emptiness are completely mingled in one state. But the ultimate nature of this state is beyond conception, for our ordinary minds can only think dualistically. Thought involves distinctions. And thought is involved specifically in the subject-object distinction. This is true of the thinking which gives rise to the three realms.

To understand and realize the state of enlightenment, something special is needed. Ordinary thought processes must stop, and the mind must be mingled with emptiness. Meditating in a non-conceptual, non-imaginative, non-dualistic way is the means of mingling with emptiness. As the great blissfulness and equanimity is developed in this way [through skillful means and wisdom] one will gain a special mental power. This is similar to the state of enlightenment, but is not exactly the same. At this point, one has the perfect understanding of the relative, for one is free of all defilements. As Buddha Sakyamuni said in *The Lankavatara Sutra*, if the eye has no defects, one will see clearly. The noble ones or realized masters never fall victim to illusions. All is pure. All faults are transformed into perfections. One no longer judges in terms of good or evil.

The *samatha* state taught in the Mahayana is one in which there are no eight states of liberation, no perceptions, no objects of the five senses. This state is the vehicle that carries one to enlightenment. This happens because this state produces a special meditation body or power of meditation, which Buddha described as decorated by the different powers. Special causes bring about special results. And the result of this state, since the state is non-conceptual, will bring about a result that is also without conception. This is the wisdom of enlightenment. In ordinary life, people are constantly making distinctions, such as, this is a cup, this is a vase, etc., and thinking in terms of gender, names, caste. But these distinctions do not exist on the absolute level. The wisdom of enlightenment is free from this. As Dharmakirti taught, realization never exists together with imagination. Therefore, realized beings, knowing the nature of external objects, will not grasp at them or cling to them. This realization which is based on egolessness and nondualistic awareness can only be gained through practice. Then little by little one gains the ultimate state.

How does this happen? If one persists in experiencing desire, suffering and fear, the mind will become more and more deeply rooted in that. These negative experiences are a result of dualistic-conceptual thinking. But if one turns from them and develops the wisdom mind, the mind will instead become deeply rooted in wisdom. And the mind, free from illusion, will have the power to see things as they really are.

Meditation, in accordance with the pith instructions, leads the yogi or yogini further and further along the path. Logical analysis is forced to come to an end, and relative emptiness is realized. But the ending of concepts leads only to relative emptiness. As one is led further into meditation, the meditation also must end. And this is the attainment of absolute emptiness.

But how do we know that the enlightened state of buddhahood is not nothing? Buddha's knowledge can be understood by analogy with our knowledge of the atom. When we analyze the parts of the atom, we know their nature to be emptiness. We know, nonetheless, the tables and chairs that the atoms compose. Similarly, the mind of the Buddha, though totally one with emptiness, totally non-conceptual and non-dualistic, nevertheless, knows all relative truth. So, in order to understand the relative perfectly, it is necessary to first mingle one's mind with the absolute state, enlightenment.

So, as one practices more and more, even though one starts with thoughts, one's mind will be transformed into a thoughtless state. One will understand everything. Nothing will be spoiled or wasted, this is what is meant by the phrase "eaten by jackals." Briefly and simply, a great equanimity state or emptiness state exists free from all notions and thoughts. If one wants to know perfectly and totally the nature of that state of thoughtlessness, one has to give up thought. For with thought, we cannot understand fully the nature of that state. We know this through an analysis of the inadequacies of inference and perception. But states of thought can only be transformed into the state without thought through familiarity with meditation and through the proper instructions, i.e., pith instructions. When one reaches that ultimate state through the experience or familiarization of meditation, at that time, one will understand all objects of knowledge. One will be transformed into what one is learning. So, when people practice non-conceptual meditation and practice, and become very expert reaching the ultimate state, all of the three realms become their objects conducive to happiness.

So, in all of samsara, there is nothing to accept and nothing to reject. All are the luxurious objects of Buddha Sambhogakaya. This can be understood by natural reason. Because of this, the Buddha Union Tantra says that all yogis and yoginis are the Buddha, Bhagavans, the Vajrasattva, the Thus Gone Buddha, and the Tathagatas. Everything in the three realms is transformed into Buddha Sambhogakaya forms. So, there is nothing to accept or reject. All is in the equanimity state. And *The Assembly of All the Gods Tantra* says that, if the yogi or yogini has a perfectly purified mind, and has an understanding of equanimity, then the four elements, fire, water, earth and wind, whatever exists, including all the sentient beings, are the proper objects for these yogis to use. For they are maintaining the great blissfulness of the mahamudra and mingling their minds with the true nature again and again. Everything is then transformed into the great equanimity. Everything is one's own mind— there is no distinction of subject and object, and there is perfect understanding of the true nature of phenomena, as their minds maintain the meditation

and the state of great bliss.
Again, in the *Buddha Union Tantra* (it is said):

Whatever comes by way of the different organs, eye, ear or tongue, enjoy these as they come, without having the notion of maintaining the true nature state or not maintaining the true nature state, with that understanding all will be brought into the great union with Buddha. This is the great union with Buddha.

Again from the tantra *All Condensed Thought* it is said, "in brief, what is really Buddha? All the five items of luxury are the buddhas." That means one has to achieve enlightenment with the five luxuries, without giving any of them up. And then, the Buddha Samantabhadra Tantra says that all forms, sounds, etc., are buddhas. Therefore, never accept or reject what one perceives but rather with skillful means, perceive all in a state of equanimity. With that meditation and understanding, every phenomenon has become part of one's practice, so one does not have to give up anything. Therefore, this wisdom with realization will certainly develop from the power of meditation, as reason shows. This is the source of all the good qualities. If you meditate like this, all ordinary and supreme accomplishments will be achieved. By this result, you will perform many different benefits for all sentient beings.

This benefit will continue as long as samsara exists. It will work for the good of sentient beings. Thus, those who seek enlightenment should with joyful effort, give up all pride and ego-clinging and understand the great blissfulness combined with wisdom and skillful means. For this wisdom and skillful means is the supreme understanding which will lead to enlightenment and the nature of all phenomena. This is the power of the realization of great blissful emptiness. This was composed by the great Acharya Shantarakshita. It is a Vajrayana text of the attainment of suchness, which shows how if one has the great blissfulness mingled with skillful means and wisdom, one is going to attain enlightenment very quickly and directly. And there is no need to give up luxuries if one mingles these with skillful means and wisdom. This method is here explained to the disciples by means of true reasoning in this section composed by Shantarakshita.

TATTVASIDDHI

the attainment of suchness

by

SHANTARAKSHITA

DERGEY EDITION: SUTRA KA

The Attainment of Suchness by Scholar Shantarakshita, translated, proofread and published by the Indian scholar Atisha, and the monk Rinchen Zangpo. Later, by request, the section on logic was proofread and edited by the scholar Kumarakalasha (*'bro dge slong shakya'od*).

THE TRANSLATION COMMITTEE

Khenchen Palden Sherab Rinpoche
Khenpo Tsewang Dongyal Rinpoche
Marie-Louise Friquegnon & Arthur Mandelbaum
in collaboration with Geshe Lozang Jamspal

Translation of the *Madhyamakalankara* into Sanskrit
by Geshe Lobzong Jamspal

SHANTARAKSHITA

Folio 52 (Asian Classics Input Project #26B)

In the language of India, this is called the *Tattvasiddhi* treatise. In the language of Tibet, *De kho na nyid grub pa*. To noble, youthful Manjusri, I pay homage. Having bowed down to the source of happiness and great bliss, the Vajrayana, I will explain the attainment of suchness, in order to avert all ignorance. There are those whose habitual tendencies have caused them to be disconnected from the great bliss of the Vajrayana. These people are accustomed to phenomena created by exaggerated mental constructions due solely to habits of mind. Their minds are robbed by the wind of thought construction [*rtog pa*]. Through quarreling, stirring up the muddy swamp of degenerate times, their minds become without exception stained by this. Such people do not possess the truly skillful means to cross over the ocean of samsara.

Because of following artificial conventional thinking, their wisdom is polluted, and their impoverished minds fall into a thorny mountain ravine. Through the very hidden power of the demon of thought construction [*rtog pa*] the mind becomes completely disturbed. Those in such a state do not rely closely on teachers. They do not have the pith instructions on how to meditate in the correct way and as they travel along the path, will take innumerable kalpas to realize Vajrasattva's glorious great bliss.

Those who possess the skillful means of the Vajrayana can accomplish the practice without difficulty in this lifetime through the objects of sensation. From the beginningless past and into the endless future, all things either animate or inanimate have no inherent existence. Nevertheless, all sentient beings naturally have the characteristics of consciousness and self-awareness, possess great merit and the means to realize enlightenment. In order to dispel the fog of cataracts from all those who do not know how to realize that holy of holies, the Vajrayana, I offer this brief clear account, consisting both of the words of the Buddha and correct reasoning. In general, the method consists in combining [the experience of] objects of the senses, forms etc. with wisdom and skillful means, enjoying things in the proper way, obtaining a special result, and thus achieving realization.

Folio 53 (#27A)

The sage should certainly recognize this. Because of the special accumulation (of causes and conditions), a special result will arise. This has been taught by the most renowned scholars. For example, the *churura* is a fruit that is astringent but when [the seed] is soaked in milk and planted in soil or in a pot, thus combined with other causes, it will definitely produce a plant with sweet fruit. In this way, combining special causes will bring about a special result, and one can know this through direct perception. In a similar way, the yogi generates the great mudra from the forms of objects. As to the blessings of mantra and mudra, a very special result will arise. Thus holy beings understand that in this way.

Nothing arises through a single cause, but rather from a confluence of several causes. For this reason, why would there be a single thing which cannot be enjoyed? From special causes, a special effect arises. [For example], the causes and conditions of omniscience [buddhahood] cannot be understood by the mind. But by a special combination of causes, a special result is obtained. Just as in the case of the *churura* [*skyurura*] seed soaked in milk producing sweet fruit, then forms, etc., through special causes, also could clearly produce this [special result of omniscience]. Other than through these special causes, how could this be attained?

If one begins by analyzing clearly through reason how one knows with certainty how special causes produce effects, then, in this way, one will be able to show how special causes, when combined with desires and made to encompass them, will pervade desire with the intrinsic nature of reality.

In this way, having that other special cause [non-attachment and non-dualistic experience], clearly when brought together [with other causes and conditions] in a similar way to the *churura* example, there will be no cause for obstacles. By these other special causes brought together in combination, a special result arises, since none of the particular [necessary] causes were impeded or incomplete.

Folio 54 (#27B)

Thus, only that [particular result] will follow. In order to obtain certainty about pervading and pervasive, you must examine the nature of the result. If pervasion is established for certain, then [the conclusion] is certainly correct. Similarly, it is stated in *The Circle of the Concealed Moon Drop* that[17]:

Through a mind with wisdom and method, how could this not be done? By always being without doubt, one will gain the power to use the five senses in special ways to perform all kinds of activities.

This is similar to the way various kinds of medicines can be combined in order to [produce a potion that will] catch snakes. [The snakes smell the medicine and become intoxicated.]

Thus, continually, without satiation [yogis and yoginis can unite] the lust of passionate attachment with the enjoying of song and music and are never satiated with these desirable objects. One who can accomplish this without any hesitation, will succeed (enlightenment). One with stable *bodhicitta* and no hesitation will change these attachments into passionless wisdom. In this way, knowing the essence and relying on evidence, such a person will certainly accomplish enlightenment. Thus, it has been said:

The sage, having analyzed this view in detail, must proceed with a very skillful mind. Otherwise, it is sixteen times worse than entering into fire. If one has the wisdom mind, and relies on the goddess, one will achieve realization. Otherwise, one will fall into the hell realms. This has been said.

Otherwise [the five objects of the senses– *gzugs la stsogs pai yul*] forms, etc., will be the cause of obscurations which will prevent practitioners from realizing how not to be reborn in the lower realms.

Although it is true that forms [and other objects of the senses] are the causes of obscurations, it is not possible to show [as some have claimed] that forms are sufficient to cause rebirth in the lower realms. Why is this so? It is because misery [*nyon mongs pa*] is a direct result of the ego and the ego's attachments and desire for possessions. Therefore forms, etc., are not the cause. The [root cause] is really the distinction [between self and others], because when there is consciousness of self, there will be consciousness of others. From this distinction comes all attachment and anger. From dualistic [thinking], that relates to all [the other poisons], all flaws arise.

Folio 55 (#28A)

Thus, whoever thinks that the self actually exists, will experience every kind of misery. But, whoever is very practiced in the realization of egolessness, will never taste such ills. If the objects themselves were the causes of all desires, then how could the same object produce a contradictory reaction of purity or impurity in different people? These erroneous judgments are due to the power of what is familiar [*sgro btags pa nyid*].

How could this produce knowledge? Only exaggerated knowledge is being generated. Since through exaggeration certain causes are considered to produce certain effects, why not accept that through the transformation of particular causes there will be a special result through this cause of [the realization of] reality*. For example, three persons (lit. three subjects) will see the body of a dead young woman in different way. The renunciate will see it as repulsive, the ordinary person as lovely, the dog, as food. In that way, three different types of thought construction [arise]. Different beings have different conceptions.

So, if one completely transforms one's thought constructions in a special way, they will not necessarily become the cause of bondage in samsara. If one no longer clings to the three spheres, giver, giving, and [recipient] [subject, action, and object], not perceiving in this way, one will be completely purified. For that reason, the threefold spheres, by this complete cause will all be transformed into mantra and mudra. Because of this thorough transformation of samsara, by mantra, etc., and other objects of the senses [*gzugs la stsogs pai yul*], one will only generate unsurpassable results, i.e., liberation.

When one purifies poisons etc. through the alchemy of mantra and mudra, one produces a special result. Otherwise for the foolish one [poison] would mean death. Similarly, objects blessed by mantra and mudra gene-rate a very special result. One should understand this with certainty. It is also said in the *First Glorious Tantra* that the poisons of attachment, anger and ignorance can be transformed.

Someone relying on this most excellent practice, transforming the three poisons of attachment, anger, and ignorance, will be able to keep the mind in equanimity.

*"To view the five aggregates as the five Dhyana Buddhas is not really to exaggerate, but rather to utilize a cause that can bring about the realization of reality," to quote Khenpo Tsewang Dongyal Rinpoche

Folio 56 (28B)

Relying on this practice for the purpose of obtaining nectar,
we can turn these very poisons into nectar.

So it was said in the *Ratnakuta Sutra* (*Three Precious Stacks Sutra*).

For example, Buddha said:

Kasyapa, the manure of the big cities if used by the farmer will be put to good use in the sugar cane and grape fields.

So it is said.

And thus, Kasyapa, similarly the Bodhisattva, uses the manure of his defilements to produce benefits leading to omniscience.

Buddha also said:

Oh Kasyapa, people protected by mantra and medicine, even when they take poison, will not die. So similarly, those bodhisattvas, protected by wisdom and skillful means, will completely terminate the poison of emotions and will not fall down.

Also the great Lord teacher, Nagarjuna, said:

Oh Protector [Buddha], you gave up defilements as well as habitual tendencies entirely. You achieved nectar through the nature of defilements.

Thus, it is said in the Question of Upali:

The Bodhisattva's desires, through his great purpose, benefit sentient beings, because his desires make him affectionate to them. So it was said.

Different results appear through the combination of different [causes]. [Thus, the cause] of realization of the non-substantial nature [*bdag med*] of phenomena will result in a person never being burdened with attachments. There is no other way to gain the fruition of great bliss. Because of this path of nourishment and activity, etc., it is clear that one can achieve perfect bliss. Because would not one agree that similar things transform into what is similar? How could [things] arise from other than what is similar?

Thus *Samvara Tantra* says that:

The Buddhas, as well as myself, are all heroes. Therefore, I should practice uniting myself with the supreme deities. The yogi cannot achieve enlightenment through reflections or imitations.

Folio 57 (#29A)

Striving diligently for bodhicitta, the yogi will become a deity through complete self-abandonment, and not through the torments of asceticism. Only by experiencing bliss can you capture bliss. This (yogi) is the future Buddha.

This is not attained by unnecessary oaths and vows, nor is doing difficult ascetic practices necessary, nor ascetic vows. One will not succeed through ascetic practices, but rather one will gain bliss through enjoyment.

Buddha said that because of forms, etc., this completely transformed bliss arises. It is said that in a like manner the cause of the supreme bliss arises from this perfectly transformed touching. And this will bring forth its own result. You may think this contradicts the precepts, and cannot be accepted. But that is not so, for having this special touching [is harmonious with] the precepts, because through it one obtains a [special] result.

To those who argue that Buddha has prohibited this, one must reply that there is no problem because the object is only a hindrance to those who Buddha taught can not transform this [touching], as they lack skillful means and wisdom. Because having really attained the result of transformation through the special teaching about touching in the scriptures, how would this contradict the scriptures? Because of this, one might say that the body is an obstruction, but since one has completely attained the result of the special teaching of the scriptures, they [activities of the body] are transformed.

How would this be a contradiction? Because of this, the body is not an obstruction. The object [body] is only a hindrance to those who lacking skillful means and wisdom are completely clinging to desire. They do not know the teachings about total grasping and they cling to ego. They do not know at all the teachings about how to bring about this transformation of this special touching. Such people grasp completely without understanding this special kind of contact– touching objects. Thus, objects having been [grasped in this way] may lead to rebirths in the lower realms. Buddha also said:

To a fully ordained monk who is still clinging to phenomena, or one who clings to old traditions, or an intellectual, one should not show how to make contact with the true nature. Buddha considered it an obstacle for them. [*From the Guhyasamadra*]

The path of the ten virtuous actions is for those that give up non-dual wisdom. One should have the wisdom to accept desires. So it has been said.

This is said also in the *Vairocana Tantra*:

Buddha, the great hero, in order to help the Sravakas, when explaining the teachings, taught wisdom without skillful means when teaching the precepts. But by totally combining wisdom and skillful means,

Folio 58 (#29B)

through diligently searching in this way, through this very special result, one will completely experience the dharma of absolute truth [*don dam pai chos kyi de*] (*dharmadhatu*).

Achieving this absolute realization of reality [*go na nyid*], one will not share in even the smallest fault.

Thus, by thinking about this in a special way, one will gain this unsurpassable result, because one does not have a polluted mind. Through this special mind one will not distinguish between doing what is meritorious and what is non-meritorious, since that distinction does not actually exist in the object.

Aryadeva said that:

The meditation of the bodhisattva will by the power of all his thoughts [kun rtog] transform all virtue and non-virtue into virtue. Thus it was explained.

Therefore, you should think that all is virtue, whether meritorious or non-meritorious. Because these [thoughts] are tamed by mind, then, because of this special cause, mind will attain a special result since the meri-torious and non-meritorious are a result of thought. So, if there is a specially motivated thought, through employing forms, sounds, etc., then one will certainly obtain a result that is special and definitely different. One would not wish to assert otherwise. This is why the Buddha said that:

If one has faith that everything is like a magical display, for those endowed with faith, everything can be properly enjoyed. They are wrong, however, who claim that those monks who are without faith, who are unworthy to receive alms (because not able to use them correctly, as with this practice) are worthy of enjoying this. (from *Samvara Tantra.*)

All phenomena have the nature of the sky. Yet, the sky has no characteristics.

In the three realms without exception, all is like a magical display. Like magic, it can be seen and touched, yet it cannot be veridically perceived. In this manner, not having conceptions, the yogi through the practice of mudra, is able to purify all three realms by this special mind. Thus it is said in the *Assembly of All Gods Tantra* that:

In this way, one is completely perfected by this union. Otherwise, the foolish are bound by that with which the enlightened one is playing.

Folio 59 (#30A)

And it is like a [mere picture of a] lamp. And it was also said to practice the secret way to emancipation, by enjoying objects non-conceptually. Otherwise one becomes careless. Through this, all aspects, continually, are beyond conception. The mind in meditation without conception is without doubt [or hesitation]. In all aspects, all the time, a mind that is without doubt can enter into all activities, and will not become bound by them. If one engages in all these enjoyments, the heroic mind will not be bound. With a mind free of concepts, one can practice enjoyments without exception. By practicing all the enjoyments of the senses, remaining in this mental state one will not become bound. All these forms are completely empty. Through the aspect of empty eyes, the holy ones, who have no doubt, will see them non-conceptually.

And it was also said that this engagement is completely empty. And through the aspect of the eye of emptiness, objects are similarly seen non-conceptually, pure, without conception.

All is like the sky [empty space]. Mind is also like the sky [empty space]. By relying on non-conception, freedom from doubt arises.

And it was also said that since all dharmas have a sky-like intrinsic nature of space, the mind is also like the sky. If one asks, what is the yogi's asceticism? The answer is, to engage in all activities with no hesitation, non- conceptualization, and skillful means. This is the best of all asceticism.

How is this all asceticism? A mind that is free of concepts and practices non-conceptually performs the best ascetic practice. All activities with objects done by a mind without concepts practicing without hesitation, is the supreme perfect ascetic practice. Relying on objects with a mind that does not assert existence, there is no harm, nothing to blame. Those ascetic practices are difficult to improve on. One really combines all things with wisdom uniting with reality, while remaining in an awareness of the emptiness of concepts. One is oneself the Great Ascetic [Buddha]. Form is transformed by wisdom, by non-discursive mind. Without a doubt, one should enjoy non-conceptually. Then one will be an ascetic. If one enters into this with a mind of wisdom and skillful means, then one will attain enlightenment and will have great gifts.

Folio 60 (#30B)

Thus Buddha said in the *Buddha Yoga Tantra* (*Sangye Naljor*):

With really joyful effort [mngon brtson pa], maintaining this connection [non-conceptual enjoyment], the yogi will direct his or her efforts in this way. His or her mind completely in a non-conceptual [state] will reflect all forms from the mirror of wisdom. If aspects are perceived in this way, arising from the mirror of wisdom, with one's own mind free of conceptions, all aspects are [reflected] from the mirror of wisdom. The mirror-like display is similar to a [collection of] magic dreams, or bubbles of water, and optical illusions [all non-substantial].[18]

When one perceives this way, as the Buddha said, one is declared to be a master.

When one views the changes in compounded things as lightning and a city of the *ghandarvas*, it has been taught that one is powerful among sentient beings.

Therefore clearly, as to attachment, nothing exists to which one can be attached. But when one views reality as magic, through having this special enjoyment through the complete arising of this perfect bliss thoroughly perfected by this view of reality, one obtains completely a special fruit. Why would one not accept this? One relies on the insubstantiality of all things, which are just appearances. By the force of practicing these special meditations, and becoming accustomed to them, you will gain bliss and a happy mind, etc. A special result is generated; the unsurpassable result. How could anyone disagree about this cause of true nature? This is found in the *First Glorious Tantra.*

Through this accomplishment, through the gaining of true nature, one becomes Buddha and also all the heroes. Through identifying with the deity, through this happiness, one will succeed, but harsh ascetic practices will dry up one's very bodies. These sufferings will disturb one's mind, and it will become distracted. Rather if the mind relies on [the bliss of] the body, it will be transformed by this bliss. It will not be disturbed by suffering. Because sufferings will cease, the mind will transform.

And in the *Beyond Samsara and Nirvana Vajra Tantra*:

In that way, one will succeed. The body will not be in torture. From this state of concentration, happiness will be vast.

Folio 61 (#31A)

Otherwise by fasting [cessation] and severe ascetic practice, etc., by tormenting the body with troubles, one becomes distracted. It has been declared that through these difficult practices, [such] lower beings will not succeed.

So it has been explained. It was also said in the glorious *Guhyasamadra*:

One will not succeed through relying on vows of unendurable ascetic practices. But if one practices the joy of all desires, relying on this, one will accomplish [enlightenment] quickly. Don't beg for food, reciting mantras. Don't enjoy begging. Rather enjoying all, say the mantras perfectly without losing the limbs [syllables].

Keeping body, speech and mind in bliss, one obtains enlightenment. If not, certainly at the time of death, one will stay in hell and burn. So Buddha said.

Therefore, like a great crystal jewel, which has the nature of clear light, forms, etc. [sense objects], functioning as special causes in combination, will clearly result in this special happiness. If the essential characteristics of this happy mind are wisdom and skillful means, then by the special force of this, one will completely transform within this ultimate state.

Through this wisdom, art [*bzo*], and special skill [*sgyu rtsal*], e.g., [training of the body as in gymnastics, etc.] one will experience objects in this special way. And all these combined, experienced in this special way, because of this supreme meditation, will enable the yogi [through the power of continual meditative experience] to attain the supreme eternal self nature.

Therefore, by this, according to our Buddhist view, you will be like the Sugata, going beyond samsaric attachments. Even in samsara, contact with good people can bring relief from suffering, fear, and craziness [*smyos pa*]. By this special activity of touching, happiness will come. In the same way, the supreme special cause has intrinsic value, and should not be mistaken for imagination [*dmigs pa*]. By all this, suffering will disappear as a result of this special characteristic of happiness.

Folio 62 (#31B)

If the result [of this training] is a mind characterized by happiness, etc., when one has clearly been transformed by that power, then suffering, which is contrary to happiness, cannot abide in such a mind. Because it is certain that the persistence of these habits of mind will prevent [*agogs*] suffering which is contrary [to happiness], suffering cannot return to a mind that has become happy. When one becomes more experienced, through touching and so forth, the opposite of happiness will not arise, and the mind will not change to a state of suffering. Whenever through repetition the force of bliss manifests, one will achieve [more and more] happiness and bliss. Due to bliss, suffering and sorrow will be reversed.

Because of this supreme attainment of meditation, the result will be a gathering of one's own good qualities. If one achieves happiness through practicing skillful means, this is an antidote [against suffering]. Suffering will not be able to arise and make obstacles. For example, cold is the opposite of heat, and if it meets with heat, it cannot increase. In the same way, since two opposite things cannot co-exist in the same ground [*gzhi*], suffering cannot co-exist in the same mental stream when happiness is present, because they are not harmonious.

Through the practice of this mental and other [physical] happiness, then it is correct to say that no remainder of suffering will ever be found. If the contrary of the ultimate mental state does not exist, then by this understanding [*goms bar*], through this special familiarization, one can go to the ultimate state. Similarly if one has knowledge, art and skill [in gymnastics, etc.], through that understanding, then you will not have ignorance. If you obtain this special [realization] you should understand that there will be no reversal.

Some believe that earth meditation is unchanging so there is no reason to believe my type of meditation is not unchanging. If one meditates in this way, how can one think one's meditation will change again? For one has entered completely into a state of non-dualistic meditation. Similarly, for example, as in earth meditation, one will not reverse because one is relying on that special happiness and happiness of mind by which one has achieved one's own true nature. No matter whatever faults [have been committed], if mind has entered into this state, there is no chance of reverting

Folio 63 (#32A)

back to one's former mistakes. Because of this aftermath of meditation, suffering will not arise again. It is impossible because one has come to the ultimate limit. Otherwise, one could not say that after this, one was liberated from samsara. Remaining in this ultimate state precludes suffering. For if someone is ultimately liberated, one cannot assert they must be born into samsara. This cannot occur because there are no more causes of the habits of ignorance. Such a person will not be reborn except for the sake of others. One who is born only for the sake of others is not a samsaric person. However, because of the power of previous aspirations, a person is able to enter into samsara. But the power of habitual tendencies will not affect them. Thus, he or she will not take rebirth in samsaric suffering– because of reaching perfect bliss, mental anguish [*sdug bsnyal gyi sems*] will not occur again.

Thus, such persons are completely pure, like the color of a crystal jewel. One who relies on this experience, by the power of its special, noble nature, will never revert from the characteristics of this state. People's minds become pleased with whatever object becomes familiar and in which they take pleasure. Their minds become like a wish-fulfilling jewel, which takes on the color of the object it reflects, and will not reverse its color.[19]

Because one has these special qualities, bringing about a very special result through these special causes, the opposite cannot be produced. From the force of previous times, how will what will come after not be exactly like that? If events did not occur in this way, it would not be fitting for people to rely on their intentions being fulfilled.

Also, it is said in the *Victorious Mother* [a *Prajnaparamita* text],

Furthermore by the great saintly bodhisattvas making offerings of celestial scents to the Tathagatas and the Tathagata's stupas,

Folio 64 (#32B)

....and by the virtuous activities in the Buddha fields where I received perfect enlightenment, may all creatures experience the special teachings of the divine realms. Moreover, Subhuti, by their great intention, through the five qualities of the object of desires [offered] to the Buddha, may all, including the sangha of the Sravaka and all sentient beings, through the perfect understanding and the virtuous root of positive activities, when they have achieved enlightenment in the Buddha fields, spontaneously achieve the five sense qualities of the desirable objects. Furthermore, Subhuti, the disciples, the saintly great bodhisattvas, the Buddha's sangha, the Sravakas and all sentient beings will be given these five desirable qualities and will gain great merit. Thus, it has been said.

This happens by the power of habitual tendencies due to practice, and one will see the karmic result. Similarly, one sees the result in the world of nature, when the *matulunga* [a sweet lime tree] is stained with resin [*gya kyeg*], etc., it resembles that [resin]. Therefore, when mind has also connected with the sensations, it will experience pleasure, etc., and by that will develop discriminative knowledge, make progress and move forward in that direction [towards more pleasure]. This is because the mind is attached to this special pleasure and because of that becomes solid [strong]. For example, the *datura* [cotton seed– a hallucinogen] and pomegranate, etc., when combined with other causal conditions, have the power to produce a special result, and similarly, the mind will achieve a special and very superior benefit from this special pleasure of touching [the great seal]. Thus, by this special blissful mind, etc., one will obtain higher and higher results [due to this great blissfulness], and the opposite [suffering] can never arise.

Folio 65 (#33A)

Therefore, Buddha said in the *First Glorious Tantra* that:

One should not allow suffering and a mind devoid of pleasure to arise.

In the *Assembly of All Gods Tantra* [it was said that]:

Gods, and asuras and demonic beings, are not generally capable of this discriminating wisdom, but by having the elements of the teaching, they can experience happiness, if they have this practice. Those who have discriminating wisdom can go as a lamp blown out. That is going to the Nirvana state.

The irresistible power of Nirvana will not leave even the ashes of the bodies of the gods behind.

Such a practitioner has no body and, similarly, has no five sense organs nor any objects of the five sense organs. Then, there are also no *dhatus*, no principles of mind [five conscious senses], and no mental states.

The mind of pride no longer exists. Since sentient beings do not exist, there is no wisdom. This is like the state of deep sleep. There is no intellectual discrimination, no ego.

There are no conceptions, no activities [conduct], no forms, no qualities. This is Nirvana. Those who wish for freedom are freed from these aspects.

One comes to know that the characteristics of samsara have no intrinsic nature. One knows the nature of reality. Don't desire enlightenment. Then when you are free from hope and fear you will wake up. Then you will wake up and will know the true nature to be without inherent existence. Those will not attain Nirvana who have no joyful effort. They will always have an inferior mind. They will have just wasted activities [*gson*]. [Such people] do not get perfect enlightenment. Because they are frightened, they rob themselves [of enlightenment].

In doing this, they produce mental afflictions (*stug*) in themselves. Acting in this way, they cannot increase their buddha bodies through blissfulness.

If one has no diligence, one will have no strength of heart and will not persevere. Then one will not be enlightened.

This is the very lowest of states, [but] those who have gained enlightenment have abandoned their very bodies, and by trying very hard to make an effort [joyful effort], through this diligence, will wake up [Tib. *sad*]. Then all their senses will be liberated.

Folio 66 (#33B)

By thoroughly enjoying of all one's senses, one will not be bound [in samsara]. This was said.

Also in the *Perfect Destroyer of Doubt Tantra* etc.:

A person who does not have the realization of the absolute [without discipline], even if they aspire to a great result, how can habitual tendencies be abandoned?

The mind will only be purified through the practice of the yogi. The [yogic] views are different [from that of the renunciate]. Therefore, even if you are intelligent, you are lost, completely awakening into nirvana like a butter lamp that is blown out.

There is no greater waste than this. By not enjoying the accomplishment that arises from the blessing of one's own body that arises from direct perception, one remains in nirvana.

There is no weaker courage than this. By that cause of [limited] awakening, one can enter into nirvana having thoroughly abandoned unlimited bliss. Then one should ask what it is all worth. This has been said.

And it is said [*Assembly of All Gods Tantra*]:

When mercury and fire are touched together, what will become of that object? It disappears, but there is clearly no burning. The smoke has also disappeared. By crushing dung and applying it, it [the mercury] will again collect. Similarly, the great wisdom mudra should be understood like this. Thus it has been explained.

Achieving that, and applying that, one will never reverse from that. For example in liberation, etc., the nature of the cause of ultimate reality, bliss and blissful mental states, are the proof of that nature. By this meditation that you do, by the power of this meditation, you will reach the ultimate state and never reverse. For example, just as wisdom, practical knowledge of handicrafts and dexterity are attained, through this meditation done through wisdom and skillful means [enlightenment comes with the great mudra]. Through that special touching, bodily blessings and a blessed mind arise.

This is the evidence of going to the ultimate state. In this way, how could one be separated from the ultimate state?

Folio 67 (#34A)

Through this special familiarization, by its force, one will attain suchness through this irreversible nature. Also, nothing else will reverse it, because the intrinsic nature has been attained.

Because of the special nature of this burning, its self-nature [that of being a tree] will not again arise. Also, a tree, [unlike] gold, cannot become a tree again through a specific cause.

In this case of a tree no transformation whatsoever will take place. When gold is burned by fire it is liquid, but when separated from fire, it will have other qualities. Similarly, when water [boils] it is like fire, but when it cools, it goes back to its natural state. Similarly, gold when cooled, goes back to its natural state. By wanting qualities of certain objects, mind will fasten on these objects, and become more and more like them, and will not reverse.

Whoever reaches that sublime state, undergoes a transformation of their evil qualities. So, for example, a very pure Brahmin with powers, very clean and so forth, may reverse. Although very ascetic, lacking compassion, he may change. My blissful mind, however, having achieved certainty, becoming more familiar with these powers, never ceases to be blissful, and there is no cause that can stop it. And this is the cause of the cessation of suffering.

Folio 68 (#34B)

If there is no cause that can stop it, suffering will be experienced. Some wise people see there is no benefit in suffering, and abandon it. And searching for its cause, they will abandon attachment to the cause. Since wise people do not want this [suffering], they would be crazy [not to completely abandon it] immediately. Because even in the ordinary sense, not to mention the ultimate way, by avoiding contact even in a small way [with the causes of suffering], one will benefit and avoid suffering. Having this view, one will not find oneself [involved in] the opposite of happiness: suffering. Similarly, people know not to keep [poisonous] snakes or touch thorns. Thus, by giving up the suffering and cause of suffering, by the power of this special training, one can learn the truth through obtaining this special result. Because of the nature of this, through the abandonment [of the cause of suffering], mind learns to give up [suffering], and from the very start, will not stray from the way.

Having been habituated to this way of thinking, one will abandon even the thought of not abandoning [suffering]. This cessation of habits, is the result [of happiness], and can be established by natural reason. Bliss will lead to higher bliss, because each has the same nature. This similarity results from special meditation. [By meditating on ugliness, all appears ugly. By meditating on happiness, all appears happy.]

By accustoming oneself to wisdom, one becomes wiser, etc. Therefore, it is not something unproven and is not uncertain. By becoming accustomed to bliss and mental happiness, etc. one will not enter into [suffering] that is its opposite. This does not contradict natural reason. [Having this special happiness of mind and body, would you not agree that suffering can not occur?] These points are well known to everyone.

Each person when studying [each kind of] wisdom will clearly attain the result accordingly. By wisdom, art and skill, etc. each person through practice will attain the result of that practice. One stops passion through meditation on impurity; anger is replaced through love and ignorance is replaced through the understanding of interdependent co-origination. Thus, it is said that all attachment is completely changed only by detachment, because it is the opposite of attachment.

Nevertheless, one might argue that it is also true that through the experience of attachment one can be free of attachment, by experiencing more passion. [Through this special technique] you can be freed from passion [attachment subduing attachment]. If this is attained, suffering will be stopped. Because of this, the root tantra declares that all the buddhas are replete with desire.

Folio 69 (#35A)

Some say that when attachment is removed by detachment, one becomes desireless, thus they do not agree. But when you cultivate your desire (by this special training), you become desireless. Because of this wisdom of passion, there will be no trouble.

In the *Mulatantra*:

[Thus] one is victorious over attachment with or without attachment. This was said by Buddha.

The intrinsic nature of passions is neither a natural nor a created negativity. Otherwise, no one could attain the stage of stream-winner [first stage of realization], because the stream-winners are engaged [on the path to enlightenment] without having abandoned their attachments. Buddha said this in the *Chapter on Discipline.* The bodhisattva can go against even the ten virtuous actions for the sake of others. For example, if a woman desires the bodhisattva to the point that she will throw away [*ador ba*] her life if she does not obtain him, then, in order to serve, the bodhisattva should satisfy her wish in the interest [*gzung ba*] of saving her life. Similarly, if the bodhisattva sees someone committing a great sin, if the bodhisattva kills that person, he or she does not go to hell, but accumulates great merit.

Buddha said this: if attachment, etc., were negative by nature, then, why would one not say these beings go to the lower realms? If desire and so forth were by nature evil, then why would they not go to the lower realms? Rather one says merit arises. Because the acts are not negative by nature then they can be transformed, and through the different circumstances involved, develop different qualities. For example, the *ketak* flower if eaten by the incense elephant when digested produces [excrement like] musk. But, if another [ordinary] elephant eats it, when digested, it will naturally become foul. If this happens, it is not the fault of the *ketak* flower. Likewise, passion, attachment, etc., can also be purified in this way by means of the special purifying power of intention which remains in a pure stream, giving rise to a special result. For example, if milk is drunk by a snake, when the milk is digested, it becomes the snake's poison. If milk is drunk by other kinds of beings its nature becomes nutritious (nectar). Similarly, attachment when experienced by a mind trained in a special way will produce a special [beneficial] result, because it is not negative by nature.

Folio 70 (#35B)

Applying this reasoning, relying on this special contact, one will get a special result. This is similar to the *ketak* flower [which cleanses muddy water]. This resembles the special attachment existing in the [mental] stream of the noble ones, and can be demonstrated through reason.

As for the relationship of the enjoyment of the mental stream of the special ones [bodhisattvas], this will produce only the attainment of the special result, because it is the final complete set of causes and conditions, the final moment of the actual accumulation of the cause. Anything naturally related is connected to it so that the result is produced if it is subject to no obstacles or blockages. [For example, if the eye is healthy and there is light, one will be able to see objects which have the nature of being visible.] If there are some obstacles, then one cannot be sure the result will occur. But if the proper causal conditions are present, one can rely on the result occurring. If obstacles could arise, then something else could happen. And if there is a special transformative power acting on the cause, if it is unimpeded, then one need not rely on other activities. This is clearly reasonable.

There is no uncertainty that the effect will follow the cause when all the causal conditions are present. No obstacle can intervene, because there is no intervening time for this. For example, those expert chemists who are engaged in extracting the essence from medicinal [substances] can, because of their skill, impart a special form [of health]. For example, the forces of mercury, etc., and copper, etc., when combined will develop new qualities, and will never revert again. Similarly, one should understand [in this way how the afflictive emotions [*kleshas*] can be permanently transformed]. Otherwise how could copper and mercury be altered? Otherwise things would not have the ability to change.

It is like the supreme gold-making elixir, for it transforms this unclean body we have assumed into the priceless jewel of the body of a buddha. Therefore, firmly seize this awakening mind, because of this merit, the sage will have a happy mind.

Folio 71 (#36A)

Even if one remains, for the sake of others, in samsara, how could such a compassionate one be unhappy? Thus it has been explained.

Also, those who know the productions of the essence– taking practice [*chud kyi len, bcud kyi len*], use its special medicinal qualities, and attain for themselves great achievements such as the five clairvoyances.[20]

In that way, remaining in samsara, they enjoy thoroughly, until the end of samsara, the special objects which arise purely, making aspirations, striving for the benefit of others, and thoroughly accomplishing the essence of qualities through the alchemy of *bodhicitta.* Why would you not accept this alchemy of *bodhicitta*?

There is no way of achieving enlightenment by throwing away the six realms and the afflictive emotions [*nyon mongs*].[21]

For you are not just seeking benefit for yourself when transforming the emotions. Thus, make an effort firmly to attain enlightenment in this way. You must not just burn away the afflictive emotions like a small piece of grass.[22]

By grasping your afflictive emotions, through mindfulness and knowledge, you will gain all the good qualities. Because by abandoning the afflictive emotions one comes near to enlightenment. Having absorbed and transformed the *kleshas* [afflictive emotions], one surely comes close to enlightenment. In that way, you will not, in the future, make mistakes. You will be born in the world again and again, within a field of good qualities.

When one has taken birth in the stream of samsara's realms, achieved these qualities, and remained within the ultimate wisdom, then, will the reaching of this ultimate state be with thought or without thought? How could thought come from the power of no thought? Or non-thought from thought? They are opposites. However, if you think that one comes close to non-conceptual wisdom by removing the habitual root and branch emotions, that is not correct.

Folio 72 (#36B)

What other way would there be to reach the non-conceptual other than through the removal of the root and branch emotions? There is no satisfying evidence.

There is none through direct perception because one does not have the ability to connect that which appears to the senses [in the mind] with the [external] object. It has been shown that the knowledge of the grasper and the grasped cannot be separated. Thus one fails to understand that there is no adequate ground of inference [*rjes su dpag pas*] able to connect them. Thus in accordance with our former procedure, there is no proof or evidence. 2) [Through reasoning in terms of result reasoning, or in terms of the same nature of things in question– *rang bshin rtags.*] But, through inference we know the sign through that which is related to the sign. [But how could] liberating knowledge arise from subject and object when it arises from dualistic thinking [which makes use of conventional signs]? This offers no proof of the non-conceptual, because the object itself is a hindrance. Through logic one cannot achieve any result through [working with] objects in this way, because the cause and effect are really unconnected. Duality and non-duality exist at the same time, so one cannot be the cause of the other. And if the cause is gone, the result cannot come.

Nor can it be known through invisible reasoning [Logic of nonapprehension or invisible reasoning– *ma dmigs pai rtags*], because the subject is not the sort of thing that could be perceived [because non-conceptual]. Thus as previously said, reasoning will not work. Reasoning about cause and effect is not correct. This is true, because since there is no cause, there is no result. Thus nothing is produced. If the cause is not gone, the result will not be produced. Because things arise instantaneously, time does not tarry. If there were no change, everything would be permanent. If there were no instantaneous activity, objects would be like sky flowers. How could they arise? Thus for instance [as Nagarjuna says]:

If the seed is not gone, how does the sprout arise? It is said by omniscient Buddha that all results arise like magic.[23]

Thus, whatever Buddha the protector said about the birth, arising, and transitory nature of sentient beings is a temporary truth.

In the absolute state, nothing is developing or existing. [Therefore, although we cannot say exactly how non-conceptual wisdom arises from the transformation of experience, there is no proof that this is impossible]. Because production and producer are not in contact [lit. are not agreeable] cause and effect do not really exist. It [the non-conceptual] is very hidden [mysterious] and cannot be logically demonstrated.

Folio 73 (#37A)

[One cannot say that cause and effect] really exist, because there cannot be a coherent account of their relationship. One cannot elicit a proof of their existence through the use of perception. Nor can one have logical proof of this rather than its opposite [because] it concerns the ultimate wisdom. [Logic too is ultimately unreal.] This logic would be accepted by others (non–Buddhists) as well. This knowledge is non-conceptual. How could you express it in words? Thus it is said:

Understood properly, objects neither arise from themselves, nor from others, nor from both. They cannot be said to exist, to not exist, nor to both exist and not exist. From what source can things happen in that way?

This insight is beyond logic. One could never assert the existence of a space lotus, neither with nor without thought construction. If one has the thought of the absolute meaning, then, [thought] has become that which is without thought. The person who understands the meaning of this is not committed to the existence of the space lotus and the like. Space lotuses really do not exist. What kind of knowledge could one usefully attain in this way [through concepts like space lotuses]? The existence of such things cannot be demonstrated. Because of inter-dependent co-origination, production and producer gain reality, and thoughts and objects are completely known [conventionally] through thought constructions. For this reason, the three realms are explained as analyzed [in terms of] the causal conditions of grasper and grasped [subject and object]. As it is said in the *Lankavatara Sutra*:

The exalted ones see no mistakes [neither subject nor object], because on the absolute level there are no mistakes.

Because if they perceived mistakenly, this would be a mistake. Otherwise, not abandoning these mistakes, the cataracts would not be gone. Thus it is said.

Why regress from reality? Why regress from reality to conceptual analysis when one can produce the result of the meaning of reality through the highest, best meditation?

Folio 74 (#37B)

Having been transformed, there is neither a gap nor no-gap [between the relative and the absolute]. The nature is the same, because one relies on the practice of meditation on such happiness, and so forth.

Similarly, having the excellent knowledge of subject and object, one knows objects purely [through] subject and object. And one obtains ceaselessly in one's own mind the self-nature of reality through the net of concepts and what arises from them. Therefore, remaining with this, one understands completely the meaning of these characteristics without exception, because one has mingled skillful means and wisdom completely.

[Skillful means and wisdom is not found in the Sanskrit text.] By mingling wisdom and skillful means, one has achieved full awareness of things as they are [on the relative ultimate level]. For that reason, in the *Laikavatara Sutra*, it is said that:[24]

The Great Vehicle is not my vehicle, no syllables, no sound, without the [four] concentrations, [eight] liberations, no appearance, and no object of practice.

Yet the Great Vehicle is a vehicle for those who have the power to control the meditation which accomplishes the self-supreme body of mind meditation, adorned excellently with the flowers of power. Thus it is said.

One explains everything through realization of the particularity of the cause and the particularity of the effect. Nevertheless, after examining names and categories, grasping and excluding [inference], there may be complete agreement or clarity [about concepts such as the nature of the compounded [impermanence], nevertheless the appearances of subject and object are not clear and manifest.

Renowned Acarya Dharmakirti also taught that in samsara, whatever knowledge arises appearing clearly, following from the careful distinctions of subject and object, is due to logical analysis. Therefore names and categories are distinquished and are clearly apparent. [Different from worldly knowledge, the direct perception of enlightened beings is non-dualistic and does not rely on conventional characteristics, etc.]

Acarya Dharmakrti taught that one must thoroughly analyze subject and object, through analyzing names and categories, relying on the perfect knowledge of subject and object, which arises from experience of objects. Then if one confirms this with categories of establishing and reversing, becoming accustomed to this type of experience [through meditation], then one must agree this will not block clear perception of reality.[25]

If there is smoke, there is fire.
There is smoke
Therefore there is fire.

Conversely,

If there is fire, there is smoke..
There is no smoke.
Therefore there is no fire.

Folio 75 (#38A)

Also, having accomplished this familiarization, the proof is in the meditative experience. Desire, misery, fear and madness, thus, have been similarly explained [as resulting from habitual tendencies]. Yet, if the complete understanding of the appearance of subject and object is similarly transformed by the ultimate transcendental wisdom, then there will be complete comprehension. Similarly, without this absolute ultimate level, this comprehension cannot happen. Furthermore, if you know all objects without exception to be empty, then this knowledge remains completely without exception separated from the net of concepts. By the wisdom of non-appearance, similarly it is completely cut away from this net of concepts. If this is the case, does this contradict the idea of categories?

Nothing that has the nature of being partless can be perceived, is perceivable, nor has a perceiver. These three are not acceptable [the absolute is beyond distinctions]. This true nature which we understand in our hearts has some similarity [to our ordinary modes of perception].

Similarly, when subject and object are completely distinguished and [this analysis] is taken as far as it can go, the very special nature arises. Through the logic applied to the nature of all things, everything without exception is completely understood. In this way, the power of that [knowledge] is not eaten by ravens [useless– like unwanted food left to birds]. There are those who disagree, holding that, since all compounded thoughts etc. are known to be empty, they should be discarded.

However one can, in harmony with the conventional knowledge used by the ongoing generations of families of all sentient beings, and through one's increasing familiarity with meditation, transform what one learns from the senses, as well as all mental states. One becomes similar to that with which one has become accustomed, and comes to understand things in those terms. So, if very pure, great ascetics meditate on impurity, [habitually] remaining in the great [equanimity] state, similarly through meditation, the impurity will be transformed, and the three realms will all be their enjoyment. This is simple logic.

Folio 76 (#38B)
In The Buddha Union Tantra, it is said that:

All yogis are Bhagavan, Vajrasattva, and Tathagata. Whatever is in all three realms is intimately enjoyed by them.

And, also in the Assembly of All the Gods Tantra:

All the elements of phenomena and all that pertains to sentient beings may be used as enjoyment, if the yogi maintains a pure mind.

Meditating on the great mudra and repeating the great [mantra], each [syllable] of all of these words is the self [nature]. Mingling [applying] in this way, meditate.

Furthermore, no matter how many sentient beings reach the ultimate state of meditation, when they familiarize themselves with the self-nature of this connection, all things which arise connect with this meditation. And, through this meditation, all things contained in the three realms have the qualities of bliss, a blissful mind, etc.

For that reason, again, in The Buddha Union Tantra:

Whatsoever appears through the senses [lam gyur] is the true nature, whether it is meditated on as such or equally if it is not meditated on as such, and one is united with all the buddhas.

One also finds in *Collection of All Realization Tantra*:

All the scriptures explain the qualities of the five objects of desire as Buddha.

Also in the *Guhyasamadra Tantra* it is said:

Form, sound, the characteristics of objects, you must know, upon analysis are really the deity itself.

Thus, it is also said:

Therefore, these objects [of the senses], transformed through the highest meditation, are the very objects which have been analyzed. If you meditate in this way, through the power of this you will develop wisdom together with concepts, and by the strength of that, certainty arises, which is the result of the attainment of all these qualities.

Relying on this special nature, staying without exception with these qualities, seeking all the results of accomplishment, and also all the special ones, remaining in samsara for the sake of all sentient beings, with diligence abandoning all pride, by making the effort to know, one will know all that is knowable.

Folio 77 (#39A)

Thus, in this way, one reaches realization.

The Attainment of Suchness by scholar Shantarakshita, translated, proofread and published by the Indian scholar Atisha, and the monk Rinchen Zangpo. Later, by request, the section on logic was proofread and edited by the scholar Kumarakalasha (*'bro dge slong shakya'od*).

COMMENTARY
ON
MADHYAMAKALANKARA
the ornament of the middle way

Khenchen Palden Sherab Rinpoche
and
Khenpo Tsewang Dongyal Rinpoche

This commentary was transcribed from oral transmissions given by the authors to Marie Louise Friquegnon over a ten years period in the 80's, at various locations in India and the United States of America.

Please note: Because of the extremely concise phrasing of Shantarakshita's works, it may be useful to read the commentaries in conjunction with the root texts.

COMMENTARY ON *MADHYAMAKALANKARA*

Following in the traditional manner, we shall first discuss the *Madhyamakalankara*, divided five ways. The first indicates the author; the second, for whom the text was written; the third, the category or *pinaka* to which it belongs; the fourth, what the text explains; the fifth, the purpose for which it is intended, i.e., the type of benefit for sentient beings.

1) The author: The *Madhyamakalankara* was composed by the unsurpassed scholar, most highly realized siddha and saint, who shines like the sun and the moon, the great teacher Shantarakshita.

2) The audience: For those who wish to understand the vast and profound clear wisdom of scripture, this text provides a guide and uncontroversial proof of all Mahayana teachings.

3) The *pitaka*: The text belongs to the category of *abhidharma* (philosophy) and is based on all the Mahayana scriptures but especially on the *Lamp of the Moon Scripture. Madhyamakalankara (King of Noble Meditation Sutra-Aryasamadhirajasutra.)*

4) What the text explains: It clearly and correctly shows the nature of the two truths (absolute and relative) by means of a synthesis of the two systems, of Nagarjuna's Madhyamaka and Asanga's Chittamatra.

5) The purpose: It is intended to help students to understand, to achieve certain wisdom, and to attain enlightenment.

There are two aspects of Madhyamaka, 1. the meaning, and 2. the scripture and commentary.

1. The meaning of Madhyamaka,

This first section of the text comprises its ground, path and result. The ground of the Madhyamaka is two-fold — relative and absolute. But these two also need to be viewed in terms of an inseparable union. Similarly, there are two types of the path Madhyamaka — the path of the accumulation of wisdom and the path of the accumulation of merit. The result of the Madhyamaka is also two-fold, resulting in the union of the two *kayas, i.e.*, the dharmakaya and the rupakaya.

Madhyamaka also has two divisions — scripture and commentary.

2. Scripture

The main scriptural source is the *Prajnaparamita Sutra*. The longest form of this sutra has one hundred thousand stanzas; a short form is the *Heart Sutra*. The shortest is the seed syllable AH:

There are also the *Mother and Son Sutras* of which there are seventeen ent kinds of sutras (six mothers and eleven sons), seventeen forms of Prajnaparamita. Commentaries on this sutra include such works as Nagarjuna's *Mulaprajnamadhyamaka*.

Since this is an abhidharma text, the homage is to the noble, youthful Manjushri. According to the King of All Creation Bodhicitta Great Perfection lineage, there is a fourth *pitaka*, the *tantra pitaka*. Or there may sometimes be tantric homages respectively for each of the three standard pitakas. For vinaya, it would be to the omniscient Buddha, for sutra, to one Buddha and the bodhisattvas, and for the abhibdharma, to Manjushri. So the homage indicates clearly to which pitaka the commentary belongs. The homage of this text is to Manjushri. The translators are Surendrabodhi and Shang Yeshe De who worked together on the text in the eighth century.

3. The philosophical content of the text

Some Buddhist schools as well as some non-Buddhist schools accept that certain things truly exist. But, when any particular thing is fully analyzed, it becomes clear that it can neither be said to be one nor many. Since anything must be either singular or manifold, and if it can neither be one nor many, then how can anything be said to exist? Things are like the reflection of the moon in water. Although the reflection appears, it has no real existence. Therefore, whatever our own schools or those of others proclaim, there is no basis for the intrinsic existence of anything.

Nevertheless, there are many things which those schools do claim really exist, such as the five aggregates: atoms, a cosmic substance, or universal essence [Skt. *prakrti*], the Self or mind. Some, such as the Samkhya, claim only one phenomenon exists, which is Cosmic Substance. Advaita Vedantin claims it is the Self, or Brahman.

Yet, how would only one thing exist? Since all results occur successively and are different, their causes must also be different. If there were a unitary single cause, there wouldn't be different causes at different times, therefore all results would occur simultaneously. If Isvara [the Creator] were the cause of all things, for example, then would not Isvara have to be constantly changing [not permanent and unchanging].

Nor could we ever have knowledge of an uncompounded* permanent entity. Vaibhaishikas claim we know the uncompounded through the cessation of the six consciousnesses [eye consciousness, ear consciousness, smell consciousness , touch consciousness and mind consciousness as the sixth]. But Mipham Rinpoche points out that the whole enterprise of questioning whether cessation is compounded or not is senseless, because cessation is not a thing that can exist or not exist.[26] Cessation, by definition, is not a thing at all, but rather the absence of a thing.

The uncompounded cessation (*nirvana*) of the Vaibhaishikas can neither be uncompounded nor, furthermore, can it be permanent. Because, how could nirvana,

*"For *saṃskṛta/asaṃskṛta*, Douglas Duckworth suggests: conditioned/unconditioned

as the stopping of consciousness, be permanent, since the mind learns of nirvana progressively in stages. We know that yogis and yoginis have progressive realizations. If nirvana were permanent and uncompounded, all of these moments of realization would be the same, which is impossible.

As Mipham Rinpoche says: "Before and after, each is in its place. Thus an uncompounded reality will never arise."

Nothing compounded is really permanent. Things only seem to be that way. If you look at a cup, for example, it seems to be unchanging. But this is true only on a gross level. The cup will become discolored or deteriorate over time. We do not see these subtle changes, but they are always taking place. Similarly it looks as if the meditation of the *arhat* [a highly realized disciple of Buddha Sakyamuni] does not change. But the arhat is always changing, so subtle changes are occurring in his or her realization.

Further, if realization is dependent on causal conditions, it cannot be uncompounded. Otherwise, realization would either always be there or never be there. Nor could there be any benefit to us in a Nirvana that was unchanging, because we could never relate to it. We change; therefore, our relation to a permanent reality would also have to change. If it did not, it would not exist in relation to us. Thus, an unchanging Nirvana would be something that could not possibly be of benefit to us [like a eunuch, who can't make love, to the woman seeking a lover].

The argument could equally apply to the notion of an uncompounded permanent self, or ego. Since it cannot be one, and it is contradictory to its meaning to say it is many, it cannot exist. And it is surely clear about all we know about our bodies, thoughts, etc., that they are always changing. One cannot find anything about one's self that is permanent.

Some have argued [*Samkhyas*] for a holistic vision in which all things are pervaded by a permanent universal essence or nature. This, however, is self-contradictory. Because if this cosmic substance is permanent and unitary, how could it constitute the essence of what is changing and not singular? Nor could one essence then be further subdivided into three — lightness [*sattva* or *tejas*], activity [*rajas*], and dark or inert, *tam*, as the Samkhyas say it is. In short, a unity cannot become two. Therefore, it cannot pervade two different objects to make them what they are.

Shantarakshita then turns his attention to those schools that affirm the reality of atoms. Some [like the Hindu Vaisheshikas] claim everything is composed of atoms that are completely conjoined, similar to the Vaibhashikas who claim that atoms are surrounded by other atoms (forming a solid mass).[27]

But if there is no space between atoms, they cannot move. Further, these schools see atoms as completely partless particles, which cannot be further divided up. Being indivisible, how could they interrelate to each other to form the elements? That is, their interrelation would imply connecting portions. They must connect at least with the sides that face each other. But talk about sides is talk about sections, or parts, of the atom and that would be inconsistent with its being partless. Therefore, strictly speaking, the notion of an atom, or partless particle, is senseless.

If this is true, then the theory that the categories accepted by the Vaibhashikas [substance, quality, action, particular, general] all come from atoms, is equally shown to be senseless. All these things, like atoms, are empty in nature. This is also true, of course, of the ten sense fields, that is, the five sense organs and their five types of objects, as well as the resulting sensations and actions, which are believed by some schools to originate from atoms.

Starting with sloka 16, Shantarakshita turns his attention to problems of the nature of consciousness and its object. He is going to consider four points of view:

1. *Vaibhashika*: only the object of awareness exists; e.g., the eye knows the object directly.
2. *Sautrantika*: objects are composed of atoms; e.g., the eye consciousness knows a mental image reflected from the consciousness.
3. *Chittamatra*: only the subject exists independently.
4. *Madhyamaka*: neither the grasper, known as the subject, nor that which is grasped, known as the object, exist independently.

Mahayana philosophers consider the first two schools to be provisional teachings of the Buddha. They are satisfactory explanations as long as they are not analyzed very carefully. They both accept atoms, but the Sautrantika school denies we have direct knowledge of these atoms. Atoms cause us to have images in our minds which are our direct objects of experience.

Shantarakshita follows the general Buddhist position that mind is unlike matter which is insentient. Thus it must originate from that which is similar to it in nature — awareness.

Some Buddhists have been reluctant to admit the existence of self-consciousness or reflexive-awareness. They believe this could commit them to the acceptance of a substantial self or ego. Shantarakshita points out that this is because they are clinging to a certain model of knowledge, which is inappropriate in the case of self-awareness (sloka 17). Buddhists traditionally divided up knowledge into subject, object and activity. In the case for example, of "John knows the cat," the subject is John, the object is the cat and the activity is knowing. But in the case of John knows himself, the subject cannot be an object.

The whole point about self-awareness is that it is a state of pure subjectivity. Awareness of an object is not self-awareness, by definition. To think otherwise is to be misled by the grammatical similarity of how we speak about knowing objects with how we speak of self-awareness. But this is a purely grammatical similarity, not a real one.

Mind is simply the "clarity" aspect of being.

The difference between a non-sentient thing and a sentient being is that the latter possesses clarity and awareness, which is the nature of mind. Mind is not a substantial entity.

Knowledge of objects arises from awareness. It cannot arise from matter, which is its opposite in nature. Thus even if matter could be shown to be coherent we could never know it. As Mipham Rinpoche says, we can only know objects when they appear in our minds. Otherwise how could we know them? Knowledge then, is knowledge of the mental — which is the same nature as awareness. This is why he will argue that the Chittamatra view is true on the relative level.[28]

To summarize the Vaibhashika school

According to the Vaibhashika school, the relative truth consists of all these gross things starting from mind to matter, including time. These are relative truth, because they do not exist after analysis. One way of looking at ultimate truth for the Vaibhasikas is that reality consists in two types of partless entities, partless atoms and partless instants. Atoms are counted as absolute truth because they cannot be crushed or destroyed. As for time, there is nothing more fundamental than the partless instant [*shes pa skad cig cha med*]. These instants are indestructible moments of consciousness,, and hence are part of ultimate truth. They are indestructible because they are partless. Although both objects and thoughts are changing, only thoughts are temporal, because time is only in the mind [minutes, days, etc., which are relative and not really real]. The Vaibhashika path consists of meditation and practice in accordance with the Four Noble Truths. The Truth of Suffering consists of impermanence, our experience of suffering and the insubstantiality of our egos and objects. The Truth of the Cause of Suffering is the reason why this all develops, namely attachment. The Truth of Cessation describes cessation [or nirvana] as peace, complete satisfaction, and one's ultimate goal. One's practice is the Eight-fold Path along with the two forms of meditation: *samatha* [calming the mind] and *vipassana* [insight into the nature of reality]. The result is arhathood. Arhats create no more karma.

Critique of the Vaibhashika

What we know, then, is a product of mind, not external [objective] reality. This is a common error. It is just that they both arise from awareness. Thus the Vaibhashikas cannot be right that only objects exist [and that there is no real self-awareness]. Matter itself cannot be aware. There is no 'who' in matter that can know. If mind and its object, however, were so different in nature, they could never "touch" each other.[29]

Again, we tend to be misled by words. We give objects names that imply a lack of consciousness: table, atom, etc., and assume that these objects are totally different from mind. But these are just names; Shantarakshita will argue that there is no matter existing to which these names correspond.

Summary of Sautrantika

Sautrantikas accept two types of objects, particular objects or characteristics [*rang mtshan*] and imagined objects [*spyi mtshan*]. The first category is ultimate, the second, relative. Our perceptions are relative truth. Objects such as atoms and partless instants are real because they are functional [*don byed nus pa*]. Everything else is imagination.

Critique of the Sautrantika

Shantarakshita, in sloka 22, considers the Sautrantika view. The difference between the Sautrantika and Vaibhashika views is subtle. The Vaibhashika believe that tables, etc., are substantially existing things composed of partless atoms. We know them because our eye organs are material. Mind is merely the partless moments of consciousness, a continuous collection of which knows objects directly without self-consciousness. The eye consciousness, for example, catches the form of the table, as a hook catches a fish.

The Sautrantika view is a bit different. Although the Sautrantika accepted the atomic composition of objects, they also believed in self-consciousness.

The Sautrantikas realized there is a paradox in our concept of the atom. If it is partless, it is indivisible. Yet how can we stipulate an end to the divisibility of an extended substance? So partless atoms, they claim, are beyond conception. Further, since consciousness and matter are opposites, they can't touch each other. Consciousness knows a reflection of matter that is mental in nature.

Shantarakshita points out that whether or not your conception corresponds to the Sautrantika or Vaibhashika view, if the atomic theory is incoherent, appealing to the existence of an unknowable atom will not help. A partless atom acting in combination with other partless atoms makes no sense [as he, following Vasubandhu, has shown previously].

Although the Sautrantikas believe in the existence of atoms and that we do not know these atoms, they accept a representational theory of knowledge. That is, mental states represent distinct objects.

This creates a problem for them, because while physical objects are infinitely divisible, mental states are not spatially divisible at all. Shantarakshita argues that since they say thought is not a manifold, they cannot say it can be divided up into distinct objects.

Shantarakshita now turns to the idea that the mind knows a complete mental object all at once: a single state of mind knowing a single unified object. But if the mental object is real, this, too, is impossible. For the mental object is infinitely divisible. It is not really a unified state. How could our mental objects be an infinity of partless aspects? But if the mental object is real, how could they not be? Further, the five senses each have their own mental objects. But how can these five senses have partless aspects for their objects?

So, since if, as some Sautrantikas believe, consciousness is one and indivisible, it cannot represent distinct objects. The only way a single, unified consciousness could correctly represent reality would be if reality itself were only one thing, which is contrary to perception and common sense. This was the [mistaken] view of *na dug nyi medpa* [*sna trug nyis med pas*] or many things/one mind: one unified mind sees many things all at once (slokas 21–23). If one looked at a flowered cup, one would know it through an undifferentiated thought. But if the thought were undifferentiated, and thought is representational, the object must be undifferentiated. Thus we could never know a multi–colored flowered cup. And clearly, we do.

Shantarakshita then considers another Sautrantika view [half–egg — *sgo nga phyed tshal ba*], that thought is a temporal manifold rather than a spatial one, many states of mind rather than the same mind. In sloka 24, he examines the possibility that cognitions arise gradually, one aspect at a time, one cognition per aspect. But this happens so quickly that it seems as though thoughts arise all at once, instantaneously. So, for example, if I look at a multi-colored flowered cup, I'll see red, then green, then yellow, then the shape, etc., but this will happen so fast it will be a single perception.

This is called the half-egg view because the relation between reality and its object is considered similar to the two parts of a hard-boiled egg split in half. Mind is not thought of as a unity. Each aspect of the object has a corresponding state of mind [one aspect and one state of mind per instant of time]. There is a separate mind that knows each aspect of the object (e.g., the cup) but these perceptions follow each other with such rapidity, the illusion of a unified mind and object is produced.

But if this were the case, Shantarakshita argues the process would occur so quickly that one could not differentiate between perceptions arising at different moments. How could we know the Sanskrit word "lata" (vine) was not the word "tala" (palm tree) (sloka 25).

Shantarakshita then calls on us to reflect on the way we know (sloka 26). Our minds jump about very quickly from thought to thought. Suppose we are looking at some animals. We see a large, loud, black bird, then notice a small, yellow cat. If one saw these things one aspect at a time, our awareness would be slow and gradual. But this is usually not the case. All the different aspects of the object are captured instantly by the mind.

Shantarakshita then considers an example upon which the half-egg Sautrantikas place a great deal of weight (sloka 28). When one looks at a torch whipped about in a circle, one seems to see, mistakenly, a circle of light. But there is no circle, only the torch appearing in successive positions. Similarly, the mind perceives one aspect at a time, but so quickly, the illusion of simultaneity is produced.

Shantarakshita's refutation is based on the fact that we can only see what exists in the present. We do not really see the circle of light at all. The "perception" of a circle produced is really a trick of the mind. But neither does the mind remember the successive positions of the torch. If memory did this, the wheel would not appear so clearly. But the mind perceives it, clearly, distinctly, and all at once. Since the wheel of light is not seen in stages, one cannot use this as evidence concerning the gradual nature of perception.

The Sautrantikas say that perception occurs in the following way: One aspect of mind connects with one aspect of the object. This happens so fast that we think we see all these aspects at once as when we look at a flowered cup. But actually, it is like a firebrand that is whirled around. The resulting circle of light is an illusion. Foolish people think they perceive the object all at once, because they perceive it so quickly. The cause of the illusion of the circle of light is memory, which joins the boundaries.

The example is not correct

Shantarakshita's refutation of the example: In the case of the circle of light, one does not see anything clearly except the illusory circle of light. One does not see the torch at all. If this were the case with all objects of perception, we would not ever perceive distinctly. When we heard lata spoken quickly, we would nor be able to distinguish it from tala. When we looked at a multi-colored flowered cup, we would not be able to distinguish the red flowers from the blue flowers.

Further, memory is of the past, which quickly perishes. If perceptions happened so quickly, how could memory inform the mind by joining the boundaries between the apprehension of aspects of the object? Certainly not in a clear way, such as the bright circle of light or the distinctly flowered cup. The image would be vague — like a memory.

Why? There is only a vague connection between the object aspect of perception and the subject aspect of perception. It is not very distinct. The image that is directly perceived may be prompted by memory, but is not itself a memory. It is not directly perceived by the senses. It is a product of the mind consciousness. Therefore the Sautrantikas have not correctly explained perception as direct perception of the object or as memory.

The first Sautrantika view was that there is one mind that knows many objects. The second, or half-egg view, was that in an act of perception, in succession, there are many minds knowing each of many aspects of objects. The third view is that there are many minds at each instant, each knowing different aspects of an object

The previous view, half-egg, states that one perception is possessed by the mind at one instant. These perceptions change so rapidly that it looks like we perceive an entire object. Shantarakshita refutes this by pointing out one cannot perceive the past so if this theory were true, we could never know the cup, only single aspects of the cup. We could never put them all together. Rather, we put the aspects of the cup together, not by perception, but by memory and inference working together.

If we consider the third view, however, that many minds [mental states] at the same instant know many aspects of objects, then since each object is infinitely divisible, then there must be a infinite number of minds [mental states] at each instant. This is absurd.

Criticisms of non-Buddhist schools

Given these considerations, Shantarakshita next turns his critical eye on the views of those who claim there is only one single [unchanging] mind or knowing self. This is a different view than merely holding that there is a single mental [momentary] state that perceives an object or an aspect of an object. As Shantarakshita points out in sloka 35, many non-Buddhists such as the Naiyayikas understand the difficulties in this position. The Nyaya School divides the objects of knowledge into six categories: substance, quality, activity, general, particular, and composition. The mind in coming to know these various objects must change. The Nyaya school also recognizes that mind must be different from matter if matter is composed of unchanging permanent atoms, since consciousness is always changing.

In sloka 36, Shantarakshita argues against the view held by the Jainas and

Mimamsas that each person's mind is one, but appears many, similar to a pigeon's neck which seems to change its colors constantly. His argument is, once again, based on the idea that a mind must be transformed by what it knows. The only way a mind could be permanent and unchanging would be if its object were permanent and unchanging. But, we know a constantly changing world. Mind, therefore, must also be constantly changing.

Lokavadas

At the extreme opposite from those who hold that reality is cosmic mind are the Charvakas [Lokavadas] (sloka 37). These ancient materialists believed that direct perception was the only way to truth [one door]. Because of this they doubted the reality of causation. We only know one event follows another. We do not perceive the causal connection between them. Direct perception takes place only in the present. So only the present can be said to exist. The past and future are just names.

Further, the Charvakas believed that all things come from nature (*prakriti*). Nature, which is material, is made up of the elements, air, earth, fire and water. These elements form the body and from the body, as beer is fermented from grain, comes consciousness. Consciousness depends on the body and cannot exist without it. The only liberation from suffering that one can hope for is death.

Shantarakshita points out that this view is self-contradictory. If the only road to truth is direct perception, then one cannot hold that earth, air, fire, etc., are the essence of all things because their essentiality is not perceived.

Samkhyas

Next, in sloka 38, Shantarakshita considers the Samkhya claim that all reality can be reduced to a single principle, *prakriti* [or nature]. The Samkya believed that nature evolved in three strands or gunas: darkness, force, and brightness. Out of these were formed consciousness and twenty-four kinds of matter.

Shantarakshita argues that from a single unified essence, no duality can arise. Nature is either one or many. It cannot be both a unity and a diversity. If it is a unity, no change is possible; there is nothing with which it can interact to bring about change.

If reality were one and manifested as three, its nature would be self-contradictory. But we cannot know what is self-contradictory. So we would know nothing at all (sloka 39).

Advaitas

The next view that Shantarakshita criticizes is that of the Advaita Vedantins, or the Great Secret Soul. This is the view that all reality is really Brahman, partless, permanent and unchanging. Shantarakshita presents four arguments against this view in slokas 40, 41, 42 and 43. First, he points out that our knowledge of reality comes to us bit by bit. If reality were an undifferentiated unity, we should know it all at once. Secondly, if one were to argue that space is a unity, yet appears to be divisible, on closer reflection, it becomes apparent that space is not a thing. It is just a mental construction that provides a matrix for our measurements, directions, etc. Thirdly, even if one held that reality is a unity, which is incorrectly given various names, then, since these names are part of reality, and since names are made up of different letters, reality is once again revealed to be a diversity. And finally, the view that reality is an undifferentiated unity violates common sense for it certainly does not appear in that way.

Criticism of Chittamatra school

Shantarakshita, in sloka 44, begins his examination of the view that is closest to his own, and which he argues is generally true, but only on the relative level. This is the *Sem Tsam Pa* [*Chittamatra*] position. The incoherence and unverifiability of matter having been proved, all that seems to remain as a category for reality is mind. But as we have seen, it cannot be the unchanging cosmic mind of the great secret soul. What about changing mind? Consciousness, like all else, is immersed in the ocean of cause and effect. Past situations cause sentient beings to experience the world in predictable, orderly ways, the result of maturing habits. But these experiences do not correspond to anything — they are simply an illusory manifestation of the habitual tendencies of minds. Since all minds within each realm are similar, they produce similar results. That is why we usually agree on what we see, hear, etc., and why our logical methods are in agreement.

It is not at all correct to characterize individual minds as floating in a giant cosmic collective unconscious like fish swimming in the sea. Thoughts, memories, ideas of individuality, all these, are rather like waves that rise and fall in an ocean. According to the Chittamatra [the consciousness-only idealist school], consciousness, like all else, is immersed in the ocean of cause and effect. The result of past situations causes sentient beings to experience the world in predictable and orderly ways, the result of maturing habits. But these experiences do not correspond to anything — they are simply an illusory manifestation of the habitual tendencies of minds. Since all minds within any given realm are similar, they produce similar results. That is why we usually agree on what we see, hear, etc., and why our logical methods are frequently in agreement.

There are four forms of the Chittamatra view. Three in which appearance is accepted as true, [*sems tsam rnam bden pa*] and another in which appearance is not taken to be true [*sems tsam rnam rdsun pa*]. The first three have analogies with the three views of the Sautrantika.

In sloka 46, Shantarakshita begins his analysis of the Chittamatra version of the many objects — one mind view. If mind is one, and the mental objects are many, then that one mind could not reflect the diversity of objects. These objects are endlessly divisible. Even if the object is mental, rather than material, it is clearly made up of parts. And these parts are made up of parts and so on. How could a unified mental state remain one and yet be affected by such diversity? In sloka 47, he argues that a unified mental state could not relate to opposites such as hot and cold. And yet we can know something to be hot and another cold at the same time. Further, like all Buddhists, the Chittamatra believe the mind is always changing. How could the mind remain one when it is constantly transformed by the diversity of its object?

In sloka 48 he discusses the Chittamatra half-egg view. This is the position that one mind grasps one aspect of an object at a time, but this happens with such rapidity that it seems as if one sees a whole object. The example given was that of a torch, which when whipped about produces the illusion of a circle. Thus when we look at a flowered cup, we see first red, then blue, etc. But then, if this were true, the mental object would only possess one quality at a time. Nothing would have a simultaneously existing opposite. For after all there is only the mental object. For the Chittamatras there is no external physical object. If this position were correct, it would be impossible to feel simultaneously your left hand being cold in a bowl of cold water and your right hand being hot in a bowl of hot water, which is contrary to common sense. Nor could we ever perceive an entire object, for [as with Shantarakshita's criticism of the half-egg Sautrantika view] "seeing" the circle when a torch is whipped about is really caused by the mind, for seeing must take place in the present.

Nor can the theory of many objects/many minds be held consistently. If there is a separate mind for each object, and each object is infinitely divisible, then there must be an endless number of minds corresponding to each atomic part, which is absurd. And saying we perceive these objects contradicts the fact that we do not perceive indivisible parts at all (sloka 49).

In sloka 50, Shantarakshita discusses the claim that the mental object is not real. All of our experience then would be just reflections of a single mind. The Jainas also held this view, and Shantarakshita's argument against this is that it violates common sense. Jewels, for example, are clearly different from one another. How can they be a single mind? Objects have different qualities, incompatible ones. Some objects are round, some square. How could they be qualities of a single mind? If the mental object is unreal, all our perceptions are a mistake. Why, Shantarakshita argues (sloka 52), would anyone make such a claim? He understands this is because the Chittamatra school believes that absolute mind is beyond duality. So they believe it is all right to hold that what we see on the relative level is [ultimately] a mistake.

In sloka 53, Shantarakshita argues against applying the absolute to the relative. [His position is rather similar to Candrakirti's view that all words derive their meanings from their interrelation with one another, forming a net from which it is impossible to escape except through meditation.] This Chittamatra school admits that, although unreal, we know what cold is because we also know what hot is and vice versa.

Shantarakshita agrees, but then raises the question of how we are able to distinguish between the existent and non-existent. His argument unfolds in two stages. 1) It follows from the above that opposites like existent and non-existent must derive their meaning from one another, as do hot and cold. Thus on the relative level, both concepts must have meaning if either has a meaning (slokas 53-54). 2) This Chittamatra school has the problem of accounting for the difference between things like the Empire State Building which can be perceived and things like the horn of a horse and a sky flower which cannot be perceived.

The classic Buddhist position on existence and non-existence has always been that what is real is functional. In other words, a thing is real if it can enter into causal interactions. Shantarakshita returns to this early view, applying it to the relative. It becomes the touchstone of the real and unreal. On the relative level, those things are real that can enter into causal relationships. Sky flowers and horns of horses can't do this [except as ideas affecting our minds, in which case they are real ideas but not real entities].

Shantarakshita now introduces the Madhyamaka view. From the time of the earliest Prajnaparamita literature, the Madhyamaka position has been that which is free of all four extremes: 1) free of existence, 2) free of non-existence, 3) free of both existence and non-existence, 4) free of neither existence nor non-existence. This applies to the absolute. Any distinctions that are made must be made on the relative level alone.

Similarly, one cannot say that on the absolute level there is only subject or only mind. The notion of subject has no meaning without the notion of object. The notion of mind has no meaning without the notion of that which is not subject. Mind must have an object.

This does not mean that the object of mind must be matter. If matter is an incoherent concept, it cannot be the object of mind any more than the child of a barren woman. As Shantarakshita has argued elsewhere, upon close analysis, the idea of matter can be shown to be senseless.

Further, this Chittamatra school asserts that all of our common sense reality is as unreal as the horn of a horse (sloka 56). It can be named but doesn't exist. But only the existent can function as a cause. We are aware that earthquakes, volcanoes, etc. affect us. If they were unreal, they could not do this. They could not even arise in our minds. One hand cannot clap; similarly, the object cannot be identical with the subject.

Further, if there were only mind with no external reality, from where would thoughts arise? Mind would be like a pure crystal (sloka 59). How could it have any experiences? And even if these experiences were said to be deceptions, where is the deceiver? What is the origin of these deceptions?

Thus Shantarakshita concludes that, upon analysis, it becomes clear that this fourth Chittamatra position is incoherent. Thoughts must arise from a source other than the subject's mind.[30]

However, considering the arguments previously given by Shantarakshita, what are we to conclude? The theory of materialism has been refuted. The representational theory of knowledge, where the mind represents an external object, has been refuted. The view that mind and object are the same has been shown to make no sense. What is left?

At this point in the argument, it might be useful to outline the direction of Shantarakshita's thought:

On the unanalyzed relative level it is correct to make distinctions between real and unreal, hot and cold, table and chair, large objects and atoms, etc. These concepts form a network of meaning in which each term depends on others for its usefulness to us.

On the analyzed relative level, when we examine external reality closely, we discover that entities such as atoms, matter, elements, and compound material objects cannot exist. Nor can a single element such as nature [*prakrit*] exist. But internal reality is in no better shape. The notion of one mind is incoherent, but so is the notion of many minds.

Further, it is impossible to maintain that the mind depends on nothing else. If this were the case, we could not account for the orderly arising of thoughts. So, there is interdependent co-origination. Mind depends on this.

Nor is it possible to deny awareness. To do so is self-contradictory, because there must be awareness to deny awareness. So, on the pure relative level, one can assert the reality of awareness and interdependent co-origination.

On close examination, however, we discover that on the absolute level, causality [cf. Nagarjuna's critique] is itself is an incoherent concept. Further given the fact that awareness is pure subjectivity, it can never be known correctly as an object. So it is unknowable. Thus on the absolute level, truth is beyond conception. We call it emptiness.

In presenting this argument, Shantarakshita is following the traditional divisions of experience accepted by Chittamatra and Madhyamaka thinkers:

1) [Tib. *Kun tag (kun brtags)*]: conventional, habitually constructed experience.
2) [Tib. *Shan wang (gzhan dwang)*]: power of another or causality.
3) [Tib. *Yong drub (wongs grub)*]: nature of emptiness.

In slokas 61 to 63, Shantarakshita summarizes his general view. When analyzed, our experience of things on the gross level shows that objects can neither be single nor many. Since no entity can have a separate independent existence [recalling his previous critique of atoms, elements, and nature], then neither can a collection of separate entities. Since the only possibility is that objects are one or many, then there is something wrong with the way we know things. Our knowledge results from our habitual tendencies to think of things in certain ways, rather than from an accurate view of reality itself. And there is no beginning to these habitual tendencies. The causal conditions which cause us to conceive of phenomena in these misguided ways stretch endlessly into the past (slokas 65 and 66).

Thus no opponent can really refute Shantarakshita by arguing that things exist or do not exist (sloka 68). For Shantarakshita does not assert anything whatever concerning the ultimate existence or non-existence of things. Existence and non-existence are just relativistic concepts, and cannot correctly be applied on the absolute level.

There is one more subtle point that needs to be considered about this outline. There are two kinds of interdependent co-origination — pure and impure. Impure interdependent co-origination describes our understanding of how the world works on the unanalyzed relative level. A seed, for example, is the root or primary cause of a tree. But it must work together with other conditions such as air, soil, water, light, etc. But all of these notions such as seeds, etc., are concepts which when fully analyzed turn out to be incoherent. Causal relations, too, are a result of habitual tendencies. The planting of a seed under optimum conditions is always followed by the plant, so we think there is a necessary connection between the two. But this connection is, in fact, not discoverable. One event simply follows another and we call it cause and effect.

Pure awareness, then, cannot be said to depend on this illusory causality. Rather, it depends on pure interdependent co-origination. Here we begin to approach the heart of the matter. Reason is leading beyond itself to what will later be known through direct yogic perception [non-dual gnosis of the ultimate nature].

Although Shantarakshita does not put this in precisely these terms, the following is implied. Awareness, that is, objectless awareness, is the seed of enlightenment itself — the *tathagatagarbha*. The *tathagatagarbha* is the pure interdependent co-origination, which through *tendrel* [*rten 'brel*, synchronicity] brings all beings to enlightenment.

The tathatagarbha is the display of primordial wisdom. And pure inter-dependent co-origination, the orderly production of the enlightenment state, is the condition for developing the thought of enlightenment. This is the connecting point with the philosophy of the *Tattvasiddhi*, for through the experience of great bliss we are pushed beyond conception and experience by the conditions productive of enlightenment.

Starting with sloka 63, Shantarakshita puts aside his discussion of the absolute level and turns his attention to the relative. The relative level has three main characteristics. 1) It seduces the mind into accepting its reality, because on the unexamined level it looks perfectly convincing. 2) It is constantly changing, as instant by instant it disappears and is replaced by the arising of the next instant. Nothing is permanent — phenomena are an endless stream of birth and death. 3) All that exists is functional — that is, anything real functions as a cause in the system of interdependent co-origination. This stream of causes stretches endlessly throughout past, present and future. Every result comes about in this way, relying on causes immediately before it.

There is, therefore, no permanent cause. Some argue that Isvara [the Lord] is a permanent cause. But what reason do they have for their view? No one has ever found a permanent cause.

So that is all you can say about the relative. It is constantly changing in accordance with cause and effect, and when you analyze even this, you find its nature is emptiness. Other than this, Shantarakshita has no opinion about it. So there is nothing to refute in his system. For it rests squarely on the ultimate. And on the ultimate level, existence and nonexistence are categories which do not apply, for this level is beyond distinctions.

So, in sloka 69, Shantarakshita brings us back to an examination of the absolute. In sloka 70, he forestalls a possible criticism that he can say nothing about the absolute at all, since it is beyond conception. He points out that nevertheless there is some similarity between what he says and the absolute because the absolute is beyond distinctions and complexities and his method of reasoning breaks down distinctions and complexities. Further, there are two levels of the absolute, one of which is accessible in accordance with the capabilities of ordinary people. There are, as well, two ordinary ways to the absolute. One is through reasoning. Another way lies through selfless virtue and devotion. The only way to the higher absolute level is beyond ordinary capabilities, for it involves the spontaneous opening of the wisdom mind. This is the way of direct yogic perception.

So the absolute is beyond birth and dissolution, all concepts, all opposites (sloka 71). On the highest level, the absolute that can be spoken of is not the absolute. Nevertheless, reason is useful, for it can cut through the exaggerations that obscure the absolute. Ultimately, what reason points to can be verified by direct experience.

How can reason do this? The answer lies deep in the theory of Buddhist logic, designed specifically for debate. No argument can proceed without a common ground of agreement [*chos chan*, ground of the argument]. For example, if we are to carry on an argument about whether or not rabbits have horns, we must agree on what we mean by a rabbit. As Shantarakshita points out in sloka 78, on the relative level he accepted the apparent nature of phenomena and their generally accepted properties, so debate can begin at that point.

From where does the relative arise? From cause and effect, of course. But what is the nature of cause and effect? Our world is made up of our expectations, our habits. Not just our personal ones, but those of our species. We inherit our modes of perception, our way of thinking [logic] and our conceptual systems. The sum of this inheritance is the *alaya* [the storehouse consciousness]. All comes from the alaya as from a seed. It grows gradually, not all at once (sloka 81). Nothing is permanent. Thus, from these habits of thought, the self also arises, but it, too, is impermanent. It, like all phenomena, is *tendrel*, part of the system of interdependent co-origination.[31]

Because, on the relative level the system of cause and effect works well for us, we can use it to transcend the relative. This is why the accumulation of wisdom and merit can lead to the absolute (sloka 85). But for the result to be pure, the cause must be pure. Therefore, the motivation for practicing virtue cannot be to make money, etc. If you do this, you will make little progress. Only by not grasping at relative phenomena will you achieve a great result.

Before leaving the *Madhyamakalankara*, we should reflect once again on the purpose of this teaching, and how it can be put to good use on the path to enlightenment. The purpose of the teachings on the Madhyamaka is to bring about the realization of emptiness. This is equally true for the Prasangika Madhyamaka school which stresses the role of *reductio ad absurdum* arguments and the Svatantrika Madhyamaka school which stresses the use of result reasoning.

For both schools, reality is emptiness. We should connect to that nature by relaxing into it, without extreme views [nihilism and eternalism], and without grasping or clinging.

Because all phenomena are interdependent, there is no core existence. All are related, all are connected, all are in a state of change. Each is dependent on all others, and supports the others. That is how samsara and nirvana both function.

Nothing within an interdependent system truly exists. Everything within the system is like a reflection, mirror images, bubbles, dreams, mirages. It is like the moon reflected in water. These are the examples the Buddha and other great masters used to awaken us from our hard-headed grasping dualistic minds. Through these teachings the great masters bring forth a realization of great emptiness. This is not the same as holding on emptiness. Rather, with equanimity, and full of great confidence and joy, the great masters meditate on this meaning and obtain realization.

Absolute truth cannot be encompassed within ordinary logic. Absolute truth is beyond conception, beyond categories. When one has the realization of ultimate absolute truth one no longer distinguishes between absolute truth and relative truth. Both merge in a single state because there is no duality, no grasping. Just relax in the natural state. As the great teacher Santideva said in the ninth [wisdom] chapter of the *Guide to the Bodhisattva's Way of Life*, absolute truth is not an object of conception, of mind.

Similarly the great Shantarakshita said in the *Madhyamakalamkara*, since there is no birth, there is no rebirth. Playing this game of existence/non-existence ushers us beyond duality. Thinking of or playing with the words existence and non-existence will smash our regimented dualistic conceptions. Once duality and grasping are eliminated, we are not compelled to make divisions. Nature is not divided. There are no divisions or fabrications. At the ultimate level, even emptiness and non-emptiness are fabrications. This is the same as the Dzogchen view. Therefore there is nothing on which to meditate. No meditation is the great meditation. There is no conceptual constructed meditation in absolute truth

Dzogchen teachings often speak of the self-liberated state. Everything is self-liberated. There is no need to liberate it. Forceful liberation is conception, construction, illusion. Liberating and non-liberating, as well as emptiness and non-emptiness, are mental fabrications from the absolute point of view. From the ultimate absolute point of view, these are boundaries that mind creates for itself. They are dualistic, grasping. For that reason Chandrakirti said in his famed *Madhyamakavatara*, "Sentient beings are bounded by conceptions. Buddhas are not bounded by conceptions. If you relax in the absolute state, you will release the knots, the boundaries."

Practicing on the Madhyamaka teachings is no different than Dzogchen practice. Start with strong devotion, joy, appreciation and bodhicitta. The prayers in the ritual texts express love, compassion, joy and devotion that echo the beautiful qualities of our minds. They invoke one's hidden qualities. As is often said in the Vajrayana teachings, they will cleanse the dullness of channels, winds, nervous systems and mind and bring freshness. Thus with these beautiful thoughts and prayers, unite the two truths together in the Madhyamaka state.

The true nature is a union of the absolute and relative. So when you meditate, just relax. Don't think, "I'll only do this. I don't like that." During meditation just relax your mind in the great dzogchen or great emptiness. In the post-meditation state, perform every sort of good deed, the deeds of the paramitas. This is known as the two accumulations of wisdom and merit united together without any sorting out, without saying this is good or bad. Even the Vaibhashika and Sautrantika schools are based on impermanence, and thus on the two truths.

In the Mahayana teachings, because the two truths are in union, the ground is in union, Because the accumulation of wisdom and merit are in union, the path is union. Following this, the result will be union. For the two kayas, dharmakaya and rupakaya, are in union. This is full realization and achievement of enlightenment.

There is little difference between the Svatantrika and Prasangika Madhyamaka schools. Both are Mahayana and very special. They are the very ground of Dzogchen and Mahamudra teachings, but this is not only a teaching. It is a practice. So when you have time, do a little practice on the meaning of emptiness. Review the different arguments. The nature of Dzogchen and Mahamudra is the same. Both roads lead to the same goal. Relax and meditate on the true nature.

So as the great master Longchenpa said about all practices, begin with bodhicitta and devotion, practice the Madhyamaka without grasping or clinging, and with a good will dedicate the merit for the good of all.

REMARKS BY MIPHAM RINPOCHE ON THE TEXTS OF MADHYAMAKALAMKARA AND MADHYAMAKALMKARAVRITTI.

Mipham Rinpoche

Je Tsongkhapa says that the root text comprises both the verses and the autocommentary in prose. The commentary, being also the statement of the great master Shantarakshita himself, is extremely eminent and meaningful, and it is good to expound it at the same time as the root verses, regarding them both together as the root text.

Although there is nothing contradictory in such a proposal, and although this great being must surely have had some special purpose in explaining the matter so, the fact is that it is not usual for teachings to be expressed in such an alternating manner, sometimes in verse, sometimes in prose The normal procedure is for the commentary to do no more than explain the root verses.

If I had used the autocommentary itself as a basis for my own explanation, the result would, on account of its extreme prolixity, have been difficult for others to assimilate. I have therefore refrained from following the autocommentary word for word. Nevertheless, since the present work covers all the important points discussed therein, it may serve as a basis for understanding all the meanings that it contains. It would, however, be good in due course to consult the autocommentary as well as Kamalashila's Commentary on Difficult Points.

The Madhyamakalankara was translated from Sanskrit into Tibetan by the Indian scholar Surendrabodhi (lha dbang byang chub) and the monk translator and editor Yeshe De. The translation was later revised and checked for verbal accuracy, and its meaning established in the course of exposition.

[Padmakara p. 377, The colophon of the translators]

Colophon from Madhyamakalamkaravritti.

།འདི་ལ་རྗེ་ཙོང་ཁ་པས་ཚིགས་བཅད་
ལྷག་གཉིས་ཀ་རྩ་བར་བཞེད་པ་ནི། འགྲེལ་པ་འདི་འང་ཤིང་རྟ་ཆེན་པོ་རང་གི་གསུང་ཤིན་ཏུ་དོན་
གྱི་སྙིང་བྲུ་ཕུལ་དུ་བྱུང་བ་ཞིག་ཡོད་པས་རྩ་འགྲེལ་ལྷན་དུ་འཆད་ཉན་བྱུང་ན་ལེགས་པས་རྩ་བ་ཡིན་ནོ་
ཞེས་གསུངས་ནའང་དོན་གྱི་འགལ་བ་མེད་པ་སོགས་བདག་ཉིད་ཆེན་པོ་དེས་བསྟན་པ་ཐུགས་ལ་གཞག་
པའི་དགོས་པ་ཁྱད་པར་བ་ཡོད་པར་གདོན་མི་ཟ་ཡང་། སྤྱིར་ནི་དོན་རེས་འགའ་ཚིགས་བཅད་
ཀྱིས་བསྟན་པའམ། རེས་འགའ་ཚིག་ལྷུག་པས་བསྟན་པ་ལྟ་བུའི་སྲོལ་མ་མ་ཡིན་པར། རྩ་
བ་ཚིགས་བཅད་ཀྱི་དོན་དེ་སླར་ཡང་འགྲེལ་པས་བསྒྲལ་ཏེ་བཤད་པ་ཁོན་ཡིན་པ་འདི་ལྟར་ལགས་སོ།
།དེས་ན་འདིར་རང་འགྲེལ་ཉིད་འགྲེལ་བའི་ལུགས་སུ་བྱས་ན་ཚིག་ཤིན་ཏུ་མང་བས་གཞན་དག་འཇུག་
དཀའ་བའི་ཕྱིར་འགྲེལ་པའི་ཚིག་འབྲུ་གཉེར་བ་མ་ཡིན་ཀྱང་། དོན་དུ་འགྲེལ་བའི་གནད་ཀུན་
གསལ་པོར་བཀོལ་ཡོད་པས། འདི་ལ་བརྟེན་ཏེ་འགྲེལ་པ་ཉིད་ཀྱི་ཚིག་གི་ནུས་པ་རྣམས་ཀྱང་
སྤྱོད་ནུས་པས། སླར་ཡང་རང་འགྲེལ་དང་དཀའ་འགྲེལ་གཉིས་ལའང་བལྟ་བར་བྱས་ན་ལེགས་
སོ།

དབུ་མའི་རྒྱན་འདི་ནི་སློབ་དཔོན་ཞི་བ་འཚོ་བདག་དང་གཞན་གྱི་གྲུབ་པའི་མཐའི་རྒྱ་མཚོའི་ཕ་རོལ་ཏུ་ཕྱིན་སོན་པ། འཕགས་པ་ངག་གི་དབང་ཕྱུག་གི་ཞབས་ཀྱི་པདྨ་རྙོག་པ་མེད་པའི་ཟེའུ་འབྲུ་སྤྱི་བོས་ལེན་པས་མཛད་པ་རྫོགས་སོ། །

अयं मध्यमकालङ्कार आचार्यशान्तरक्षितेन स्वपरसिद्धान्तसागरपारंगतेन आर्यावलोकितेश्वर-निर्मलपादकेसरमूर्धग्रहीतेन विरचितः समाप्तः ।

རྒྱ་གར་གྱི་མཁན་པོ་ཤཱི་ལེནྡྲ་བོ་དྷི་དང་། ཞུ་ཆེན་གྱི་ལོ་ཙ་བ་བནྡེ་ཡེ་ཤེས་སྡེས་བསྒྱུར་ཅིང་ཞུས་ཏེ་གཏན་ལ་ཕབ་པའོ། །

अनूदितः संशोधितश्च भारतीयोपाध्यायेन शीलेन्द्रबोधिना तथा भोटदेशीयानुवादकैः भदन्तज्ञानसेनादिभिश्चेति शुभमस्तु ।

MADHYAMAKALANKARA

The Ornament of the Middle Way

by

SHANTARAKSHITA

Translated into English from the Tibetan by Marie Friquegnon and Arthur Mandelbaum in in collaboration with Geshe Lozang Jamspal·

SHANTARAKSHITA

1

Whatever my schools and others assert,
All things are completely free of
The intrinsic nature of one and many.
Therefore, they lack intrinsic nature, like reflections.

2

Because results are brought about in close succession,
There is no permanent single cause.
If each result is different,
Then causes are not permanent.

A CRITIQUE OF THE VAIBHASHIKA BEGINS:

3

That object of knowledge arising from meditation,
Which some (the Vaibhashika school) assert to be uncompounded,
Even in their system, cannot be one,
Because it is connected with successive cognitions.

4

If one knew the former cognition
Had the same nature as what followed after,
Then the former would be just like the latter,
And the latter would continue to be along with the former.

5

If the uncompounded object
Does not remain in the past or future,
Then one should recognize that, like one's knowledge of it,
The uncompounded object has only instantaneous existence.

6

Each thing arises
By the power of each previous moment.
Therefore objects cannot be independent of conditions.
Mind and mental states arise in the same way.

7

If one were to say that things occasionally
Arise by their own power, independently,
Then since it does not depend on another,
It should always remain either existing or non-existing.

8

What benefit is there whatever
In analyzing that which is impotent [nonfunctional]?
What benefit is there in lustful [women] debating
Whether or not a eunuch is beautiful?

9

It cannot be demonstrated that a person
Is either instantaneous or non-instantaneous,
Therefore it is clearly known
That it lacks the nature of one or many.

10

Since they [atoms] are connected in many directions,
How could pervading things be one?
Also since [parts of bodies, etc.] are covered or not covered [by each other],
Gross forms cannot possibly be one.

11

If sticking to, or else surrounded [by 10 atoms in the10 directions]
Or even completely [inseparable] with no gap,
A single partless atom is embedded in other atoms
And faces another atom.

12

But if one says that they face one another and are partless,
They would be the same.
In this case would they not fail to increase and
Become earth, air, water, and so on?

13

Seeing that the sides of the atom facing others are different,
If one accepts this,
How can the extremely subtle atom
Be considered as partless and one.

14

Each partless atom is thus proved to be without inherent nature.
Therefore the eye, substance, and so forth [composed of atoms]
About which my own schools and others have much to say
Should be understood as having no intrinsic nature.

15

Thus if the nature of atoms which compose
Such things as generalities and particulars,
If all of these are combined together like this,
How can they have intrinsic existence?

16

Consciousness arises
From what is completely opposite.
Not from that which is insentient,
But rather as self-awareness.

17

Because its nature is unique and partless,
It is impossible for it to have a three-fold nature.
Therefore self-awareness does not have
The aspect of subject and object.

18

This is the nature of consciousness.
Thus self-understanding is possible.
But how could it know the nature of objects if
As you have asserted, the nature of objects is different?

19

You cannot explain how consciousness
Knows others, as well as knowing itself
Because you have asserted
That subject and object are different.

20

The features of subject and object in this [your] theory
Appear to be different in substance from each other.
But they are similar being both reflections of the mind,
And the conventional distinctions are in a sense tied on to them functionally.

CRITICISM OF SAUTRANTIKA BEGINS:

A. ONE MIND/MANY OBJECTS:

21

For those who do not hold that consciousness
Is transformed by the representation of the object,
Then in their system, there would be no ability to know
An aspect of an external object.

22

[If you claim] one mind is not many, then
It cannot be divided into many aspects.
But then, the view of mind as undivided
Has no power to explain knowledge of many objects.

23

Without being free from diversity,
Consciousness would not be single.
But if it is different, one rather than many,
How could knowledge be one with its object?

B. CRITICISM OF HALF EGG:

24

[You say] perceptions of white and so forth
Have arisen gradually,
Because they arise quickly, foolish people
Think they experience these simultaneously.

25
But the sound of the word vine [lata],
Arises very quickly.
If [the syllables] were perceived simultaneously.
Then why would not [the syllables] be heard simultaneously?
[also tala]

HALF EGG:

26
You say that thought is of the mind alone and
Is not known gradually.
However [in my view], since they do not remain for long,
All mental states also arise quickly [successively].

27
[Opponents say] All the parts of an object of perception,
Are not grasped gradually but [all together].
Yet for all the different parts,
As they arise, they only appear to be simultaneous.

28
A firebrand whirled around once
Appears [deceptively] as a wheel.
Although it appears clearly,
It cannot be connected by perception.

29
In that way, the joining of the boundaries
Is done by memory,
Since there is no perception of the past,
There is no perception of the object [circle].

30
In this way, the object
Perished, and therefore cannot clearly appear.
Therefore the circle that appears
Is not clearly perceived.

C. Against many objects known by many minds:

31

[Some argue that] when one sees a drawing displayed,
Since it has many aspects, there are many states of mind [in a single instant]
In what way could this happen through one [mental state]alone?
This is how such views arise.

32

In that case, how could whiteness, and so forth
Which are known in a single way,
Have differences, such as a top, middle, and bottom?
Each of these would have to become multiple objects of knowledge [which is absurd].

End of criticism of the Sautrantika

33

A bit of white etc., atomic in nature,
In itself, single and partless,
Which appears to anyone's consciousness,
I do not feel exists.

34

[The Sautrantika correctly claim] that the elements of the five consciousnesses,
Have their own way of perceiving accumulations [of atoms].
The perceiving mind and [its objects] mental states
Are the sixth category.

35

Even non-Buddhists recognize
That consciousness cannot be considered as a singularity
Because it perceives substances
Which have [a plurality] of qualities.

ARGUMENTS AGAINST JAINAS AND MIMAMSAKAS

36

[Others argue that] in nature like a many faceted cat's-eye jewel
[Mind] reflects all the properties [of objects].
But if mind is grasping these many objects,
How can it be one in nature?

37

[The Charvakas say that] the accumulations of earth [air, fire and water together]
Are the basis of all objects and sense organs.
But this belief is not consistent,
Because they say there is only one truth [through perception] and the accumulations [of elements] are not perceived.

REFUTATION OF THE SAMKHYA VIEW:

38

Energy and so forth (the three gunas) they claim are the nature of sound and other things,
And are the basis of all objects and senses.
But this cannot be known by a single consciousness,
Because it has a threefold nature.

39

[If as the Samkhyas say] there are three aspects of a thing [the gunas],
But [reality] has a single aspect
They are inconsistent.
And how can reality be characterized this way?

ARGUMENTS AGAINST THE ADVAITINS:

40

Without external objects, and knowledge alone [Brahman],
What appears as various or permanent,
Whether simultaneous or successive,
Is very difficult to justify.

41
All knowledge about space etc.
Is just names for appearances.
But 'space' is comprised of letters
That are clearly a manifold.

42
Some say there is a single mind
To which a diversity of knowledge appears.
Yet it is not correct to hold that such a view could be [correct],
Because it [has already been shown] to be impossible.

43
Because manifolds appear to consciousness
All these cognitions are clearly diverse.
Similarly since different appearances are perceived as a manifold,
It is not correct that consciousness is one.

44
Similarly, [Yogacharins say] continuously from beginningless time,
Mind is composed of illusions brought about by maturing habits.
All the parts appear to us erroneously,
And are illusory by nature.

45
But yet although this [the Yogacharin view] may seem alright,
Is it really true?
One would agree
Only when one thinks on the unanalyzed level.

Criticism of the Yogacharin/Chittamatra—Mind Only view:

I. Subject and object are different
A. Against one mind/many aspects

46
So perfect consciousness should become many,
Or these objects should become one
But since they are distinct from one another,
Then this certainly generates a contradiction.

47

If there are not many distinct objects,
Then moving and not moving (opposites) and so forth,
Would all move with a single motion?
This would be undeniably an absurdity.

B. Half egg:

48

Also in the case of any doctrine that objects exist externally,
If the aspects are not separate [perceived as if simultaneous],
All phenomena would be one.
And nothing could be said to remove the absurdity.

C. Many minds/many objects:

49

If according to the number of reflected features,
One assigns states of consciousness
Then [states of] consciousness would be as numerous as the atoms,
This analysis would be difficult to circumvent.
[Features like blue are accepted as atomic.]

II. Subject and object are the same

A. Refuting the view that all is a reflection of one mind:

50

If as you [Yogacharins/Chittamatrins] say, all things are one,
Is this not to agree with the sky-clad ones [Jainas]
But multiplicity cannot have the characteristics of oneness,
Similar to the way a multi-faceted jewel is not one.

B. *Against the Chittamatra View that Distinct Appearances Are Unreal:*

51

But if one [a Chittamatra] holds that a manifold's true
nature is single
But appears to have multiple nature
How could these many qualities happen
Such as covered or not covered and so forth.

52

If they believe the perception of forms is in error,
And that forms do not exist independently,
This is because forms do not exist on the ultimate level.
Therefore the perception of forms is a mistake.

53

But how could it be that [forms] do not exist [apart from mind]
When we clearly perceive
That they are different from one another,
And [according to the Chittamatra] knowledge is not like this.

54

There cannot be any knowledge
Of what does not exist.
Just as there is no pleasure in what is unpleasant,
And no white in what is not white.

55

In such a way one cannot agree
[That the Chittamatra's] view of knowledge is logical,
Because this is not itself real knowledge,
Anymore than a sky flower and so forth, could be.

56

Non-existent features have no power,
And cannot be designated, like the horn of a horse,
Non-existent, it could not appear to consciousness
One could not assert correctly that it had that power.

57

Because [in this case] how could these noticed features
Be related to consciousness?
Being non-existent, they are not similar in nature, and also
Could not arise in consciousness.

58

If there is no cause whatsoever one cannot
Explain why [images] arise occasionally.
If there is a cause,
The mind cannot avoid being controlled by others.

59

If the object does not exist, but only the mind,
Without an object, developing by itself, then
Like a pure crystal glass,
The mind would not perceive at all.

60

Then if you think all cognitions are illusory,
How is this illusion perceived?
If images arise in the mind by the power of this illusion,
Then it is still the power of another.

END OF CRITICISM OF THE CHITTAMATRA POSITION

61

Investigating the properties of things, this and that,
[It becomes clear] that none has the nature of oneness.
[But] since no single thing exists by itself,
Then a collection of single things cannot exist either.

62

Things must be classified as one or many,
Nor can they have another classification
That includes both properties,
Because one and many are mutually exclusive.

63

Therefore these objects,
Are devoid of anything but conventional characteristics.
If someone asserts they are [ultimately] true,
Then what can I do about it?

64

That which is agreeable when unexamined,
Phenomena– both arise and decay, and
All things have the ability to function.
One should understand the conventional nature of all these objects.

65

That which is agreeable when unexamined,
Relies for its cause on an antecedent cause, which itself is caused by a former.
And the support of that past cause is that which was previous [to it].
All results are similarly brought about.

66

It is not correct to hold
There is no cause on the level of conventional appearance.
But if you claim this proximate cause is ultimately real,
You should explain it [without contradiction].

67

Following the nature of all things
Through the path of logic,
The assertions of others are dispelled.
Inferior debaters have no place to stand.

68

Those who do not assert anything to be existent or nonexistent
Nor both existent and nonexistent,
Not even very diligent opponents
Can successfully criticize.

69

Therefore on the absolute level
Nothing can be proved to exist.
Thus it was said by the Tathagata,
"Nothing whatever arises".

70

This is harmonious with ultimate truth,
And thus it has been called 'ultimate truth'.
Truly it is free from all
The accumulations of mental elaborations.

71

Since arising and so on does not exist,
Non-arising and so forth is impossible.
And thus since their reality is refuted,
Not even the sound of their names is possible.

72

[Others say] since that which you are trying to refute does not exist,
Reasoning about it cannot be correct.
But, however, [I reply] relying on your intellect
It will all be true on the relative, not the absolute level.

73

Now having realized this [the solidity of these arguments].
The nature of reality [emptiness] should be directly perceived.
Then why do not even simple people
Recognize the nature of things?

74

No, because from time without beginning,
The mind stream of beings has been burdened
Through accepting the reality of deceptive appearances.
For this reason, all sentient beings lack correct perception
[of reality].

75

Some come to know through
Cutting reification, evidence and reasoning.
Powerful yogis
Perceive directly and clearly.

76

By giving up all the different conceptions
Proclaimed as doctrines, and accepting those things
Known by the learned, women and children, all
Will be able to recognize what is really provably true.

77

The mode of proof and what is proved
Will exist completely on the relative level.
If not, the basic ground of agreement would not exist.
And how could refutation be possible?

78

As for myself, I never disputed,
The relative reality of the nature of appearances.
Having established this view of things,
One will not be confused about the relation of premise and conclusion.

79

Therefore continuously from beginningless time,
All certain investigation of existence and non-existence
Comes from the conformative seed of thought construction
And is known through inference.

80

By the force of entities,
Nothing arises, because they are non-existent.
The self-nature of things in themselves,
I have opposed extensively.

81

Because arising gradually and therefore not suddenly,
Nothing comes from what is chance or eternal.
Therefore because of this process, because of habitual patterns,
[Consciousness] arises from the start in its own manner.

82

Therefore the views of eternalism and annihilation
Are very far from the view of this doctrine [the middle way].
Perishing and arising also continue
Like the seed, sprout and twig, and so forth.

83

The wise who recognize the insubstantiality of phenomena,
And practice that which is without self-nature– emptiness,
Abandon the obscurations and defilements
Which come from mistaken views.

84

Cause and effect on the relative level,
I did not reject as spurious.
So on this level it is not confusing to maintain
The laws of defilements and purifications.

85

In this way, since cause and effect have been maintained,
Then since this dharma is established,
The stainless accumulations
Are consistent with this doctrine.

86

Through a completely pure cause
There will arise a completely pure effect.
Similarly, from a perfect view, morality
And all its pure branches will arise.

87

Similarly, from an impure cause,
An impure effect arises. Just as
From the force of wrong views,
Sexual misconduct, and so forth, arises.

88

Perception of objects is
Destroyed by valid arguments,
Therefore, they are erroneous
Like a mirage, and so forth.

89

If one's practice [of the six paramitas]
Arises under the power of the view which objectifies objects
Like practices arising through the false notion of "I" and "mine,"
They will be weak.

90

By not conceiving of things as real,
A magnificent result, [giving and so forth] can arise,
Because it arises from a nourished cause,
Like a sprout coming from a healthy seed.

The Relative Level is Mind

91

Causality is also only mind.
Whatever is established by the mind,
Remains mind.

The Absolute Level is Emptiness

92

In relying on Mind Only,
One knows that external objects do not exist.
Relying on this doctrine [Madhyamaka],
One will know as well the highest state, the selflessness of all things,
[including mind].

93
By riding the chariot of the two methods,
Grasping the reins of logic,
This is how the exact meaning
Of the Mahayana is attained.

94
Even those such as Vishnu and Shiva never experience
The cause of remaining in the limitless.
Even those who are crowned in the world [Sravakas and Pratyekabuddhas]
Absolutely never can taste this.

95
This perfectly pure nectar [enlightenment],
The result of pure compassion
Is experienced only by Buddha,
And enjoyed by no others.

96
Therefore by reaching mistaken views,
Those who believe in wrong tenets,
Arouse great compassion
In the minds of those that follow the system of the bodhisattva.

97
Those who possess the treasure of knowledge
Find no essential truth in the doctrine of others.
Thus great respect arises in them
For the Protector.

This completes the ornament of the doctrine of the Madhyamaka, composed by the mentor, Shantarakshita, who crossed the ocean of the doctrines of his own school and those of others, and who has taken the stamen of the lotus from the stainless feet of exalted Noble Lord of Speech (Manjushri).

This has been translated and corrected by the Indian abbot Surendra Bodhi and the Tibetan monk Bande Yeshe De.

About the Authors of the Commentaries

Khenpo Tsewang Dongyal Rinpoche

Khenchen Palden Sherab Rinpoche
(May 10, 1942-June19th, 2010)

Venerable Khenchen Palden Sherab Rinpoche is a renowned scholar and meditation master of Nyingma, the Ancient School of Tibetan Buddhism.

He was born on May 10, 1942 in the Dhoshul region of Kham, Eastern Tibet, near the sacred mountain Jowo Zegyal. On the morning of his birth a small snow fell with the flakes in the shape of lotus petals. Among his ancestors were many great scholars, practitioners, and treasure revealers.

His family was semi-nomadic, living in the village during the winter and moving with the herds to high mountain pastures where they lived in yak hair tents during the summers. The monastery for the Dhoshul region is called Gochen and his father's family had the hereditary responsibility for administration of the business affairs of the monastery. His grandfather had been both administrator and chantmaster in charge of the ritual ceremonies.

He started his education at the age of four at Gochen monastery, which was founded by Tsasum Lingpa. At the age of twelve he entered Riwoche monastery and completed his studies just before the Chinese invasion of Tibet reached that area. His root teacher was the illustrious Khenpo Tenzin Dragpa (Katog Khenpo Akshu).

In 1960, Rinpoche and his family were forced into exile, escaping to India. Eventually in 1967 he was appointed head of the Nyingmapa department of the Central Institute of Higher Tibetan Studies in Sarnath. He held this position for seventeen years, as an abbot, dedicating all his time and energy to ensure the survival and spread of the Buddhist teachings.

Rinpoche moved to the United States in 1984 to work closely with H.H. Dudjom Rinpoche, the supreme head of the Nyingmapa lineage. In 1985, Venerable Khenchen Palden Sherab Rinpoche and his brother Venerable Khenpo Tsewang Dongyal Rinpoche founded the Dharma Samudra Publishing Company. In 1988, they founded the Padmasambhava Buddhist Center, which has centers throughout the United States, as well as in Puerto Rico, Russia and India. The primary center is Padma Samye Ling, located in Delaware County, New York. Padmasambhava Buddhist Center also includes a traditional Tibetan Buddhist monastery and nunnery at the holy site of Deer Park in Sarnath, India.

Rinpoche travels extensively within the United States and throughout the world, giving teachings and empowerments at numerous retreats and seminars, in addition to establishing meditation centers.

Khenchen Palden Sherab Rinpoche's three volumes of collected works in Tibetan include:

Opening the Eyes of Wisdom, a commentary on Sangye Yeshe's *Lamp of the Eye of Contemplation*;

Waves of the Ocean of Devotion, a biography-praise to Nubchen Sangye Yeshe;

Vajra Rosary, biographies of his main incarnations;

The Mirror of Mindfulness, an explanation of the six bardos;

Advice from the Ancestral Vidyadhara, a commentary on Padmasambhava's *Stages of the Path, Heap of Jewels*;

Blazing Clouds of Wisdom and Compassion, a commentary on the hundred-syllable mantra of Vajrasattva;

The Ornament of Vairochana's Intention, a commentary on the Heart Sutra;

Opening the Door of Blessings, a biography of Machig Labdron;

Lotus Necklace of Devotion, a biography of Khenpo Tenzin Dragpa;

The Essence of Diamond Clear Light, an outline and structural analysis of *The Aspiration Prayer of Samantabhadra*;

The Lamp of Blazing Sun and Moon, a commentary on Mipham's Wisdom Sword;

The Ornament of Stars at Dawn, an outline and structural analysis of *Vasubandhu's Twenty Verses*;

Pleasure Lake of Nagarjuna's Intention, general summary of Madhyamaka;

Supreme Clear Mirror, an introduction to Buddhist logic;

White Lotus, an explanation of prayers to Guru Rinpoche;

Smiling Red Lotus, short commentary on the prayer to Yeshe Tsogyal;

Clouds of Blessings: an explanation of prayers to Terchen Tsasum Lingpa;
and other learned works, poems, prayers and sadhanas.

In English:
Turning the Wisdom Wheel of the Nine Chariots
Khenchen Palden Sherab Rinpoche's works in English co-authored with his brother Khenpo Tsewang Dongyal Rinpoche:
Ceaseless Echoes of the Great Silence: A Commentary on the Heart Sutra;
Prajnaparamita: The Six Perfections;
Lion's Gaze: A Commentary on the Tsig Sum Nedek;
Commentary on the Buddha Sadhana by Mipham Rinpoche;
Dark Red Amulet: Oral Instructions on Vajrakilaya Practice;
Discovering Infinite Freedom: The Prayer of Küntuzangpo;
Light of Fearless Indestructible Wisdom;
Door to Inconceivable Wisdom and Compassion;

Essential Journey of Life and Death;
Four Thoughts that Turn the Mind from Samsara;
Guhyagarbha Tantra;
Illuminating the Path: Ngondro Instructions According to the Nyingma;
La Luz de la Tres Joyas;
Liberating Duality with Wisdom Display: Eight Emanations of Guru;
The Buddhist Path;
Beauty of Awakened Mind: Dzogchen Lineage of Shigpo Dudtsi;
Anuyoga: Exploring the One Taste of the Three Mandalas.

Khenpo Tsewang Dongyal Rinpoche

Khenpo Tsewang Dongyal Rinpoche

Venerable Khenpo Tsewang Dongyal Rinpoche was born in the Dhoshul region of Kham in eastern Tibet on June 10, 1950. On that summer day in the family tent, Rinpoche's birth caused his mother no pain. The next day, his mother Pema Lhadze moved the bed where she had given birth. Beneath it she found growing a beautiful and fragrant flower which she plucked and offered to Chenrezig on the family altar.

Soon after his birth three head lamas from Jadchag monastery came to his home and recognized him as the reincarnation of Khenpo Sherab Khyentse. Khenpo Sherab Khyentse, who had been the former head abbot lama at Gochen monastery, was a renowned scholar and practitioner who spent much of his life in retreat.

Rinpoche's first Dharma teacher was his father, Lama Chimed Namgyal Rinpoche. Beginning his schooling at the age of five, he entered Gochen monastery. His studies were interrupted by the Chinese invasion and his family's escape to India. In India his father and brother continued his education until he entered the Nyingmapa Monastic School of northern India, where he studied until 1967. He then entered the Central Institute of Higher Tibetan Studies, which was then a part of Sanskrit University in Varanasi, where he received his B.A. degree in 1975. He also attended Nyingmapa University in West Bengal, where he received another B.A. and an M.A. in 1977.

In 1978, Rinpoche was enthroned as the abbot of the Wish-fulfilling Nyingmapa Institute in Boudanath, Nepal by H.H. Dudjom Rinpoche, and later became the abbot of the Department of Dharma Studies, where he taught poetry, grammar, philosophy and psychology. In 1981, H.H. Dudjom Rinpoche appointed Rinpoche as the abbot of the Dorje Nyingpo center in Paris, France. In 1982 he was asked to work with H.H. Dudjom Rinpoche at the Yeshe Nyingpo center in New York. During the 1980's, until H.H. Dudjom Rinpoche's *mahaparinirvana* in 1987, Rinpoche continued working closely with H.H. Dudjom Rinpoche, often traveling with him as his translator and attendant.

In 1988, Rinpoche and his brother founded the Padmasambhava Buddhist Center. Since that time he has served as a spiritual director at the various Padmasambhava centers throughout the world. He maintains an active traveling and teaching schedule with his brother Khenchen Palden Sherab Rinpoche.

Khenpo Tsewang Rinpoche has authored a book of poetry on the life of Guru Rinpoche, *Praise to the Lotus Born: A Verse Garland of Waves of Devotion*, a biography of His Holiness Dudjom Rinpoche, *Light of Fearless Indestructible Wisdom: The life and Legacy of H.H. Dudjom Rinpoche*, and a two-volume cultural and religious history of Tibet entitled *The Six Sublime Pillars of the Nyingma School*, which details the historical bases of the Dharma in Tibet from the sixth through ninth centuries. At present, this is one of the only books yet written that conveys the dharma activities of this historical period in such depth. He has also written a commentary on His Holiness Dudjom Rinpoche's Mountain Retreat instructions, *Inborn Realization*, and also *Light of Fearless Indestructible Wisdom: A Brief Account of the Life of Kyabje Jigdral Yeshe Dorje. His Holiness Dudjom Rinpoche.* Khenpo Rinpoche has also co-authored a number of books in English on Dharma subjects with his brother Khenchen Palden Sherab Rinpoche, including *Ceaseless Echoes of the Great Silence: A Commentary on the Heart Sutra; Prajnaparamita: The Six Perfections; Door to Inconceivable Wisdom and Compassion; Lion's Gaze: A Commentary on the Tsig Sum Nedek; and Opening Our Primordial Nature.*

Authored by Khenpo Tsewang Dongyal Rinpoche: *Light of Fearless Indestructible Wisdom: A brief account of the life of Kyabje Jigdral Yeshe Dorje, His Holiness Dudjom Rinpoche.*

He has also written a commentary on His Holiness Dudjom Rinpoche's *Mountain Retreat Instructions, Inborn Realization.*

ABOUT the AUTHORS of the COMMEN

TATTVASIDDHI IN SANSKRIT

आचार्यशान्तरक्षितविरचिता

तत्त्वसिद्धिः

॥ नमः सकलकलुषापहारिणे श्रीवज्रसत्त्वाय[1] ॥

वज्रयानं नमस्कृत्य महासुखसुखाकरम् ।
तत्त्वसिद्धिं प्रवक्ष्यामि सम्मोहविनिवृत्तये ॥ १ ॥[2]

एतस्मिन् वज्रमहायाने ये केचिद् अनुपचित-कुशल[3]–वासनासन्तानाः, समारोपित[4]-भावभावनाः[5], स्वविकल्पानिलप्रेर्यमाण[6]-मतयः, सकल-कलिकालकलङ्कपङ्कपटल-मली(म)स-मानसाः, असमधिगत-संसारसागर-तरणोपायाः, स्वविकल्पानल्पसङ्कल्पितधियः, विषमग्रन्थिस्थानदैन्यपतिताः, दुर्बोधग्रहावेशवशाकुलितचेतसोऽनुपासिताचार्याः, परमार्थभावनोपदेशरहिताः, श्रीमन्महासुखवज्रसत्त्वत्वम्, अनल्पकल्पासंख्येनापि मार्गान्तरेणाधिगम्यं[7] वज्रयानोपाययुक्तानाम् इहैव जन्मनि अनायाससाध्यस्थिर-सर्वभाव-[स्वभावम्], अनादिनिध(न)म्, अनालयम्, अखिलसत्त्वसन्तानं, स्वसंवेद्यस्वभावम्, महापुण्यहेतुम्, अधि[8]गमलक्षणं, तदुपायभू(तं) च महावज्रयानं समस्तयानोत्तममागम[9]लक्षणं न प्रतिपद्यन्ते, तेषाम् अज्ञान-तिमिरपटलविनिवृत्तये युक्त्यागमाभ्याम् अभिधीयते किञ्चित् ।

तत्र प्रज्ञोपायपरिगृहीता रूपादयो विषयाः परिभोगभावमापद्यमानाः विशिष्टफलावाहका भवन्तीत्यवश्यमेव प्रेक्षावद्भिरभ्युपगन्तव्यम् । विशिष्टा

---

1. [नम आर्यमञ्जुश्रियै कुमारभूताय]–भो
2. ग्रन्थकृत्कृतं मङ्गलाचरणम्
3. ० [मूल]–०
4. भावाः भावना–क
5. सं
6. –[हृत]–भो
7. ० णानधिगत–क ख
8. अभि–सं
9. आर्य–क ख

(2)

हि सामग्री विशिष्टमेव फलं जनयतीति सर्ववादिप्रसिद्धम् । यथा-पृथिव्यादिभ्यः समुत्पन्नमामलकफलं कषायरसमनुभूयते, पुनः क्षीरावसेकादिमधिकं कारणमासाद्य तदेव मधुरतया प्रतीयते । तदेवं-यथा कारणान्तराभिसंस्कृतं कारणं विशिष्टफलावाहकत्वेन प्रत्यक्षेणैव दृश्यते, एवमेते[1] रूपादयो विषया महामुद्रानिष्पत्तौ मन्त्रमुद्राधिष्ठितानां योगिनां विशिष्टतरं फलमुत्पादयन्तीति सद्भिरवधेयम्[2] । यतो न वै किञ्चिदेकं जनकमपितु सामग्री जनिका, तेन विशिष्टात् कारणा [न्तरा] द् हि विशिष्टमेव कार्यमुत्पद्यते, अचिन्त्यत्वाद् हेतुप्रत्ययसामर्थ्यस्य सर्वविदाम् । [प्रयोगः]–तत्र य इमे विशिष्टकारणाभि[3]संस्कृतास्ते विशिष्टमेव कार्यमारभन्ते, यथा क्षीरावसेकेना[4]मलकादयो मधुरफला भवन्ति, (तथा) विशिष्टकारणाभि[5]-संस्कृता रूपादयोऽ [पि], इति स्वभावहेतुः । तदत्र विशिष्टकारणान्तराभिसंस्कारमात्रानुबन्धस्वभावः[6] कार्याभिमतो [भावो] व्यापक [स्वभावः], कारणान्तरा[7]भिसंस्कारस्तु व्याप्यमेव[8] । [तेन] यद् यद् विशिष्टकारणान्तराभिसंस्कृतस्वभावम्, तद् तद् असति प्रतिबन्धके अकारण[9]वैकल्ये विशिष्टकारणान्तराभि[10]संस्काराद् विशिष्टमेव कार्यं भवति इति, तन्मात्रानुबन्धित्वात् ।

तस्य[11] तस्मात् सिद्धे व्याप्यव्यापकभावे व्यापके साध्ये व्याप्यं हेतुः । तद्यथा-व्यापके वृक्षादिके साध्ये व्याप्यं शिंशपादिः हेतुः । सिद्धत्वाद्[12] व्याप्यव्यापक-भावस्य न कल्पे[13]दत्र कारणं व्याप्य-व्यापक-भावात् परम् । एवमिहापि ज्ञेयम् । अत एवोक्तम्—

1. ऐते–सं
2. अवसेयम्-सं
3. आदि–सं
4. क्षीरार्णवसेकेन–क ख ग
5. कारणाभिः संस्कृताः–क ख
6. ०स्य,·····०स्य–सं
7. अन्तर–सं
8. रतेन–ख ग
9. [हेतौ] भो
10. कारणान्तरादिभिः–ख घ
11. तस्य–भो*
12. सिद्धत्वाद्–भो*
13. कल्पेत्-भो*

(3)

अशेषयोगतन्त्रेषु गुह्यचन्द्रतिलकादिषु ।
नास्ति किञ्चिदकर्त्तव्यं प्रज्ञोपायेन चेतसा ॥ २ ॥
निर्विशङ्कः सदा भूत्वा भोक्तव्यं पञ्चकामकम् ।
ओषधीचूर्णसंयोगादुरगस्येव बन्धनम्[1] ॥ ३ ॥
कामिनो नित्यरक्तस्य गीतवाद्यरतस्य च ।
कामसौख्यैरतृप्तस्य सिध्यते नात्र संशयः ॥ ४ ॥[2]
बोधिचित्तं दृढं यस्य निःसङ्गा च मतिर्भवेत् ।
विचिकित्सा नैव कर्त्तव्या तस्येदं[3] सिध्यते ध्रुवम् ॥ ५ ॥
सुनिरूप्य सुसञ्चिन्त्य प्रवेशं कारयेद्[4] बुधः ।
अन्यथाग्निप्रवेशोऽस्य कलां नार्हति षोडशीम् ॥ ६ ॥
तत्त्वं विज्ञाय तत्त्वेन योऽधिमुक्तिं निषेवते ।
स सिध्यत्यन्यथा तस्य[5] महानिरय[6]पातनम् ॥ ७ ॥

न चैतच्छक्यते[7]वक्तुं यथैते[8] रूपादयो विषयाः क्लेशप्रसूति-हेतुत्वादपायहेतव इति। क्लेशानाम् आत्मात्मीयग्रहाभिनिवेशपूर्वकत्वात् न रूपादयो निमित्तम्, येन

आत्मनि सति परसंज्ञा स्वपरविभागात् परिग्रहद्वेषौ ।
अनयोः सम्प्रतिबद्धाः सर्वे दोषाः प्रजायन्ते[9] ॥८॥[10]

तस्माद् यस्यात्मदर्शनं तस्यैते क्लेशाः सम्भवन्तीति। यस्तु नैरात्म्य-

---

1. मारणम्–क ख ग घ
2. ३–४ श्लोकौ 'श्रीचन्द्रगुह्यतिलकनाममहातन्त्रराज'स्य देगेभोटसंस्करणे जखण्डे २५६ तमे पृष्ठे स्वल्पपाठभेदेन प्राप्येते, अन्येषां निर्देशो न शक्यः।
3. [इह]–भो
4. [कुर्यात्]–भो
5. तस्य–भो*
6. निलय–ग
7. शक्यम्–ख घ
8. एते–भो*
9. क ख ग त्रिषु गद्यमयम्, भोटे पद्यरूपम्।
10. प्रमाणवार्तिके-प्रमाणसिद्धिः २२१–२२२।

(४)

सात्मीकरणात् समासादितनैरात्म्यरसः[1], तस्य नैते तथा भवन्ति ।

यदि पुनः विषयाः सर्वदा[2] रागहेतव एव तदा कथं सम्यक्परीत-ज्ञानमपि जनयन्ति अशुच्यादिभिराकारैः, अभ्यासबलात्, तेन यथासमारोप-मेव तत्त्वेन विज्ञानमुपजनयन्ति । एवं [विषयाः] विशिष्टसमारोपाद् विशिष्टपरिणामाच्च विशिष्टफलनिष्पत्तौ हेतुभावं प्रतिपद्यन्त इति किं [न] इष्यते ? यथा—

परिव्राड् - कामुक - शुनामेकस्यां प्रमदातनौ ।
अशुचिः[3] कामिनी भक्ष्या इति तिस्रो विकल्पनाः ॥१॥[4]

न च एतेऽपि विशिष्टसमारोपाः तथापरिणामाच्च संसारबन्धहेतुका भवन्ति इति, त्रिमण्डलपरिशुद्धत्वाद् देय-दायक-परिग्राहकाप्रतिलब्धेः । [यस्माद् त्रिमण्डलपरिशुद्धेः मन्त्र-मुद्रापरिणामः] तस्मान्मन्त्रादिभिराहित-विशेषा रूपादयो विषया अनुत्तरमेव फलं कुर्वन्ति । [यथा[5]] विषादिकं[6] मन्त्रादिभिः संस्कृत्योपभुज्यमानमन्यदेव रसायनादिकं फलमावहत इति, तदन्यथा बालानां नियमेन पञ्चत्वं[7] करोतीति । एवं विषया अपि मन्त्र[8]-मुद्राधिष्ठिता विशिष्टतरमेव फलं विकुर्वन्तीति सुतरामवबोद्धव्यम् । तच्चोक्तं **श्रीपरमाद्ये**—

रागो द्वेषश्च मोहश्च त्रयैते विषमं गताः ।[9]
विषत्वमुपयान्त्येव विषमत्वेन[10] सेविताः ।[11]

---

1. मानसः-ख ।
2. [सर्वथा]-भो
3. [शव-] भो
4. द्रष्टव्यः श्लोकवार्तिके-शून्यवादः ॥ ५९ ॥
5. तदादि-सं
6. मदादिकं-ग घ
7. पञ्चस्कन्धम्-ख ग घ
8. मनु-क ङ
9. [त्रय एते हि विषं गताः]-भो
10. विषमेण-सं
11. विषयत्वमुपयान्त्येते विषमेन तु सेविताः-ख घ ।

(5)

अमृतत्वं पुनर्ये च अमृतत्त्वेन[1] सेविताः ॥ १० ॥[2]

पुनश्चोक्तं **रत्नकूटसूत्रे**–[3] 'तद्यथा **काश्यप** ! इक्षुक्षेत्रेषु शालिक्षेत्रेपु[4] संकरकूट[5] उपकारीभूतो भवति, एवमेव [यो] बोधिसत्त्वस्य क्लेश [संकरकूटः सः सर्वज्ञतायाम्] उपकारीभूतो भवति ।' 'तद्यथा **काश्यप** ! मन्त्रौषधिपरिगृहीतं विषं न निघातयति[6] [7]एवमेव प्रज्ञोपायसमन्वितो बोधिसत्त्वः [क्लेशविषै]र्न विनिपात्यते ।'[8] पुनश्चोक्तम् **आचार्यनागार्जुनपादैः**

वासनामूलपर्यन्ताः क्लेशास्तेऽनघ[9] ! वर्जिताः ।
क्लेशप्रवृत्तितो[10] यावत्त्वयाऽमृतमुपार्जितम् ॥ ११ ॥[11]

पुनश्चोक्तम् **उपालिपरिपृच्छासूत्रे**—'रागो बोधिसत्त्वस्य महासत्त्वार्थतायां संवर्तते, सत्त्वानुरागत्वाद्[12]' इति ॥

सामग्रीभेदात् कार्यभेद-दर्शनाद् धर्मनैरात्म्यावबोधाच्च न तत्राभि-

---

1. अमृतत्वाय–ख घ
2. देगेभोटसंस्करणे 'त' खण्डे २२० तमे पृष्ठे ।
3. **काश्यपपरिवर्तः** (रत्नकूटे 'छ' खण्डे भोटदेगेसंस्करणे १३० तमे पृष्ठे । संस्कृत-भोट-चीनभाषासु शङ्घाईतः १९२६ तमे ईशवीये वर्षे प्रकाशिते श्री ए० बी० वान् स्टाल-होल्सटीन-सम्पादिते 'आर्यकाश्यपपरिवर्तनाममहायानसूत्रे' ७९ तमे पृष्ठे प्राप्तं पाठान्तरम् एवम्—'तद् यथा अपि नाम **काश्यप** यं महानगरेषु संकरकूटं भवति स इक्षुक्षेत्रेषु मृद्वीकाक्षेत्रेषु च उपकारीभूतो भवति, एवम् एव **काश्यप** यो बोधिसत्त्वस्य क्लेशः स सर्वज्ञतायाम् उपकारीभूतो भवति ।
4. [मृद्वीका]–भो
5. [महानगरे कूट]–भो
6. निपातयति–क ख घ ङ
7. काश्यप–सं० +
8. 'ज्ञानोपायकौशल्यपरिगृहीतो बोधिसत्त्वस्य क्लेशविषं न शक्नोति विनिपातयितुम्'–**काश्यपपरिवर्त**शङ्घाईस्थपाठान्तरम्–पृ० ७८ ।
9. [नाथ]–भो
10. [स्वभाव]–भो
11. वासनामूलनिष्ठेन त्यक्तं क्लेशाशुभं त्वया ।
 क्लेशस्वभावकमपि कृतं पीयूषमेव च ॥ **निरुपमस्तवे**पाठान्तरः ।
12. रत्नकूटे 'च' खण्डे १२६ तमे पृष्ठे–भोटदेगेसंस्करणे ।

(6)

निवेशः कथञ्चिदपि सम्भवति, केवलं[1] त्वनुत्तरमहासुखफलावाप्तेः नान्यत् साधनमस्ति, तत्तैरेव[2] सुखैराहार[3]विहारादिभिस्तत्फलमभिमुखीक्रियते यस्य[4] पुरः[5]सरं त्रिभवः स सादृशः स्यात्। कथमन्यादृशोद्भूतः तादृशः स्यात्। अतएवोक्तं सम्बरतन्त्रे[6]—

आत्मा वै सर्वबुद्धत्वं सर्वशौरित्वमेव च।
स्वाधिदैवतयोगेन तस्मादात्मैव[7] साधयेत् ॥१२॥
न योगः प्रतिबिम्बेषु निषिक्तादिषु जायते।
बोधिचित्तमहोद्योगाद् योगिनस्तेन देवताः ॥१३॥
स्वमात्मानं परित्यज्य तपोभिर्न च पीडयेत्।
यथासुखं सुखं धार्यं सम्बुद्धोऽयमनागतः ॥१४॥
नातिशौचं[8] न नियमो न तपो न च दुष्करैः[9]।
तप[10]श्चारैर्न नियमैः सुखैर्हर्षैश्च सिध्यति ॥१५॥

यथा, भगवता रूपादयः तन्निर्जाताः सुखपरिणामनाः अनुत्तरफलहेतुरुक्ताः तथा स्पर्शनिर्जातसुखपरिणामना अपि[11]। यदि[12] आगमविरुद्धत्वान्न भवती(ति) चेद्, आगमः-स्पर्शविशेषसुखसंसेवनात् तत्फलमावहतीति।[13] तत्र विरोधः तस्य प्रतिषिद्धत्वादिति चेत्, [न], प्रतिषेधस्यनियतविषयत्वात्। ये हि प्रज्ञोपायरहिता आत्मात्मीयग्रहाभिनिवेशेन परिणामनानभिज्ञाः

---

1. केवलम्-भो*
2. तदर्थान्तिरैरेव-ख ग घ
3. सुखाहारादिभिः-ख
4. यस्य-ख घ हस्तलेखेषु न
5. पुरःसरम्-भो*
6. [सम्पुटतन्त्रे]-भो
7. [आत्मानं प्रसाधयेत्]-भो
8. [स्नानं]-भो
9. [दुष्करम्]-भो
10. अहङ्कारैः-क ख ग घ
11. [इयमपि तादृशी]-भो
12. तद्यथा-भो, ग घ
13. न-ख +

(7)

स्पर्शविशेषं संसेवन्ते, तेषामविद्यापरिगृहीतमूर्तीनां विषया[1] अपायहेतवो भवन्तीति। तथा चोक्तं भगवता—

भिक्षुभावे स्थिता ये च ये च तर्करता नराः।
बुद्धभावे स्थिता ये च तेषां तत्त्वं न देशयेत् ॥१६॥[2]

भगवता तान् प्रति सन्धायं प्रतिषेध उक्तः। तदुक्तं च श्रीसमाजे—

दशाकुशलान् कर्मपथानिच्छन्ति[3] ज्ञानवर्जिताः ॥ १७ ॥[4]

तथा वैरोचनाभिसम्बुद्धावप्युक्तम्—

उपायै रहितं ज्ञानं शिक्षा वाऽपि हि देशिता।
श्रावकानां महावीरेणा (व) ताराय[5] तेषु वै ॥ १८ ॥[6]

न तु प्रज्ञोपायपरिगृहीतमूर्तीनां विशिष्टफलान्वेषिणां विशिष्ट[7]-परिणामनाफलमनुभवतां परमार्थधर्मतत्त्वावबोधात् मनागपि तेषां तद्दोष-भागिता भवति, किन्तु मतिविशेषेण[8] समन्विताः सन्तोषस्य[9] चानुत्तरस्य लाभिनो भवन्ति, अकलुषत्वाच्चित्तस्य। तस्मादाशयविशेषेण कृत एवायं [पुण्य] पुण्येतरविभागो, न तु यथावस्तु व्यवस्थितरूपम्। उक्तञ्च आर्यदेवेन—

सङ्कल्पाद् बोधिसत्त्वानां शुभं वा यदि वाऽशुभम्।
सर्वं कल्याणतामेति[10] तेषां वश्यं यतो मनः ॥ १९ ॥[11]

तेन सङ्कल्पकृतेषु पुण्यापुण्येषु यस्य विशिष्ट एव कारणान्तर[12]कृत-

---

1. [विषयसेवनम्]-भो, तेषां-ख च
2. आकरो न प्राप्तः।
3. कुर्वन्ति-सं
4. गु॰ स॰ तं॰ ॥ १७।१५ ॥
5. [अनुग्रहाय]-भो
6. देगेभोट संस्करणे २२१ तमे पृष्ठे।
7. विशिष्ट-सं +
8. किन्तेनातिविशेषेण-ख
9. [फलम्]-भो
10. सर्वसङ्कल्पता सेति-क ख ग
11. चतुश्शतकम्-॥ ५।५ ॥
12. कारणान्तर-सं +

(8)

सङ्कल्पविशेषः, रूपादिषु स तस्मादाशयविशेषाद् विशिष्टमेव फलं तस्य अवश्यमकामकैरपि परैरप्युपगन्तव्यम् इति। अत एवोक्तं **भगवता**--

'मायोपमा[1] धर्माः, अधिमुक्तस्य सर्वोपभोगा युज्य (न्) ते'[2] इति। पुनश्चोक्तम्—'अहङ्कार्यश्रद्धस्य भिक्षोः श्रद्धादेयम् अपरिभोग्यम्।'[3]

पुनश्चोक्तं **सम्वरतन्त्रे**[4]--

आकाशलक्षणं सर्वं आकाशं [चाप्यलक्षणम्]।[5]
मायोपमं च [वै] सर्वं त्रैधातुकमशेषतः॥ २०॥
दृश्यते स्पृश्यते[6] चैव यथा माया हि सर्वतः।
न चोपलभ्यते चैवं सर्वस्य जगतः स्थितिः।[7]
अनया मुद्रया योगी शोधयेत्[8] भुवनत्रयम्॥ २१॥

पुनश्चोक्तं **सर्वदेवसमागमतन्त्रे**---

यैरेव मूढा बध्यन्ते बुद्धाः क्रीडन्ति तैरिह।
सर्वे सम्पूर्णयोगेन अन्यथा यान्ति दीपवत्[9]॥ २२॥

पुनश्चोक्तं—

गुप्तलोकोत्तरां चर्यां विचरन्त्यविकल्पतः[10]।
प्रमादश्चान्यथा जायेत् विकल्पस्तत्र युज्यते॥ २३॥
निर्विकल्पेन भावेन सर्वाकारेण सर्वदा।
सत्त्वमास्थाय निःशङ्कः तदा सिद्ध्यत्यसंशयम्॥ २४॥

---

1. [मायाद्युपमा]-भो
2-3. आकरो न प्राप्तः।
4. [सम्पुटतन्त्रे]-भो
5. गम्यलक्षणम्-क ख ग घ
6. दृश्यते-सं
7. द्रष्टव्या-साधनमाला-द्वि० भा० पृ० ४७०, गायकवाड, १९६८ ई०।
8. भक्षयेत्-सं
9. [महाज्ञानिनः चित्तसम्पन्नयोगिनः]-भो +
10. विचरन्-ख

(9)

मत्त्वेन निर्विशङ्केन सर्वावस्थोऽपि सर्वदा।
सर्वाचारप्रवृत्तोऽपि न बन्धमुपयास्यति ॥ २५ ॥
निःशेषाचारसञ्चारो निर्विकल्पेन चेतसा।
सर्वेन्द्रियोपभोगेन सत्त्वस्थो हि न बध्यते ॥ २६ ॥

पुनश्चोक्तम्[1]—

शून्यरूपमिदं सर्वं शून्याकारेण चक्षुषा।
पश्यतां निर्विकल्पानां सतां निःशङ्कता भवेत् ॥ २७ ॥

[पुनः] तत्र [एव]—

[सर्वाणि[2]] व्योमरूपाणि व्योमरूपेण चेतसा।
भावनान्निर्विकल्पत्वं निःशङ्कत्वं प्रजायते ॥ २८ ॥

पुनश्चोक्तम्—योगिनां कीदृशं व्रतम् ?

सोपायं सर्वकर्माणि निर्विशङ्कश्चरेत् तदा[3]।
[निर्विशङ्केन भावेन][4] व्रतानामुत्तमोत्तमः ॥ २९ ॥

तपः किमुच्यते ?

निर्विकल्पेन भावेन[5] सर्वकर्माणि सर्वदा।
आचरेन्निर्विशङ्केन तपसामुत्तमं तपः ॥ ३० ॥
विषयान् सेवमानस्य निर्विकल्पेन चेतसा।
कुत्साधितं न वा चेतस्तत्तपो दुरतिक्रमम् ॥ ३१ ॥
यस्तु सर्वाणि कर्माणि प्रज्ञया विनियोजयेत्।
सर्वं[6] शून्यपदे योज्यं तपो ह्येष महात्मनाम् ॥ ३२ ॥

---

1. ग—हस्तलेखे नास्ति।
2. तत्त्वानि—ग घ
3. [सदा]-भो
4. निर्विकल्पा यदा चर्या—सं
5. [चित्तेन]-भो०
6. [तच्च]-भो०

(10)

प्रज्ञासङ्क्रान्तिरूपेण निर्विकल्पेन चेतसा ।
निःशङ्काचारसञ्चारः तपस्तेषां महात्मनाम् ॥ ३३ ॥

प्रज्ञोपायं विनाऽन्यत्र यदि चित्तं न सङ्क्रमेत् ।
नियतं तत्समुद्दिष्टं महाबोधिप्रदायकम् ॥ ३४ ॥

योगिनामभियुक्तानां निर्विकल्पानुगामिनाम् ।
तेषां सर्वाणि भूतानि [विलासार्थं][1] च सृष्टवान् ॥ ३५ ॥

प्रज्ञादर्पणसङ्क्रान्तं तदाकारं च संस्कृतम् ।
[प्रज्ञाजाता स्मृति[2]] स्तेषां निर्विकल्पात्मचेतसाम् ॥ ३६ ॥

दर्पणप्रतिबिम्बं च स्वप्नं मायां (च) बुद्बुदम् ।
इन्द्रजालं च सदृशं[3] यः पश्येत् स प्रभुः स्मृतः ॥ ३७ ॥

तडिद्[4]गन्धर्वनगरं विपाकञ्चैव संस्कृतम् ।
तदाकारं[5] प्रपश्यन्ति तस्यायत्ताः प्रजाः स्मृताः ॥ ३८ ॥

[इत्युक्तम् ।]

तेन न कस्यचित् स्थितिरस्ति यत्राभिनिवेशः स्यात् । 'यदा चैवंभूतैरपि मायोपमैः भावैर्विशिष्टसंभोगसञ्जातसुखस्पर्श[6]-परिणामत (न?)या किञ्चिद् विशिष्टफलं प्राप्यते, तदा किं नेष्यते ।?'' न हि एते[7] स्थिराः स्वभावतः, किन्त्ववभासमात्रलक्षणाः । यदि एते विशिष्टभावनाभ्यासबलाद् विशिष्टसुखसौमनस्यादिककार्येषु आर्या[8]नुत्तरफलावाप्तिहेतुभावं प्रतिपद्यन्ते, तदा न कश्चिद्दोषः । तथाचोक्तं श्रीपरमाद्ये–

---

1. विधानार्थम्–सं
2. प्रज्ञावन्तः स्मृताः–सं
3. संदृश्य–ग घ
4. नैति–क, नेतितं–ख
5. यदाकारं–ग
6. सुखस्पर्श–सं
7. न हि ते–क ग
8. आर्य–सं +

(11)

आत्मा वै सर्वबुद्धत्वं सर्वशौरित्वमेव च ।
स्वाधिदैवतयोगेन तस्मा[1]दात्मैव साधयेत् ॥ ३९ ॥
दुष्करैर्नियमैस्तीव्रैः मूर्तिः शुष्यति दुःखिता[2] ।
दुःखाद् विक्षिप्यते चित्तं विक्षेपात् सिद्धिरन्यथा ॥ ४० ॥
मनोमूर्तिदृढत्वाच्च सर्वसौख्यं[3] दृढीभवेत् ।
दुःखंश्चलत्वमायाति निरोधं[4] वापि गच्छति ॥ ४१ ॥

पुनश्चोक्तं लौकिकलोकोत्तरवज्रतन्त्रे—

सुखेन लभ्यते सिद्धिर्न सिद्धिः कायतापनैः ।
यस्मात् समाधिसम्भूतं बुद्धत्वं सर्वसौख्यतः ॥ ४२ ॥
अनाहारादिभिस्तीव्रैस्तथान्यैश्च तृषादिभिः[5] ।
कायतापाद्धि विक्षेपो विक्षेपात् सिद्धिरन्यथा ।
हीनसत्त्वा न सिध्यन्ति दुष्करास्तेन कीर्तिताः ॥ ४३ ॥

पुनश्चोक्तं श्रीसमाजतन्त्रे[6]—

दुष्करैर्नियमैः कष्टैः[7] सेवमानो न सिध्यति ।
सर्वकामोपभो[8]गैस्तु सेवयंश्चाशुसिध्यति ॥ ४४ ॥
भिक्षाशिना न जप्तव्यं [न च भैक्ष्यरतिर्भवेत्] ।[9]
जपेन्मन्त्रमभिन्नाङ्ग[10] सर्वकामोपभोगकृत् ॥ ४५ ॥

---

1. [सुखाद्]–भो
2. [देहिनां]–भो
3. सौख्यैः–ख
4. निरोधश्चापि–ख
5. [तप आदि] भो, तथादिभिः–घ
6. गु० स० तं० ॥ ७।३–५ ॥
7. [तीव्रैः]–भो
8. ०कल्पोप–ख ङ
9. भैक्षरतो–क ख घ ङ
10. ०ङ्गः–ख ङ

(12)'

काय-वाक्-चित्त-सौस्थित्यं प्राप्य बोधिं समश्नुते ।
अन्यथाऽकालमरणं पच्यते[1] नरके ध्रुवम् ॥ ८६ ॥

नेन प्रकृतिप्रभास्वर-स्फटिकोपलसदृशे मनसि रूपादिभि-(रा) हित-संस्कारविशेष-सुखसौमनस्यलक्षण: स: तत्र प्रज्ञोपायपरिगृहीतस्याभ्यास-विशेषबलात् प्रकर्षपर्यन्तरूपता[2]मासादयेदिति । तद्यथा—प्रज्ञादि[3]शिल्प-कलादय: । शब्दादि[4]विषयानुभवसञ्जातसंस्कारविशेष [तो] योगिज्ञानम् असकृद्[5]भावनाभ्याससामर्थ्यात् समाहित[6]परमशाश्वतस्वभावं भावनाप्रकर्ष-पर्यन्त [मायात् ।] स्वसिद्धान्ते सुगतादीनामिव,[7] लोके च कामशोक-भयोन्मादादिवत् । स्पर्शादि[8]जनितसुखसौमनस्यादयश्च भाव्यन्ते, तस्मात्तोऽपि परमविशेषशालिन इति स्वभावविरुद्धोपलब्धि: । इहापि दु:खादिविरुद्धं सुखसौमनस्यादिलक्षणं कार्यम्, तच्चाभ्यासबलात् सात्मीभावमासाद्यमानमुप-लभ्यते यदा, तदा[9]तद्विरुद्धं दु:खदौर्मनस्यादिकं निवर्तयति, स्वगुणव्यूहं च ढौकते ।[10] तेन तदत्र सामग्री[11]भावनतया व्यवस्थितं [तद्विरुद्धस्य][12] दु:खादे (र) वकाशमपाकरोति । तद्यथा—शीतादिविरुद्धमुष्णादिकम् उपलभ्यमानं शीताद्यभावं प्रतिपादयति, येनैकत्र स्थाने परस्परं[13] न विरुद्ध-मुपलभ्यते, एवम् अनयोरपि सुखदु:खयोर्न चैकत्र सन्तानात्मनि कथमपि सम्भव:, तद्विरुद्धत्वात् तस्य, तेन सुखसौमनस्यादि सात्मीकरणे नैव दु:खादीनां कथमपि सम्भाव (नी) यतामारोपयति इति युक्तमुक्तम्—स्वभावविरुद्धोपलब्धि: तद्रूपाभावं प्रतिपादयति । प्रकर्षपर्यन्तगमने अभ्यास-

---

1. पतन्ति–सं
2. रूपमासा०–ख ङ
3. आदि–सं०
4. [रूपादि]–भो०
5. [निरन्तर]–भो०
6. समाहित–सं +
7. सुगतादिवत्–ग घ ङ
8. आदि–सं +
9. तद्विरुद्धं–ख
10. ढौकयते–ख
11. सात्मी–ख
12. सन्तानविरुद्धस्य–सं
13. सन्तानपरम्परया–क, सन्तानपरस्परविरुद्धयो–ख घ ङ

(13)

विशेषो हेतुः, प्रज्ञाशिल्पकलादिवत्, तद्विशेष [विरुद्धो] पलब्धेः, इत्यव-बोद्धव्यम् ।

किञ्च भाव्यमानानामपि यदि विशेषाणां तावदपि निवृत्तिरिष्यते, तदा पृथ्वीकृत्स्नादिकमपि भावनाप्रकर्षपर्यन्तवर्तिनां तथैव निवृत्तिमापादयेद् [इति] । न चेष्यते, यस्माद् ये प्रकर्षपर्यन्तवर्तितया स्वात्मलाभभावाः[1] न तेषामावर्तनम्, यथा (पृथ्वी) कृत्स्नादयः[2] । लब्धात्मलाभाः स्व[3]विशेषाश्रिताः[4] सुखसौमनस्यादयः, तस्मात्तेऽपि न व्यावर्तन्ते, व्यावृत्तौ कारणाभावात् । ये तु दोषादयो[5] व्यावृत्तिभागिनः तेषां च तदानीं [नायं भावः । तदनु दुःखोद्भवोऽपि न स्यात्, प्रकर्षपर्यन्तगमने तत्र सम्भवति, अन्यथा मोक्षानन्तरमपि] संसारः स्याद् इति न चेष्यते प्रयुज्यते वा । ये मोक्षं प्राप्तस्य संसारोत्पत्ति नेष्यन्ते[6] एव तेऽपि तदानीं कारणाभावादविद्यावासनाया विनिवृत्ताः । परार्थेन या समुत्पत्तिर्न [सा] सांसारिकी, पूर्वप्रणिधानावे[7](ध) सामर्थ्येन तत्र प्रवृत्तेः, [न वासनासामर्थ्यात्[8] ।] तेन [यथा] मोक्षानन्तरं[9] संसारः न, तथा [सुखप्रकर्षपर्यन्तगमनानन्तरं] दुःखं चित्तस्यापि [न जायते], प्रकृतिपरिशुद्धत्वात् [तदेव] मेचकमणिसदृशम् । (ततः) येन येन वास्यते तत्र तत्र चाभ्यासबलाद् विशिष्टतरस्वभावमाविष्करोति अपरावृत्तिधर्मतालक्षणम् । अत एवोक्तम्—

येन येन हि भावेन मनः संयुज्यते नृणाम् ।
तेन तन्मयतां याति विश्वरूपो मणिर्यथा ॥ ४७ ॥[10]

तेन सर्वमेतद् विशिष्टपरिणामनया परिणाम्यमाने विशिष्टफलावाहकं भवति

---

1. लब्धात्मभावन–ख
2. यथा पृथ्वीकृत्स्नादय–घ ग्रन्थे नास्ति
3. स्व–सं +, स्वविशेषभासितया–ख
4. आश्रिता–सं +
5. निर्दोषादि–घ, आदि–सं +
6. येन मोक्षं प्राप्तस्य संसारोत्पत्तिर्नेष्यते–ख घ
7. प्रणिधानावेध–घ
8. मोक्षानन्तरं–ख
9. सुखानन्तरं प्रकर्षपर्यन्तगमने–क ख घ
10. आकरो न प्राप्तः

इति। तेन न किञ्चित् नाम्यपरिणामं[1] नाम। पूर्वकर्मविधसामर्थ्याच्च तथैव तद्भवतीति, अन्यथा विशिष्टपरिणामना व्यर्था[2], [3]सर्वत्र च[4] अविश्वसनीया स्यात्। तथा चोक्तं **जिनजनन्याम्**[5] --

'पुनरपरं[6] सुभूते! बोधिसत्त्वो महासत्त्वो दिव्यानुलेपनानि ददाति तथागतेषु तथागतचैत्येषु वा। तस्यैवं भवति, अनेन कुशलमूलेन[7] अनुत्तरां सम्यक्सम्बोधिमभिसम्बुद्धे, तत्र बुद्धक्षेत्रेषु सर्वसत्त्वानां दिव्याः स्पर्शविशेषाः अभिनिष्पद्यन्ताम्। [इति परिणामना भवेत्।] पुनरपरं सुभूते! (बोधिसत्त्वस्य महासत्त्वस्यैवं भवति, मनोरथ[8])—सङ्कल्पेनैव (इष्टान्) पञ्चकामगुणान् बुद्धानां[9] भगवतां श्रावकसङ्घानां सर्वसत्त्वानां चोपनामयेयम्। तस्यैवं सञ्जानत एवं भवति-अनेन कुशलमूलेन मम बुद्धक्षेत्रे अनुत्तरां सम्यक्सम्बोधिमभिसम्बुद्धस्य[10] श्रावकसङ्घस्य सत्वानां च (मनोरथ)—सङ्कल्पेनैव इष्टाः कामगुणाः प्रादुर्भवन्तु। पुनरपरं सुभूते! बोधिसत्वा महासत्वाः सर्वसत्वैः सार्द्धं सम्यक्सम्बुद्धेभ्यो वा पञ्चकामगुणदानं ददाति' एवमादि।

इतश्च[11] वासनावेधसामर्थ्याद् [एवं] दृष्टकार्येषु वर्तते। मातुलुङ्गादि[12] फलं लोके[13] यथा लाक्षादिसेकाद् उक्तरूपम्, तथा चास्य[14]

---

1. न श्रेयेसां पदम्-क ख+, भो*
2. व्यथते-क ख घ
3. तस्मात् तस्य एवं सञ्जानत एवं भवति, मनोरथसङ्कल्पेष्टाष्टगुणाः पञ्चकामगुणाः प्रोक्ता-क ख घ, भो*
4. अन्यं-सं+
5. आकरो न प्राप्तः।
6. पुनरपरं-भो*
7. मूलेन-भो*
8. ( ) भो*
9. गुणानुबद्धानां-ख
10. ०सं-ख, [बुद्धैः श्रावकसङ्घैः सार्द्धं]-भो
11. [तथा सति]-भो
12. आदि-ख घ*
13. लोके-क*
14. चास्य-भो*

(15)

चित्तस्य [बाह्य]-स्पर्शादिसेवनात् तदेव सुखादिकं संस्कारविशेषप्रतिवेधाहित-विशेषत्वाद् पुनः तत्रैव अभिमुखीभवति। तदनुरक्तत्वाच्चित्तस्य तत्रञ्जितं च[1] तत्रैव दृढीभवति। [तदपि] यथा धत्तूरकर्पास [बीज] दाडिमादीनां कारणान्तरैराहितविशेषं [तत्र] तथैव फलं प्रतीयते, आहितसामर्थ्यात्[2]। एवं चित्तमपि स्पर्शादिनिर्जातसुखसौमनस्यादिविशेषं तदुत्तरोत्तरविशिष्ट-फलावाहकं भवति। तत्प्रतिपक्षयानानभिनिविष्टत्वात् न प्रतिपक्षोदयः तद्विमुखत्वात् [सुखित्वाच्च।] तथा श्रीपरमाद्ये प्रदर्शितं भवति[3]—

'सर्वदुःखदौर्मनस्यादिभ्योऽवकाशो न देव[4] ! देयः[5]।' ॥४७॥

पुनश्चोक्तं **सर्वदेवसमागमतन्त्रे**—

सुरासुराणां भूतानां प्रतिबोधि[6]र्न विद्यते।
कीर्तयन् तेन सर्वाङ्गमानन्दं चोपभुञ्जते ॥ ४८ ॥
अतस्तेनाति[7]गच्छन्ति निर्वाणं दीपा यथा।
निर्वाणाग्निर्महाघोरो भस्मान्यपि न मुञ्चति ॥ ४९ ॥
न तत्र तत्त्वं[8] विद्यते नेन्द्रियार्था न धातवः।
न मन [श्चैत्तकं नापि][9] नाहङ्कारो न धीरपि ॥ ५० ॥
न च [सत्त्वं][10] न च प्रज्ञा न चित्तं नैव किञ्चित्।
सुषुप्तावस्थिताकारं निर्विकल्पं निरात्मकम् ॥ ५१ ॥
न संज्ञा न च चेष्टा तु न रूपं न गुणः क्वचित्।
निर्वाणं तत्समुद्दिष्टं मोक्षं तु निष्कलं[11] भवेत् ॥ ५२ ॥

---

1. रञ्जितस्य–ख*
2. तदावेधसामर्थ्यात्–ख घ
3. [भगवता]–भो
4. देव !–भो*, नावकाशो न देव–ख घ
5. देव्यः–ख घ
6. प्रतिवेधं–सं
7. अपि–ख घ
8. न तत्त्वं तत्र–ख घ, [तनुः]–भो
9. चेतना चाथ–सं
10. तत्त्वं–सं
11. निष्फलं–सं

(16)

ज्ञात्वा संसारभावस्य[1] निःस्वभावस्वभावताम् ।
तदा प्रबुद्धो विज्ञेयो निर्वाणं यदि नेच्छति ॥ ५३ ॥
ज्ञात्वा सद्भावसारूप्यं निःस्वभावस्वभावताम् ।
निर्वाणं यः प्रपद्येत विना सिद्धिं न[2] वीर्यवान् ॥ ५४ ॥
न कृतनाश[3]श्चान्यो जायते हीनचेतसः ।
यः परां बोधिमासाद्य[4] विना सिद्धेः प्रहीयते ॥ ५५ ॥
किं तेन न कृतं पापं चोरेणात्मापहारिणा[5] ।
बुद्धात्मनः[6] शरीरस्य सिद्धिं सौख्यैर्न पूरयेत् ॥ ५६ ॥
न तस्य विद्यते वीर्यं न च सत्त्वं प्रतिष्ठितम् ।
यः परां बोधिमासाद्य[7] निर्वाणं यात्यसिद्धितः[8] ॥ ५७ ॥
[नान्यो][9] हीनतरस्तस्मात्[10] नान्यः स्याद् दुर्जनो जनः ।[11]
यः परां बोधिमासाद्य त्यजते स्वशरीरकम् ॥ ५८ ॥
तद्वीर्यं सर्ववीर्याणां यः प्रबुद्ध्वा प्रवर्तते ।
सर्वेन्द्रियोपभोगेषु रतः[12] सन्ना [पि] बध्यते ॥ ५९ ॥

पुनश्चोक्तं ~~निर्मुक्तसमुद्घातनतन्त्रे~~—

नास्ति तत्त्वव्रतं पुंसां महाफल (प्र) दं यतः ।[13]
क्वचिच्चित्ताधिमुक्तानां वासना त्यज्यते कथम् ॥ ६० ॥

---

1. सद्भावसारूप्यं–ख घ
2. स्व–सं
3. नाशादन्यो–क ख
4. आसाद्य–सं
5. आत्मापकारिणा–ख घ
6. बुद्ध्वानात्मनः शरीरस्य–घ
7. साध्य–क ग ङ
8. त्यसिद्धिना–ख घ
9. न हि–ख घ
10. तेभ्यो–सं
11. [ऽथवा]–भो
12. अतः–ख घ
13. [क्वचित्]–भो

(17)

न तेन[1] शोधितं चित्तं योग[2]तन्त्रव्रतस्थितम् ।
केवलं[3] भिन्नदृष्टित्वात् प्रबुद्धोऽपि विनश्यति ॥ ६१ ॥
न कृतघ्नतस्त्वन्ये[4] ये प्रबोधिं गता नराः ।
दीपवद् यान्ति निर्वाणं न सिद्धिमनुभुञ्जते[5] ॥ ६२ ॥
नान्यः [सत्त्वेन रहितः][6] स्वशरीरस्य जायते ।
त्रिप्रत्यक्षकामश्च[7] निर्वाणं यः प्रपद्यते ॥ ६३ ॥
प्रबुद्धकारणा[8]च्चेह निर्वाणं ये नरा गताः ।
सुखानन्तान् परित्यज्य सिद्धमिष्टं फलं तदा[9] ॥ ६४ ॥

पुनश्चोक्तम्—

पारदश्चाग्निसंयोगाद् यथाभावं प्रपद्यते ।
दह्यते दृश्यते नैव गच्छन्नो धूम एव वा[10] ॥ ६५ ॥
गोमयाधारयोगेन यथा संगृह्यते पुनः ।
ज्ञानमेवं विजानीयात् महामुद्रा[11][समं तथा] ॥ ६६ ॥

प्रयोगश्च—[ये] ये प्राप्तप्रकर्षपर्यन्ताः न ते व्यावर्तन्ते । तद्यथा-मोक्षादयः । प्रकर्षपर्यन्त [कारणस्वरूपाः] सुखसौमनस्यादयः, इति स्वभाव-हेतुः । इतरश्च—ये हि भाव्यन्ते [ते] भावनाभ्याससामर्थ्यात् समाहित-परमप्रकर्षपर्यन्तवर्तिनो भवन्ति, यथा—प्रज्ञा-शिल्प-कलादयः । भाव्यन्ते च प्रज्ञोपायपरिगृहीतानि स्पर्शविशेषनिर्जातानि सुखसौमनस्यानि, तस्मात्तान्यपि

---

1. तेन–भो*
2. यो न तत्त्वव्रते स्थितः–सं
3. केवलं–भो*
4. न तथा कृतनाशः स्यात्–क ग ङ
5. सिद्धिं [तत्र] भुञ्जते–भो
6. नान्यसत्त्वतरस्विन–क ग ङ, नान्यसत्त्वेन रसना–ख घ
7. कामेन–ख घ
8. प्रबुद्धकातराः–ख घ
9. तथा–सं, भोटग्रन्थे चतुर्थ-चरणार्थः–[सिद्धं किंस्वित् फलं तदा ?] इति ।
10. दह्यते दृश्यते चैव गच्छन्तं धूम एव वा–घ
11. महामुद्रा विधीयते–सं

परमप्रकर्षवन्ति[1] भवन्ति । स्वभावहेतुरेव । तदत्रापि प्रकर्षपर्यन्तगमन[2]-मात्रानुबन्धि सात्मीकरणं तत्त्वाभ्यासविशेषबलाद् अपुनरावृत्तिधर्मताम-[गत्वा] सादयति । न पुनस्तदन्येन केनचिद् [अपि] व्यावर्तते[3] तत्स्व-भावतामुपगतः । तद्यथा—काष्ठादौ अग्निदाहिता विशेषा न तद्व्यावर्तन्ते, दाहादि[4]लक्षणं तस्यापुनर्भावधर्मित्वात् । अत एवोक्तम्—

न पुन [र्दहनः[5]] किञ्चिद् विकारजननं[6] क्वचित् ।
विपर्ययात् पुनः किञ्चिद् यथा काष्ठसुवर्णयोः[7] ॥ ६७ ॥

हेमादौ [अग्निकृत[8]] विशेषः तत्सन्तानव्यावृत्तौ तद्विपरीतकारणतः[9] तत्स्वभावभावं सम्पादितः [यथा अग्निजलादिः[10] ।] अग्निलहुत[11] सुवर्णस्य [अस्यापि] अन्य एव कठिनस्वभावाध्यासितविशेषः सञ्जायते[12] [स्व-भावाधिवासितविशेषान्तर उत्पद्यते ।] तदत्र चेतसि विषयोपभोगसञ्जातो हर्षा[13]त्मविशेषः । तदुत्तरोत्तरं तस्यैव कारणस्य संसेवनेन परां निष्ठाम् आसाद्यमानस्य [न] व्यावृत्तिः, बुद्धेस्तत्पक्षपातात् । येन बुद्धिर्हि तदनुरक्ता सती समासादितगुणा च तदेव कारणम् आदत्ते, तद्विपरीते च विमुख्यान् [न] कथञ्चिद् व्यावर्तते । यथा[14] च—यत्र यत्र प्रकर्षपर्यन्तगमनं, तत्र तत्र[15] सात्मीभावः, तद्यथा—श्रोत्रिय (स्य) जातिभावादौ ?[16] [भावनावशात्]

---

1. ० वर्तीनि–ख घ
2. गमन–भो*
3. प्रावर्तते–ख घ, [परमप्रकर्षगमनवत्त्वं तु]–भो
4. क्लेशादि–क ख घ
5. भावतः–सं
6. [न]–भो +
7. आकरो न प्राप्तः
8. चक्षुषा दाता–सं
9. ०कारणायन्ते–ख, ०णायन्तः–घ
10. भो +
11. अन्य एव–भो*, हुत–ख घ
12. अन्यदेव कठिनस्वभावाध्यासितविशेषः सञ्जात–घ
13. हर्ष–भो*
14. तथा–क ग ङ, [तत्र च येन येन] भो
15. [तत्तत्]–भो
16. अस्पष्टः पाठः, भो*

(19)

नैर्घृण्यम्। तद्यथा -कस्यचित् श्रोत्रियस्य महाव्रतधारिणो नैर्घृण्यं भावनासात्मीकरणात् तत्साम्यमासादयति [तच्च][1] स्वसंवेद्यं सुखसौमनस्यादि सर्वसन्तानवर्ति स्वसंवेदनप्रत्यक्षं सिद्धं, तदपि तत्रैव भावनायोगसामर्थ्याद् अविच्छिन्नप्रवाहं वर्तते।[2]

[प्रवाहविच्छेद[3]] कारणाभावात् दुःखादि [प्रवाह] विच्छित्तिकारणानि न संविद्यन्ते। न हि दुःखादीनि हितरूपतयाऽवगम्य [केनचित् प्रेक्षावता] त्यज्यन्ते, न च पुनस्तदुत्पत्तिकारणमन्विष्यते,[4] प्रेक्षावान् क्वचिद् अन्यथा प्रेक्षावान् न स्यात्[5], तदन्यो मत्तकादिवत्।

तेन आस्तां तावत् प्रकर्षपर्यन्तगमनम्, किन्तु [किञ्चिन्मात्र] मेत्रनेनापि वृद्धि [स्तद्धितानुबन्धित्वात्] तद्विपरीतकारणार्थमिह कथमपि [न] सञ्जायते। न हि कश्चिज्जानन्नेव अहिविष[6]कण्टकादीन् उपादत्ते। तेन हि तत्फलावाहकमेव तदभ्यासविशेषबलात्[7] सात्मीभावमुपागतम्। तानि च हेयरूपतया बुद्धया प्रागेव निरस्तानि, तेन [तत्सन्तति] विच्छेदः। तदीय[8]स्वभावहेतुस्तत्स्वभावतां साधयति। न चासिद्धो हेतुः। भावनाविशेषेणापि[9] [विशिष्टता लभ्यते] प्रज्ञादीनां तेनाभ्यासस्तावद्[10] विद्यते। नासिद्धता नाप्यनैकान्तिकता, येन सुखसौमनस्याद्यभ्यस्यमानं न तद्विपक्षे दुःखादौ (प्र) वर्तते। न विरुद्धः, यस्मान्न साध्यविपर्ययं दुःखं साधयति। दृष्टान्तधर्मिणाम् [अपि] सर्ववादिप्रसिद्धत्वात्। येन [इमे] प्रज्ञाशिल्पकला[11]दयः प्रतिपुरुषाभ्यासतया[12] [भेद] विशेषम् आसाद्यमानाः संलक्ष्यन्ते। यदप्युक्तम्—रागप्रतिपक्षा अशुभाः[13], द्वेषप्रतिपक्षो मैत्री, मोहप्रतिपक्षः

---

1. तच्च -भो*,
2. प्रवर्तते-सं
3. विच्छिन्न-सं
4. ०ति-क ग ङ
5. प्रेक्षावान्·······स्यात्-भो*
6. विष-भो*
7. सात्मी-भो*
8. [तस्य तदभावात्]-भो·
9. अपि-भो*
10. तावद्-भो*
11. (प्रज्ञादयः)-भो
12. (अशुचि)-भो
13. न-भो*

(20)

प्रतीत्यसमुत्पादः। तत्र रागतो [विराग] विनिवृत्तिः, तद्विरुद्धत्वादिति चेन्, न[2]। [यदि तथा] ध्रुवमन्य[1]रागमात्मीकरणेऽपि[3] विरागः स्यात्। अत एवोक्तं **मूलतन्त्रे**—

अहो[4]हि सर्वबुद्धानां रागज्ञानमनाविलम्।
हत्वा रागं विरागं[5] च सर्वसौख्यं वदन्ति[6] ते ॥ ६८ ॥

न च रागादीनां प्रकृतिसावद्यत्वम्, अन्यथा न स्रोतापन्नस्य मार्गप्रतिलम्भः स्यात्, तस्य रागाद्यपरिहारेण प्रवृत्तेः। किञ्च एवमुक्तं **भगवता शीलपटले**—'बोधिसत्वेन दशकुशलान्यपि परार्थेन[7] खण्डयितव्यानि। यथा-काचित् कामार्थिनी स्त्री बोधिसत्वं प्रति प्राणान् त्यजेत्, तस्याः कामादिसेवनेन[8] प्राणसन्धारणं कार्यम्। तथैव[9] महापापकारिणं दृष्ट्वा जीविताद् व्युपरोपयति, न च तस्यापायगमनं भवेत्, बहुतरं पुण्यं प्रसवति। तद् यदि एते[10] रागादयः प्रकृतिसावद्यास्तदा कथं दुर्गतिहेतवो[11] न भवन्ति ? प्रभूतरत्नपुण्यहेतवश्च[12] कथमुक्ताः ? तेन न तेषां प्रकृतिसावद्यता, किन्तु [पुद्गल] सन्तान-विशेषाद् गुणविशेषावाहका भवन्ति। यथा केतकीपुष्पं गन्धहस्तिनोपभुक्तं कस्तूरिकादि[13]भावेन परिणमते,[14]इतरैश्च हस्तिभिरुपभुज्यमानं असेव्यभावेन परिणामयति। तेन न तत्र[15] केतकीपुष्पदोषः। तथा रागादयो [ऽपि] विशुद्धसन्तानवर्तिनो विशिष्टमेव फलं कुर्वन्ति, आशयविशेषयोगात्। यथा

---

1. ध्रुवमन्य-भो*
2. न सं+
3. (रागः)-भो
4. हत्वा विरागं रागेण-ख घ
5. (जनयन्ति)-भो
6. परार्थेन-भो*
7. संसेवनेन-घ
8. तथा-घ
9. प्राणसन्धारणं······एते-क*
10. अपायहेवः-घ
11. रत्न-भो*
12. (कस्तूरिकासदृशम्)-भो
13. परिणामयति-घ
14. (तत्)-भो
15. मनस्ति-घ

(21)

क्षीरं सर्पादिभिरुपभुज्यमानं विषादिभावेन परिणामयति, अन्यैश्च मनुजैः उपभुज्यमानम् अमृतभावमापद्यते। एवमेते[1] रागादयो (ऽपि) आशय[2] विशेषभाजिनि विशिष्टफलावाहका भवन्तीति, न प्रकृतिनिरवद्यत्वात्। [हेतु] प्रयोगः—ये ये विशिष्टसन्तानभागिनः[3] ते ते विशिष्टफलावाहकाः, यथा केतक्यादयः, विशिष्टसन्तानवर्तिनश्च रागादय इति स्वभावहेतुः। अत्रापि विशिष्ट-सन्तान-प्रयोगपरिणाममात्रानुबन्धिविशिष्टफलावाहकत्वम् अप्रति-बन्धसामर्थ्यं[4] जनयत्येव, अन्त्यकारणसामग्रीवत्। येन हि तस्य[5] स्वभावः, सोऽपि तन्मात्रानुबन्धजातं करोत्येव, प्रतिबन्धस्य असम्भवात्। [प्रतिबन्धे] सम्भवे चाप्रत्ययः स्यात्। तदत्रा[6]पि विशिष्टपरिणामान् नान्यदपेक्षत इति तन्मात्रानुबन्ध उक्तः[7]। न च तत्र [क्षेपाभावस्य] प्रतिबन्धः, [क्षेपा-भावान्तस्य क्षेपाभावान्यस्मिन्] प्रेक्षणीयस्य असम्भवात्[8]। एवं तन्मात्रानु-बन्धिनिश्चयात्[9] स्वभावहेतुरुक्तः। तथा रसायनिकोऽपि (बोधिचित्तर[10] सावेधात्?) तत्सामीभावमुपगतं भावसंविशिष्टमेव रूपान्तरं जनयति[11], तथा ताम्रादिषु[12] स्थिरीकृतपारदादि रसावेधसामर्थ्यादन्यदेवावस्थान्तरं[13] जनयते। [निर्दोषा] पुनरावृत्तिधर्मकतामुपैतीति अत्रापि विज्ञेयम्। अन्यथा ताम्रादिषु[14] न रसादीनामावर्तकत्वं[15] स्यात्। एवं [तत्] सामर्थ्य-दर्शनात् स्फुटतरमेवावगम्यते अस्तित्वम्, अन्यथा न किञ्चित् सामर्थ्यं स्यात्। तथा चोक्तम्—

---

1. एते–भो*
2. आश्रय–घ
3. भाविनः–घ
4. अप्रति‥ जनयति–भो*
5. तस्याः–ख घ
6. तन्मात्रानुबन्ध–ख
7. उक्तः–भो*
8. क्षेपाभावान्यस्य तस्याप्रेक्षणीयस्य–सं
9. नियमात्–ख
10. यथा रसोपनिबद्धोऽपि बोधिचित्तरसवैद्यः–ख
11. जायते–ख घ
12. शुक्लादिषु–ख
13. अर्थान्तर–ख
14. शुक्लादिषु–सं
15. आवेधकत्वम्–ख

(22)

अशुचिप्रतिमामिमां गृहीत्वा जिनरत्नप्रतिमां करोत्यनर्घाम् ।
रसजातमतीव वेधनीयं सुदृढं गृह्णत[1] बोधिचित्त [संज्ञम्[2]] ॥ ६९ ॥[3]

• [पुनश्च]

पुण्येन सुखितः कायः पाण्डित्येन मनः सुखि ।
तिष्ठन् परार्थं संसारे दयालुः[4] केन खिद्यते ॥ ७० ॥[5]

किञ्च, यथा रसायनिकः[6] धनिकः[7] पुरुषः कश्चिद् विशिष्टौषधिसंयोगात् समासादिततद्गुणमाहात्म्यः, तस्य[8] पञ्चाभिज्ञाः प्रवर्तन्ते, तथाऽन्ये[9] च गुणाः आसंसारं स्थितिं कुर्वन्ति, एवमेव विशिष्टविषयपरिभोगसञ्जात(र)सायनस्य[10] आसंसार-(प्र)कृत - प्रणिधिविधानस्य परार्थपरस्य[11] समाहितसकल[12]गुणगणस्य प्रतिविद्धबोधिचित्तरसस्य किमिति सत्त्वं नेष्यते ? किं च —

न बोधिं निःक्लेशां कृतगति[13]रवाप्नोति परमां
उदीर्णक्लेशश्च स्वहितमपि कर्त्तुं न लभते ।
इति प्राप्त्यै बोधेः स्थिरविहितवीर्येण भवता
न निर्दग्धाः क्लेशाः तृणलवलघुत्वं तु गमिताः ॥ ७१ ॥

---

1. गृह्णाति–ग घ ङ
2. रत्नम्–सं
3. बो. च. ॥ १।१० ॥
4. [कृपालुः]-भो
5. बो. च. ॥ ७।२८ ॥
6. रससिद्धः–क ङ
7. धनिकः–ग घ भो*
8. समासादिततद्गुणमाहात्म्यकस्य–घ
9. अन्ये–भो*
10. रसस्य–सं
11. परार्थपदस्य–ख घ
12. समाहितसकल–भो*
13. [षड्गति]–भो

(23)

स्मृतिज्ञानप्रस्ता त्रिविधगुणनिष्पत्तिलघवो[1]
गताः क्लेशा बोधेरुपकरणतामेव भवतः ।
[अनेनैवं त्वद्धीस्तदनु न कृता भ्रान्तविषया
गुणानां क्षेत्रत्वं जगति जनिधारा अपि कृताः ॥] ७२ ॥[2]

किञ्च, सविकल्पकमेव[3] तद्भावनाप्रकर्षपर्यन्तवर्ति सर्वज्ञज्ञानम्, आहोस्वित् निर्विकल्पकमिति[4] ? तत्र यदि तावन्निर्विकल्पकमेवेष्यते, तदा भावनाविकल्पसामर्थ्यान्निर्जातस्य कथं निर्विकल्पकत्वम् ? न हि सविकल्पकाद् विज्ञानात्[5] निर्विकल्पकस्य ज्ञानस्य प्रसूतिः कथमपि सम्भवति । अथ क्लेशोपक्लेशवासनाविनिवृत्तं निर्विकल्पकत्वं, तदयुक्तम्, यतः क्लेशोपक्लेशवासनानिवृत्तौ किमपरमस्ति यद् विकल्पकं स्यात्, तद्व्यतिरिक्तस्य अन्यस्य प्रमाणाभावात् । न चापि प्रामाणिका[6] काचित् सिद्धिरस्ति । तद्भावानां न प्रत्यक्षता, तस्य इन्द्रियालोकमनस्कारविषय-सामर्थ्यात् निर्जातत्वात् । न ग्राहकाकार[7] विनिर्मुक्तं ज्ञानं प्रतिपादकमस्ति, तस्य तद्विपरीतरूपत्वात् । नाप्यनुमानम्[8], तस्यापि लिङ्गलिङ्गिसम्बन्ध-ग्रहणपूर्वकत्वात्[9] । ग्राह्य-ग्राहकाकारद्वयविनिर्मुक्तज्ञानं विना भावि कार्याख्यं स्वभावाख्यं वा लिङ्गं [न] उपलभ्यते । नाप्यनुपलब्धिनिबन्धनात्तस्य प्रतिपत्तिः स्यात्, तस्याः प्रतिषेधविषयत्वात्[10] ।

तत्र कार्यहेतुस्तावदसिद्धः, कार्यकारणभावस्य ह्यनुपपत्तेः[11], यतो न विनष्टात् कारणात् कार्यमुपजायते, तस्य असत्त्वेन अजनकत्वात् । नाप्य-

---

1. [०क्लेशा]–भो
2. रत्नदासकृत गुणापर्यन्तस्तोत्रम्–भोटदेगे-संस्करणे १९९ क इति पृष्ठे ।
3. [सविकल्पकात्]–भो
4. [निर्विकल्पकात्]–भो
5. विज्ञानात्–भो*
6. अप्रामाणिका–घ
7. [ग्राह्य-ग्रहण-ग्राहकाकार]–भो
8. नाप्यनुमानात्–क
9. पुरःसरत्वात्–ख घ
10. ग्राह्य·········त्वात्–क*
11. ०भावस्येहानुपपत्तेः–ख

विनष्टाद्, उत्पन्नस्य व्यापार-समावेशकालपरीक्षायां[1] क्षणभङ्गाप्रसङ्गात्। निर्व्यापारस्य खपुष्पस्येव कुतो जनकत्वम्? अत एवोक्तम्—

न नष्टाच्चापि नानष्टाद्[2] बीजादङ्कुरसम्भवः।
मायोत्पादवदुत्पादः[3] सर्व एव[4] त्वयोच्यते ॥ ७३ ॥
येनो[5]त्पादो निरोधादि[6] सत्त्वजीवादि देशिताः[7]।
नेयार्थी सा त्वया **नाथ**! भाषिता सम्वृतिस्तु सा ॥ ७४ ॥

तेनार्थतो जन्यजनकानुपपत्तेः[8] ना [त्र] कार्यहेतुः, लिङ्गा[9]भावात्। स्वभावहेतोरपि परोक्षतत्स्वभावतया न कथञ्चिदपि सम्भवः, तन्मात्रसम्बन्धासिद्धेः[10]। अनुपलम्भस्यापि प्रतिषेधसाधकत्वान्नात्र[11] अवसरः। न[12] चापरो हेतुरिष्यते प्रमाणान्तरश्चेति कुतो निर्विकल्पकस्य ज्ञानस्य निश्चयो वाच्यः? तथोक्तम्—

स्वस्मान्न जायते भावः परस्मान्नोभयादपि।
न सन्नासन्न सदसन् कुतः कस्योदयस्तदा[13] ॥ ७५ ॥[14]

---

1. [स्थितौ]–भो
2. अनष्टात्-भो*
3. मायोत्पाद इवोत्पा०–क
4. [सर्वमेतद्]–भो
5. येन–भो*
6. [सत्काय]–भो
7. देशना–ख घ
8. जन्यजनकायन्तः–ख
9. लिङ्ग–भो*
10. तन्मात्रानुबन्धा–ख
11. नापि–सं
12. न–भो*
13. कल्पोदयस्तदा–क घ
14. **अचिन्त्यस्तवे** (९) पाठः —

न सन्नुत्पद्यते भावो नाप्यसन् सदसन्न च।
न स्वतो नापि परतो न द्वाभ्यां जायते कथम् ॥

(25)

तेन परमार्थेन तद्विज्ञानमनुपपन्नम,[1] कथं निर्विकल्पकं स्यात् ? न हि गगनाम्भोरुहादीनां सविकल्पकत्वं निर्विकल्पकत्वं वा इष्यते, नापि तत्रेयं[2] चिन्ता[3] प्रवर्तते, पुरुषार्थानुपयोगित्वात्[4] आकाशपद्मवत्[5] । तदभ्युपगमे त न किञ्चित् प्रयोजनमस्ति । [तन्निःस्वभावत्वात्[6]] न किञ्चित् [तत्]-साध्यमुपपद्यते, न च साध्यमकुर्वाणं साधनं तत्र कीर्त्यते । तस्मात् सर्वमेव ज्ञानं प्रतीत्यसमुत्पन्नं ग्राह्यग्राहकाकाररूपतया वर्तमानं सविकल्पकमिति प्रतिजानीमहे, येन ग्राह्य-ग्राहकाकारं त्रैधातुकं [विज्ञानं] प्रत्ययकल्पन-मित्याख्यातम् ।

अत एवोक्तं **लङ्कावतारसूत्रे**—

आर्यो न पश्यति भ्रान्तिं नापि तत्त्वं तदन्तरे ।
भ्रान्तिरेव भवेत्तत्त्वं यस्मात्तत्त्वं तदन्तरे ॥ ७६ ॥
[भ्रान्तिं विधूय सर्वां हि निमित्तं जायते यदि ।
सैव तस्य भवेद् भ्रान्तिरशुद्धं तिमिरं यथा ॥ ७७ ॥][7]

तत्र केवलं विपरीतपदार्थसमारोपव्यावृत्तौ[8] विशिष्टपदार्थभावना-प्रकर्षपर्यन्तगमनाद् विशिष्टफलम् आविर्भवति, सान्तर-व्यन्तर-स्वभावाभाव-स्वभावम् एकस्वभावं सुखादि, भावनाभ्यासविशेषाश्रितत्वात्, तदाकार-संवेदनवत् । तत्समानजातीयप्रवाह[9] प्रवृत्तं ग्राह्यग्राहकाकारसंविद्भेदेन [युक्तं] अध्यवसित[10] स्वरूपमविच्छिन्न [सन्तान] धर्मकं स्वचित्त-वशिताप्राप्त

---

1. अनुत्पन्नं–ख घ
2. तन्त्रे–सं
3. चित्रा–सं
4. पुरुषार्थापुरुषार्थानुपयोगित्वात्–ख
5. का(ता)रापथसरोजवत्–ख घ
6. तत्स्वभावस्य–सं
7. लं० सू० ॥२।१६६, १६७॥, १०।१२७, १२८ ॥ [ ] श्लोकः कस्मिन्नपि संस्कृतहस्तलेखे नास्ति, किन्तु भोटानुवादेषु प्राप्यते । अतः स श्लोकोऽत्र उल्लिखितः ।
8. ० व्यपावृत्तो–क
9. प्रभाव–क
10. अध्यवसित–भो०

सविकल्पकमपि यथावस्थितसकलपदार्थपरिच्छेदकम्, प्रज्ञोपायपरिगृहीतमूर्तित्वात् । अत एवोक्तं लङ्कावतारसूत्रे—

न मे[1] यानं महायानं न घोषो न च अक्षराः ।
न च ध्यानं विमोक्षो वै न निराभासगोचरम् ॥ ७८ ॥
किन्तु यानं महायानं समाधिवशवर्तिनाम्[2] ।
कायो मनोमयो दिव्य-वशितापुष्पमण्डितः[3] ॥ ७९ ॥[4]

तदेवं कारणविशेषात् कार्यविशेषप्रतिपादनेन सर्व[5]माख्यातम् । किञ्च नामजात्यादिकल्पनं[6] समारोपितम् । अर्थान्वयव्यतिरेकानुकारि[7] सविकल्पकम् अपि[8] ज्ञानं अस्पष्टाभम् उक्तम्[9] आचार्य–धर्मकीर्तिपादैरपि लौकिकप्रमाणपरीक्षायाम् । यत्र ग्राह्यग्राहकप्रतिभासो[10] भेदेन संज्ञायते, तत्रास्पष्टाभमेव ज्ञानं[11] स्पष्टाभतया भाति[12] । तद्यथा–नामजात्यादिकल्पना-रहितं ज्ञानं स्पष्टाभं भवति, ग्राह्यग्राहकसंवित्ति[13]भेदेन भिद्यते, तेन नामजात्यादिकल्पनामाश्रित्य आचार्येणा[14]प्यस्पष्टाभता दर्शिता, न ग्राह्यग्राहकसंवित्तिभेदाश्रयेणेति, तेन विषयाकारानुभवसञ्जातविशेषस्य तद्विजातीयाध्यवसायाभावः । तत्सात्मीभावमुप[15]गतायाः न स्पष्टाभताया बाधकमस्ति, साधकं च विद्यते । तत्सात्मीभावसमापत्तिलक्षणं कामशोकभयोन्मादादि [वत्] चोक्तं प्राक् ।

---

1. स–ख घ
2. वर्तिताम्–क ग ङ
3. कायं मनोमयं दिव्यं प्रसवपुष्प०–ख
4. लं० सू० । ३ । १–२ ॥, १० । १८८–९ ॥
5. सर्वम्–भो*
6. कल्पनामासमा–ख, कल्पानामसमारोपित–घ
7. व्यतिरेकान्तकारि–ख घ
8. अपि–भो*
9. [अभिहितम्]–भो
10. प्रतिभासि–भो*
11. तत्र……ज्ञानं–भो*
12. भाति–भो*
13. [विकल्प]–भो
14. अपि–भो*
15. उप–भो*

(27)

अथ ग्राह्य-ग्राहक-संवित्त्याकारतया आभास[1]मानस्य [ज्ञानस्य] प्रकर्षपर्यन्तगमने सर्ववित्त्यर्थमिष्यते[2], तन्नास्ति, कल्पनाजालसिद्धत्वात्[3] । तत्र तस्याप्यशेषाकारशून्यस्य[4] संविन्मात्रस्य कथमशेषज्ञेयपरिच्छेदकत्वम् ? न हि[5] निराभासस्य ज्ञानस्य कथमपि[6] परिच्छेदकत्वं विद्यते, युक्ति-व्याहृतं चैतत् ।

[7]एकस्यानंशरूपस्य त्रैरूप्यानुपपत्तितः ।
वेद्यवेदनभेदेन स्वसंवित्फलमिष्यते[8] ॥ ८० ॥

अथ स्वभाव एव तस्यायं यत् तत्प्रकर्षपर्यन्तगमने सर्वसंवित्तौ स स्वभावोऽस्मत्पक्षेऽपि समानः । तथा हि-ग्राह्यग्राहकसंवित्तिभेदेनभिद्यमानस्यापि प्रकर्षपर्यन्तगमने तदेव विशिष्टरूपं जायते[9] । यन्निखिलमेव वस्तुजातं यथावस्थितमेवावबुध्यते, तस्य तत्सामर्थ्यं किं काकेन भक्षितम्[10] ? किञ्च, सकल-कल्पना-कलापशून्यं तदस्तीति किमपि स्थानम्[11]अनुष्ठेयम् । सविकल्पकं तु ज्ञानं सर्वसत्त्वा[न्तः]सन्तानवर्तितया प्रत्यक्षादिप्रमाणसिद्धम्, भावनाबलाच्च सात्मीभावसमापत्तौ सर्वमेवावबुध्यते । तद्यथा हि-यद् यद् एवाति[12]-भाव्यते तत्तदेव भावनाप्रकर्षपर्यन्तगमने तत्सात्मतामापादयति-तद्यथा श्रोत्रियजातिभावादौ घृणाम्[13] । भाव्यते च सर्वमेव[14] त्रैलोक्यं तदुपभोगतया इति स्वभावहेतुः । अत एवोक्तं **संवरतन्त्रे**—

---

1. अवभास–ख घ
2. सर्वं वेत्त्यर्थं–ख
3. तत्त्वस्याकल्पनाजालविषयित्वात्–ख घ
4. तस्य–भो*, न तु तस्याप्यशेषाकारशून्यस्य–ख घ
5. हि–भो*
6. अपि–भो*
7. भोटेग्रन्थेऽयमंशो गद्यमयः, संस्कृते पद्यं निष्पद्यते ।
8. आकरो न प्राप्तः
9. स्वभाव एव·······जायते–क*
10. काकै [र्न] भक्षितम् ?–भो
11. कोषयानमनुतिष्ठेयम्-घ
12. अति–भो*
13. [श्रोत्रियाणां महाव्रतादिभिः शुद्धाशुद्धभावविनिवृत्तिः]–भो
14. सर्वमेव–भो*, सर्वमेतत्–ङ

सर्वयोगा हि भगवान् वज्रसत्त्वस्तथागतः ।
तस्योपभोग्यं[1] (त्रै) सर्वं त्रैधातुकमशेषतः[2] ॥ ८१ ॥

पुनः **सर्वदेवसमागमतन्त्रे** चोक्तम्—

चतुर्विधं च यद्भूतं यत्किञ्चिज्जगतीगतम् ।
सर्वोपकरणं[3] प्रोक्तं योगिनां सिद्ध[4]चेतसाम् ॥ ८२ ॥
महामुद्रां समाधाय महासत्त्व[5]मुदाहरन् ।
पदशः सर्वमेवाहं भावयेत् तत्त्वयोगतः ॥ ८३ ॥

इत्येवमादि-भावनाप्रकर्षपर्यन्तगमनमात्राशुबन्धि - तत्सात्मीभावः [यत्र यत्र भवति, तत्र तत्र] सात्मीभावमापादयति[6] । भाव्यन्ते सर्वदा तत्-त्रैलोक्यान्तरवर्त्तिनः पदार्थाः सुखसौमनस्यादिसाधनत्वेन [स्थिताः ।] अत एवोक्तं **संवरतन्त्रे**—

यद्यदिन्द्रियमार्गत्वं यातं तत्तत्स्वभावतः ।
असमाहितयोगेन सर्वं बुद्धमयं भवेत्[7] ॥ ८४ ॥

पुनश्चोक्तं **सर्वकल्पसमुच्चयतन्त्रे**—

पञ्च[8]-बुद्धाः समासेन पञ्चकामगुणाः स्मृताः[9] ॥ ८५ ॥

पुनश्चोक्तं **श्री [गुह्य] समाजतन्त्रे**—

रूपशब्दादिभिर्भावैः देवतानां प्रकल्पयेत्[10] ॥ ८६ ॥

---

1. तस्योपभोगतया–ख ङ, तस्योपभोग–घ
2. अशेषतः–भो*
3. [सर्वोपभोग्यं]–भो
4. [शुद्धम्]–भो
5. [महातत्त्व]–भो
6. ० मत्सात्मीभावमापादयति–घ
7. वहेत्–घ
8. [सर्वं]–भो
9. गु. स. त.
10. सेकोद्देशटीका पृ० ३० ।

(29)

नस्मात्तेऽपि तद्भावनाप्रकर्षपर्यन्तगमने तत्सात्मतामुपयान्ति. तर्हि ते च गोचरतां प्रतिपद्यन्ते[1] । तेन[2] सविकल्पकमपि ज्ञानं भावनासामर्थ्यनिर्जातं स्वभावविशेषभाजिनम्[3] अशेषगुणालयम्—

[सर्वसिद्धिफलं[4]] तद्धि सर्वलोकादिकारकम् ।[5]
आसंसारस्थितेर्हेतुः सर्वसत्त्वार्थकारकम् ॥ ८८ ॥
ज्ञातव्यं तत्प्रयत्नेन [उच्छेद्योऽहं] प्रयत्नतः ।[6]
ज्ञाते तस्मिन् भवेत् सर्वं विज्ञातं तत्त्वसंज्ञितम्[7] ॥ ८९ ॥[8]

॥ इति **श्रीतत्त्वसिद्धिनाम**-प्रकरणं प्रावृततन्त्रं समाप्तम् ॥[9]

---

1. [गोचरतां न प्रतिपद्यन्ते इति न]–भो
2. अस्य गद्यखण्डस्य पद्यरूपत्वम् अग्रे निर्दिष्टरूपेण प्रतिभाति—
   सविकल्पकमपि ज्ञानं भावसामर्थ्यनिर्गतम् ।
   स्वभाव – विशेषभाजिनमशेषगुणालयम् ॥ ८७ ॥
3. भाजिनः शेष–ख घ ङ
4. सर्वसिद्धिमयं–सं
5. [नानासर्गं]–भो
6. समुच्छेद्यं प्रयत्नतः–ख ङ, उच्छेद्यं तत्प्रयत्नतः–बहवः पाठाः
7. [ज्ञेयतत्त्वकम्]–भो
8. ८७–८९ संख्यकाः श्लोकाः शान्तरक्षितविरचिताः प्रतीयन्ते ।
9. (i) [इति आचार्यशान्तरक्षितपादकृतं तत्त्वसिद्धिप्रकरणं समाप्तम्]–भो
   (ii) तत्त्वसिद्धिनाम प्रकरणं समाप्तम् । कृतिराचार्यशान्तरक्षितपादस्य अशेष-[स्व]-पर-सिद्धान्तसागरपारस्य–ख ग ङ
   (iii) तत्त्वसिद्धिनाम प्रकरणं समाप्तम् । कृतिराचार्यशान्तरक्षितपादस्य अशेष-[स्व]-पर-सिद्धान्तसागरस्य समाप्तम् (ता) ।
   ये धर्मा हेतुप्रभवा हेतुस्तेषां तथागतो ह्यवदत् ।
   तेषां च यो निरोध एवंवादी महाश्रव (म) णः ॥–घ

52

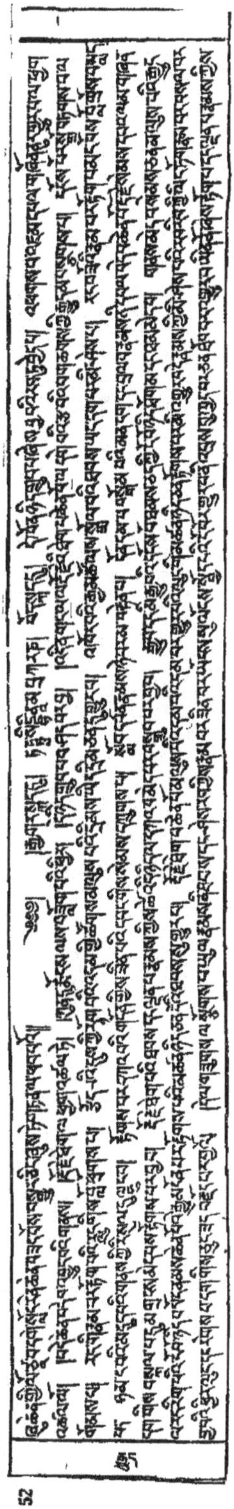

53

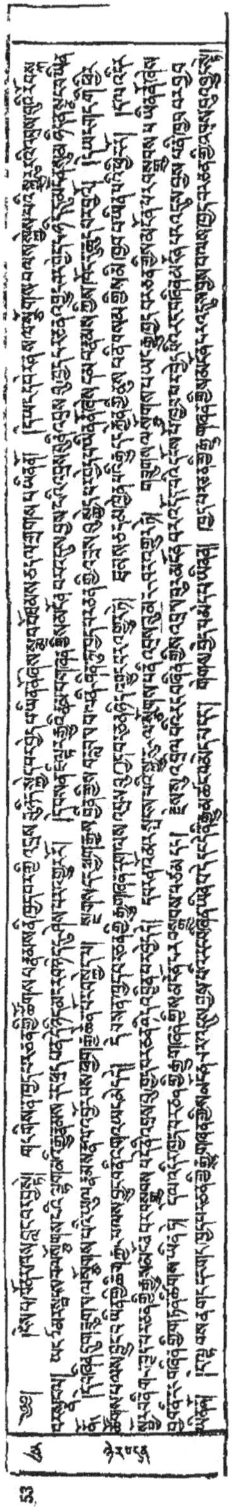

54

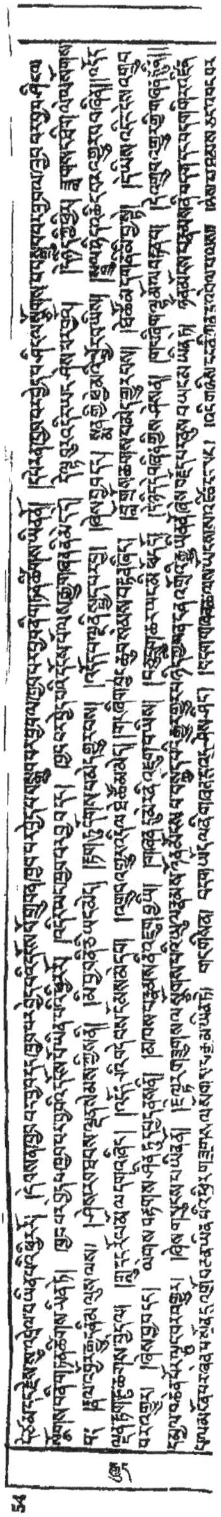

55

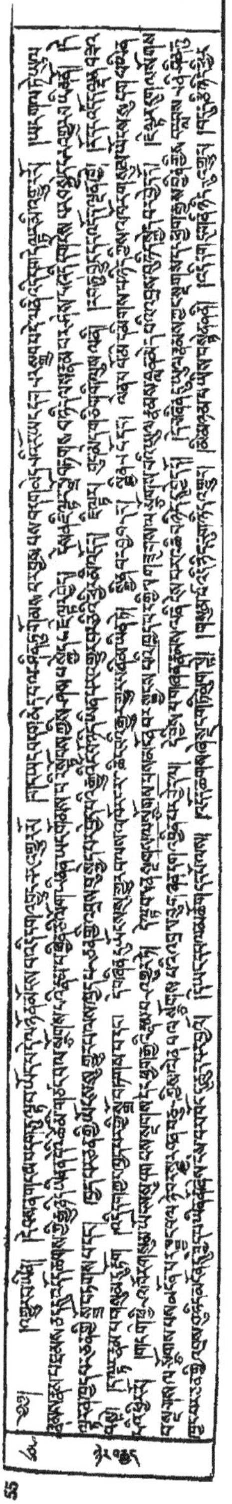

TATTVASIDDHI IN TIBETAN

55

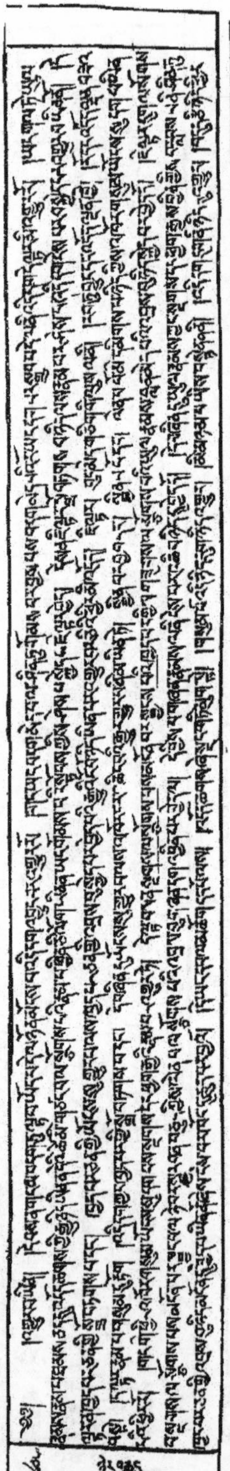

56

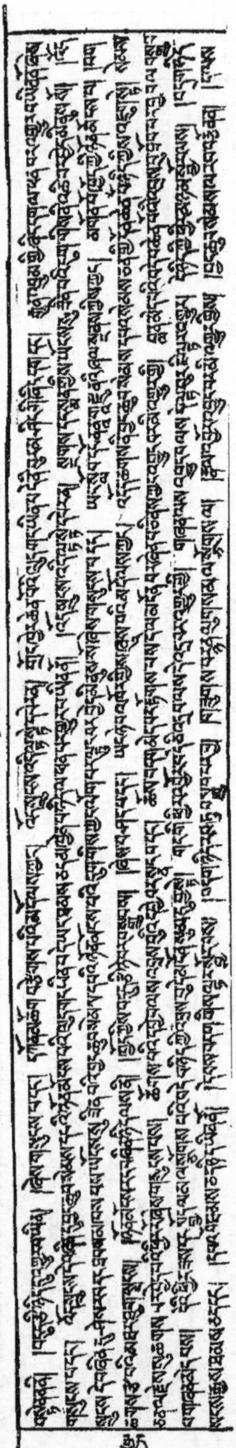

54

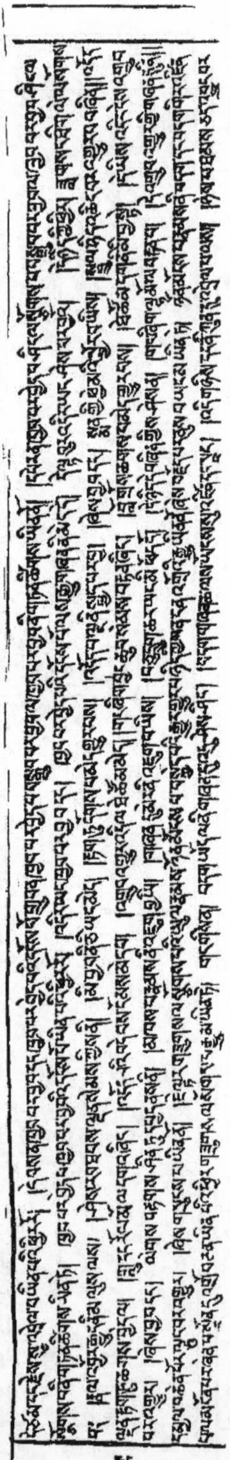

55

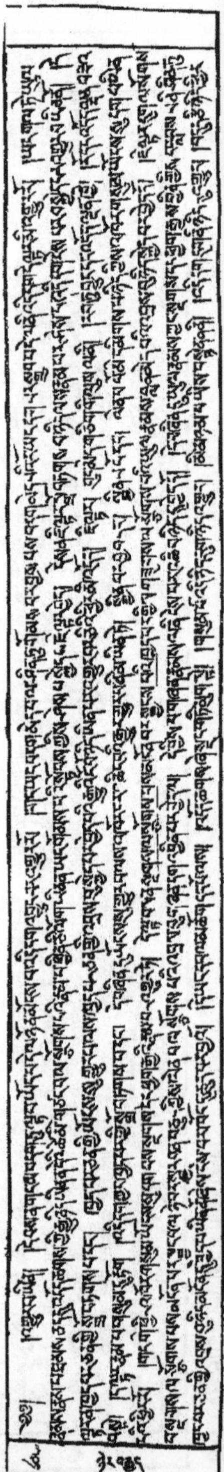

TATTVASIDDHI IN TIBETAN

56

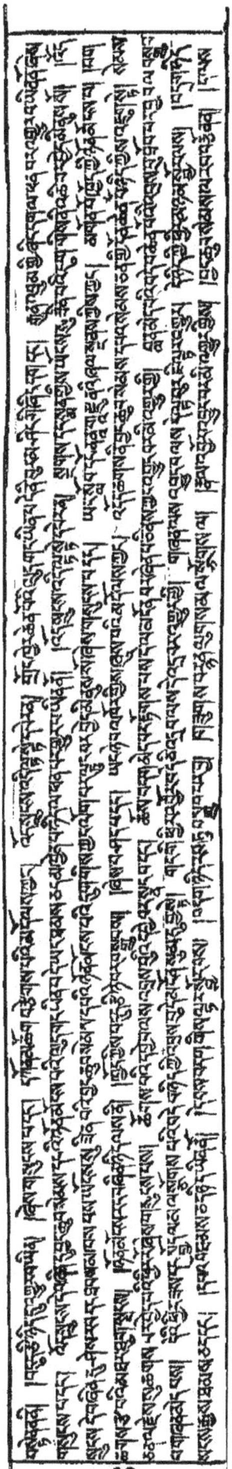

57

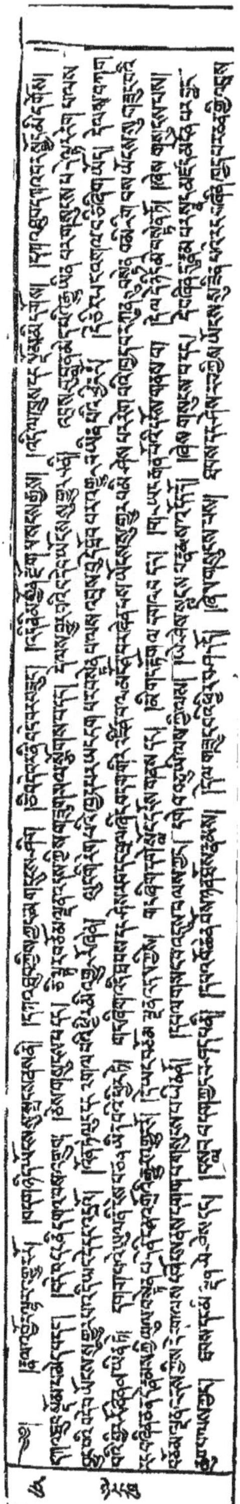

58

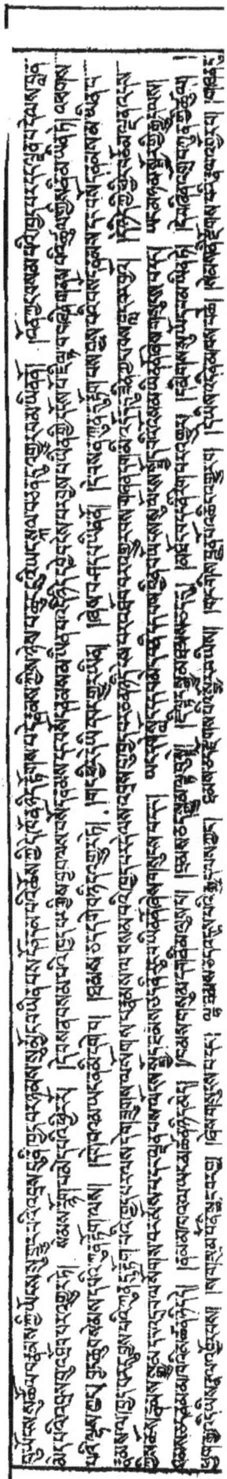

59

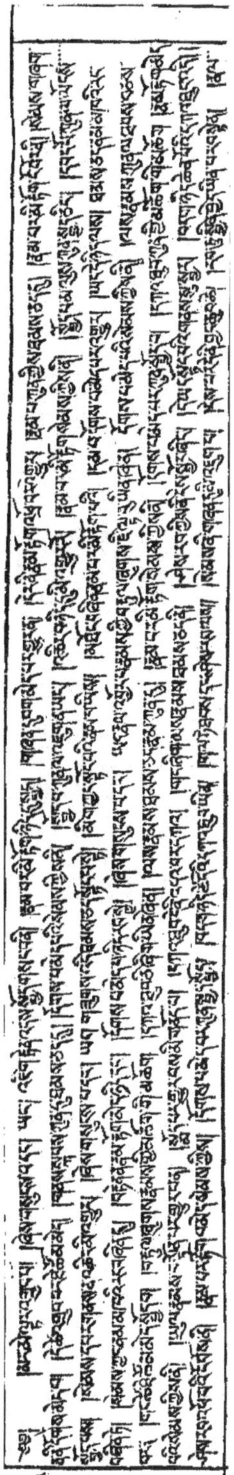

TATTVASIDDHI IN TIBETAN

60

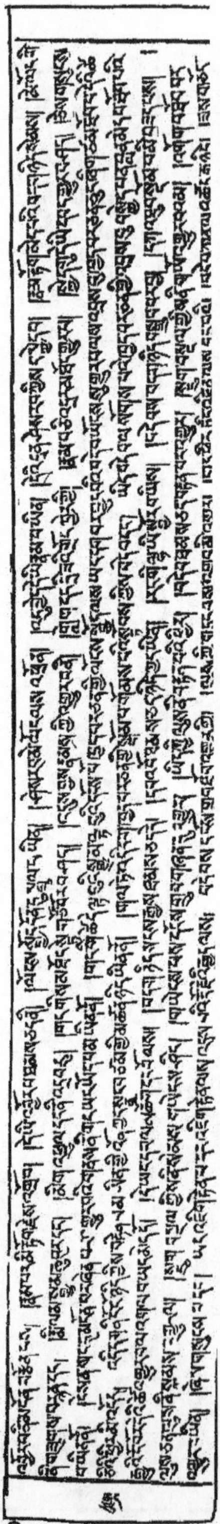

61

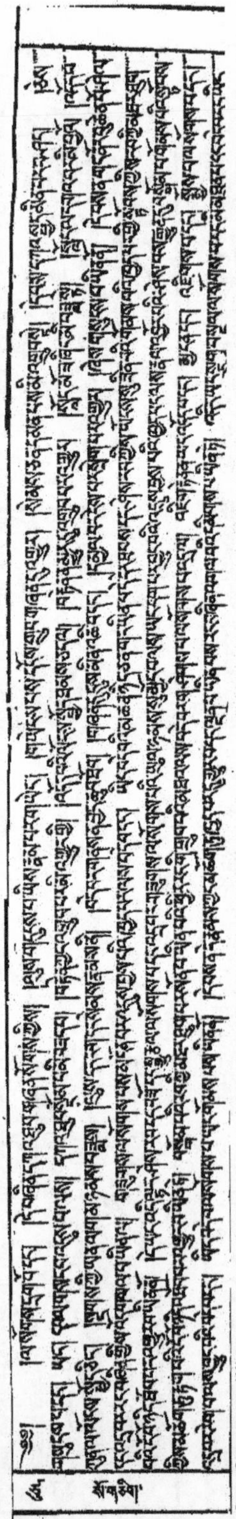

62

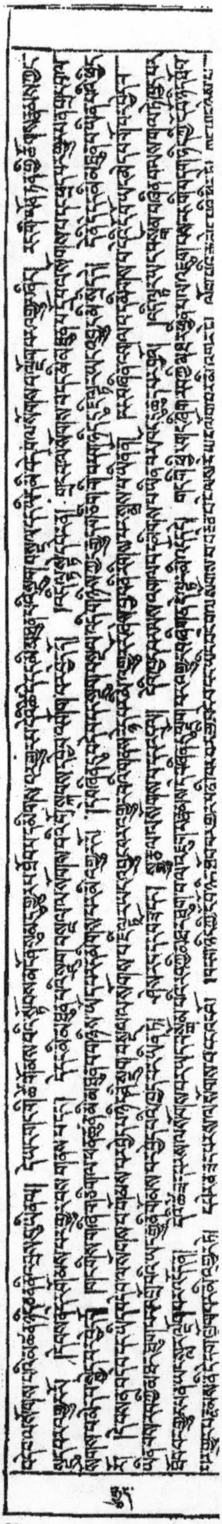

64

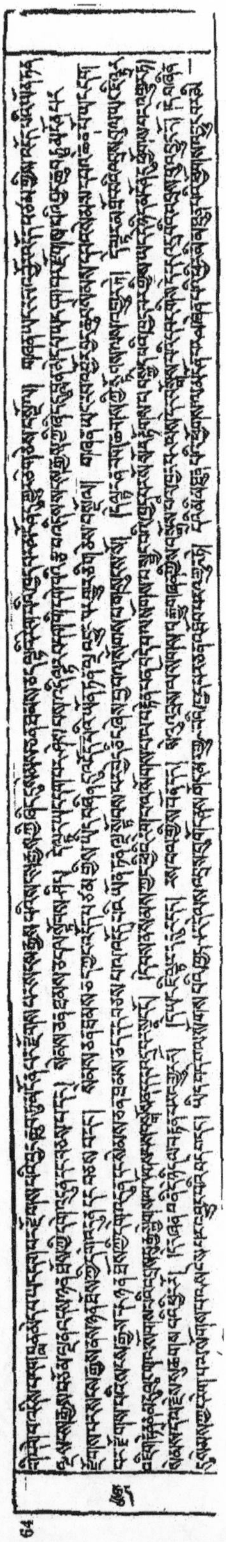

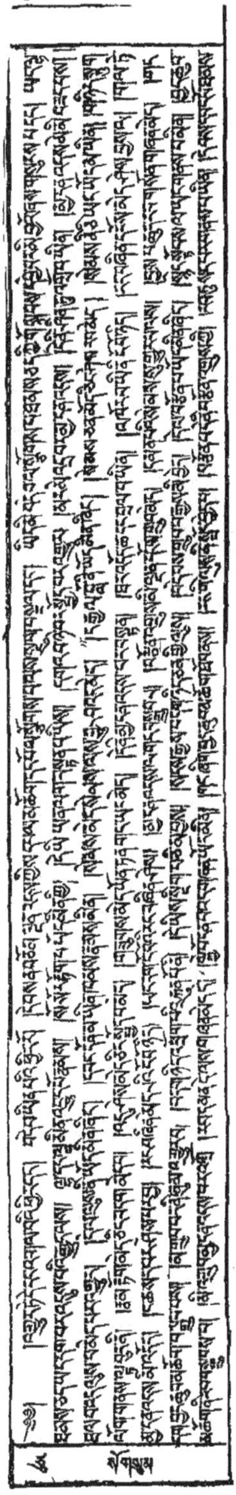

65

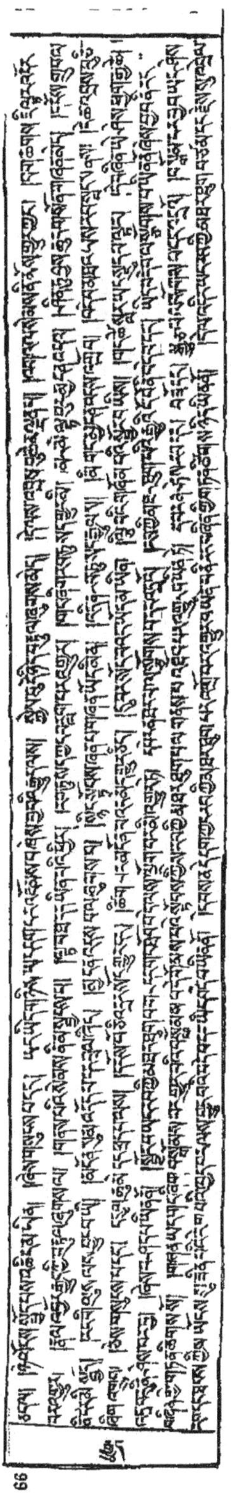

66

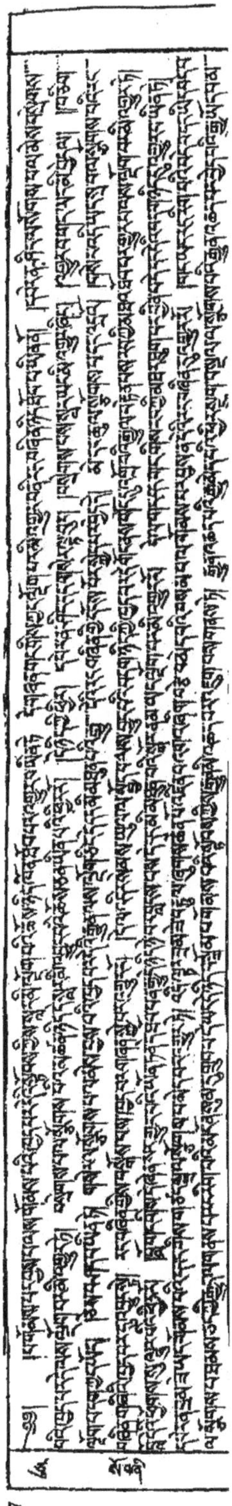

67

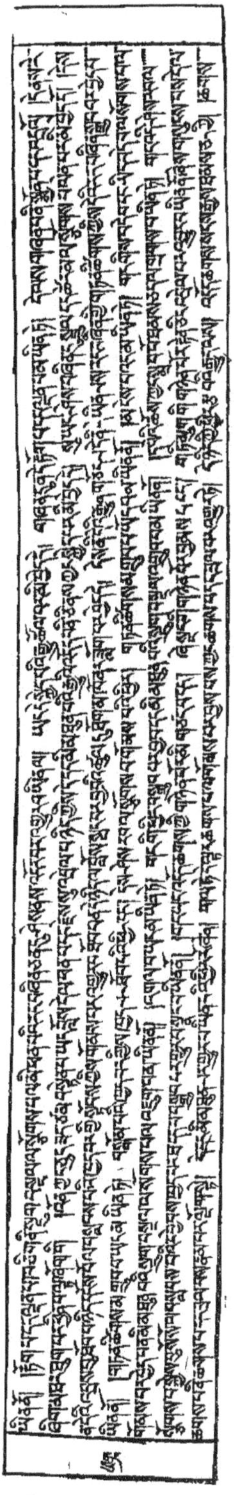

68

TATTVASIDDHI IN TIBETAN

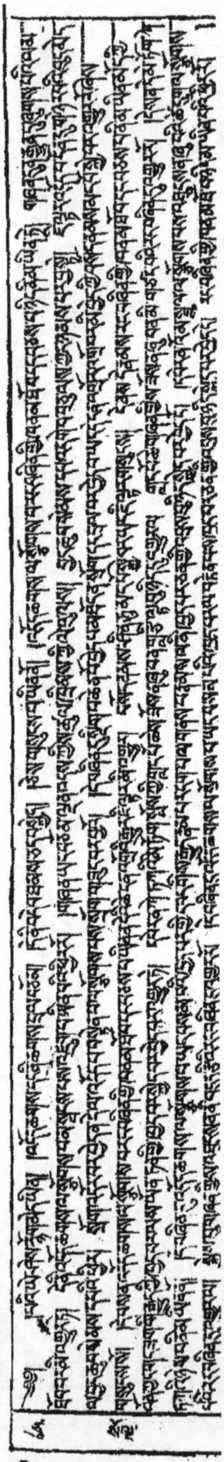

69

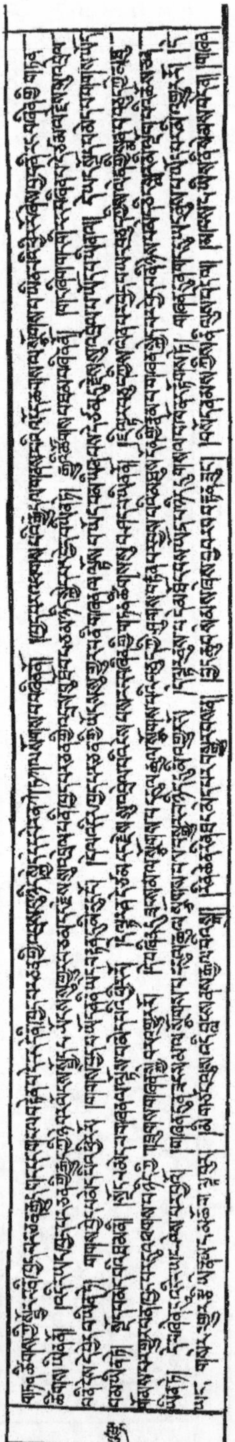

70

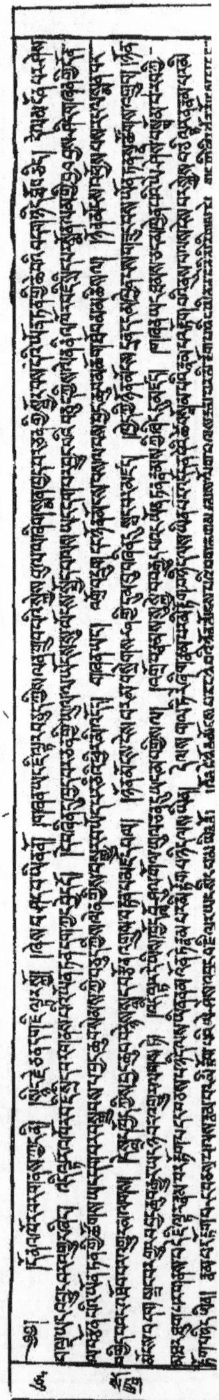

71

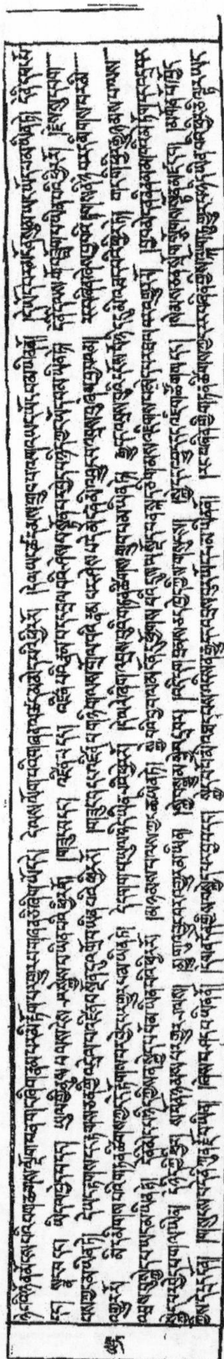

72

TATTVASIDDHI IN TIBETAN

73

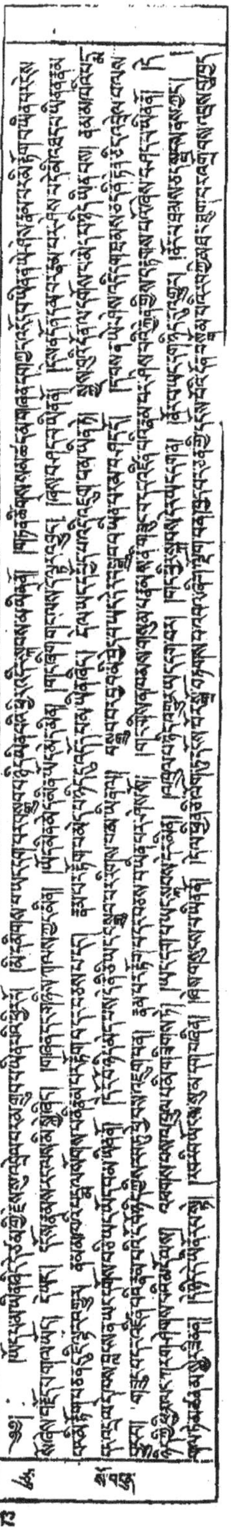

74

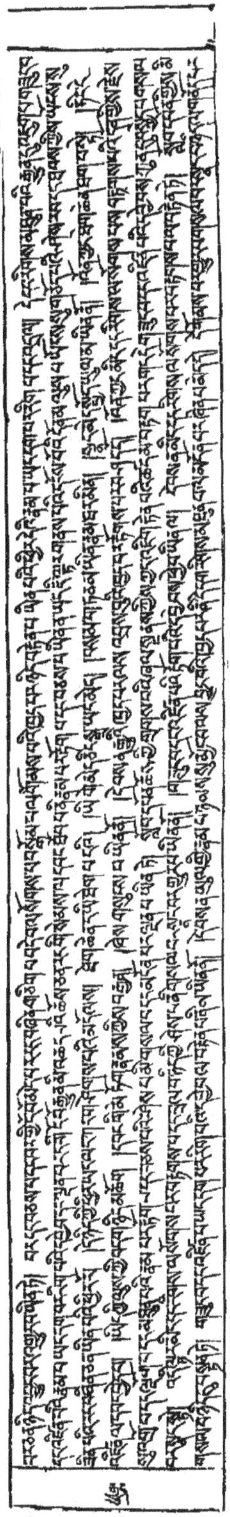

75

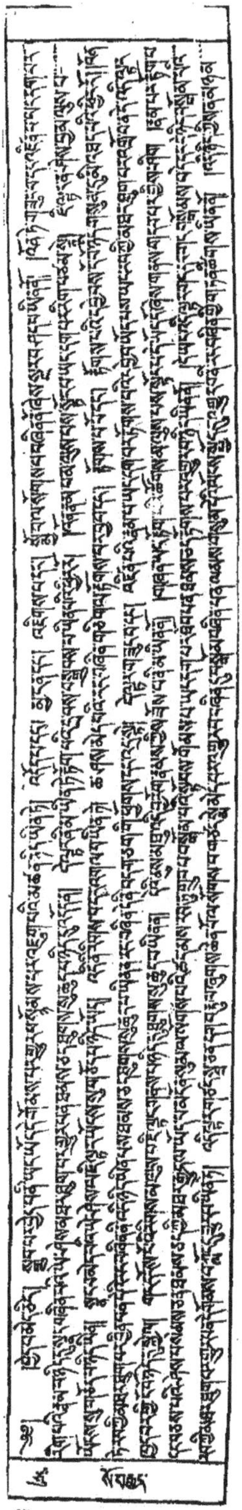

continued on next page

TATTVASIDDHI IN TIBETAN

76

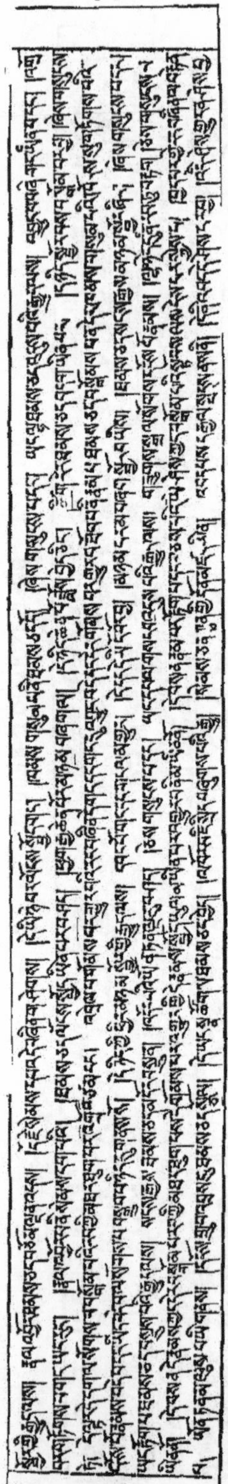

77

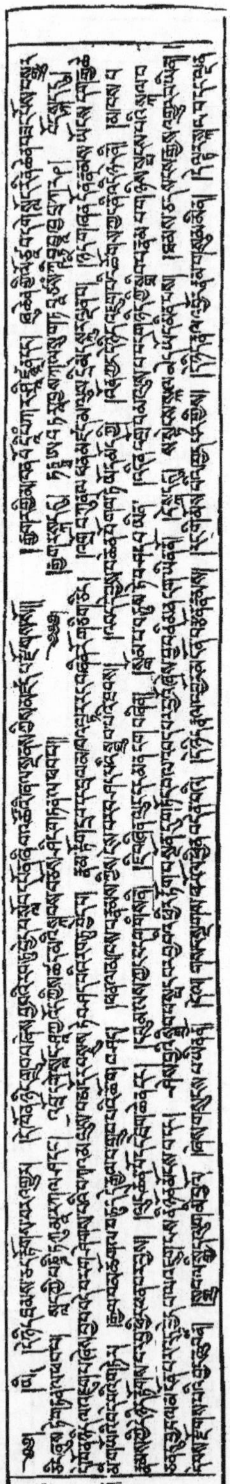

MADHYAMAKALANKARA IN TIBETAN AND SANKSKRIT

आचार्यशान्तरक्षितविरचिता
मध्यमालङ्कारकारिका

नमो मञ्जुश्रीकुमारभूताय

༄༅། །འཇམ་དཔལ་གཞོན་ནུར་གྱུར་པ་ལ་ཕྱག་འཚལ་ལོ། །

ये विशुद्धस्थिरमतिभूमिप्रतिष्ठाः
सागरवद्गम्भीरधर्मनयपारद्रष्टारः ।
अधिमुक्तिपरिभावनामहच्चित्ताः
सदा नमस्करोमि तानुत्तरप्रतिष्ठान् ॥ १ ॥

གང་དག་སྲུ་རྣམས་དག་བརྟན་བློ་མངའ་ས་ལ་བཞུགས།
ཆོས་ཚུལ་ཟབ་མོ་རྒྱ་མཚོ་ལྟ་བུའི་ཕ་རོལ་གཟིགས།
ལྷག་པར་མོས་པ་ཡོངས་བསྒོམས་ཐུགས་མངའ་ཆེ་རྣམས་ཀྱི།
བླ་བཞུགས་དེ་དག་རྣམས་ལ་རྟག་ཏུ་ཕྱག་འཚལ་ལོ།། ༡ །།

निःस्वभावा अमी भावास्तत्त्वतः स्वपरोदिताः ।
एकानेकस्वभावेन वियोगात्प्रतिबिम्बवत् ॥ १ ॥

བདག་དང་གཞན་སྨྲས་དངོས་འདི་དག།
ཡང་དག་ཏུ་ན་གཅིག་པ་དང་།
དུ་མའི་རང་བཞིན་བྲལ་བའི་ཕྱིར།
རང་བཞིན་མེད་དེ་གཟུགས་བརྙན་བཞིན།། ༡ ॥

क्रमिकार्योपयोगेन नैकात्मिकाः हि नित्यताः ।
भिन्नत्वे प्रतिकार्येभ्यः तन्नित्यताऽवहीयते ॥ २ ॥

འབྲས་བུ་རིམ་ཅན་ཉེར་སྦྱོར་བས།
རྟག་རྣམས་གཅིག་པུའི་བདག་ཉིད་མིན།
འབྲས་བུ་རེ་རེ་ཐ་དད་ན།
དེ་དག་རྟག་ལས་ཉམས་པར་འགྱུར།། ༢ ॥

भावनोत्पन्नज्ञानस्य ज्ञेयमसंस्कृतं मते ।
वादिनां तानि नैकानि क्रमिकज्ञानयोगतः ॥ ३ ॥

བསྒོམས་ལས་བྱུང་བའི་ཤེས་པ་ཡིས།
ཤེས་བྱ་འདུས་མ་བྱས་སྨྲ་བའི།
ལུགས་ལའང་གཅིག་མིན་དེ་དག་ནི།
རིམ་ཅན་ཤེས་དང་འབྲེལ་ཕྱིར་རོ།། ༣ ॥

--

पूर्वविज्ञानविज्ञेयस्वभावमनुयाति चेत् ।
पूर्वज्ञानं च पाश्चात्यं स्यात् पूर्वं च तथा परम् ॥ ४ ॥

རྣམ་ཤེས་སྔ་མས་ཤེས་བྱ་བའི།
རང་བཞིན་རྗེས་སུ་འབྲངས་ན་ནི།
ཤེས་པ་སྔ་མའང་ཕྱི་མར་འགྱུར།
དེ་བཞིན་ཕྱི་མའང་སྔ་མར་འགྱུར།། ༤ །།

पूर्वापरावकाशेषु तत्स्वरूपो न विद्यते ।
असंस्कृतो ह्यसौ धीवत् क्षणोत्पन्नोऽवगम्यताम् ॥ ५ ॥

སྔོན་དང་ཕྱི་མའི་གནས་རྣམས་སུ།
དེ་ཡི་ངོ་བོ་མི་འབྱུང་ན།
འདུས་མ་བྱས་དེ་ཤེས་པ་བཞིན།
སྐད་ཅིག་འབྱུང་བར་ཤེས་པར་བྱ།། ༥ །།

पूर्वपूर्वक्षणानां हि सामर्थ्यात् सम्भवे सति ।
नैतदसंस्कृतः स्याद्धि चित्तचैतसिका इव ॥ ६॥

སྔ་མ་སྔ་མའི་སྐད་ཅིག་གི།
མཐུ་ཡིས་འབྱུང་བར་འགྱུར་བ་ན།
འདུས་མ་བྱས་སུ་འདི་མི་འགྱུར།
སེམས་དང་སེམས་ལས་བྱུང་བ་བཞིན།། ༦ །།

क्षणिकानां च तत्रैव स्वतन्त्रोत्पादसम्मते ।
परानपेक्षतः सद्वा सदासद्वा सदा भवेत् ॥ ७ ॥

སྐད་ཅིག་མ་རྣམས་འདི་དག་ཏུ།
རང་དབང་འབྱུང་བར་འདོད་ན་ནི།
གཞན་ལ་ལྟོས་པ་མེད་པའི་ཕྱིར།
རྟག་ཏུ་ཡོད་པའམ་མེད་པར་འགྱུར།། ༧ །།

अर्थक्रियाऽसमर्थस्य विचारैः किं परीक्षया ।
षण्ढस्य रूपे वैरूप्ये कामिन्या किं परीक्षया ॥ ८ ॥

དོན་བྱེད་ནུས་པ་མ་ཡིན་ལ།
དེ་འདོད་བརྟགས་པས་ཅི་ཞིག་བྱ།
མ་ནིང་གཟུགས་བཟང་མི་བཟང་ཞེས།
འདོད་ལྡན་རྣམས་ཀྱིས་བརྟགས་ཅི་ཕན།། ༨ ||

क्षणिकं वाक्षणिकं वा पुंदर्शनं हि नार्हति ।
एकानेकस्वभावेन वियोगो ज्ञायते स्फुटम् ॥ ९ ॥

སྐད་ཅིག་སྐད་ཅིག་མ་ཡིན་པར།
གང་ཟག་བསྟན་དུ་མི་རུང་བས།
གཅིག་དང་དུ་མའི་རང་བཞིན་དང་།
བྲལ་བར་གསལ་བར་རབ་ཏུ་ཤེས།། ༩ ||

भिन्नदिशश्च योगत्वाद् व्यापकस्यैकता कथम् ।
आवृताऽनावृतत्वादेः स्थूलानाञ्चापि नैकता ॥ १० ॥

ཐ་དད་ཕྱོགས་ཅན་དང་འབྲེལ་ཕྱིར།
ཁྱབ་རྣམས་གཅིག་པུར་ག་ལ་གྱུར།
བསྒྲིབས་དང་མ་བསྒྲིབས་དངོས་སོགས་ཕྱིར།
རགས་པ་རྣམས་ཀྱང་གཅིག་པུ་མིན།། ༡༠ ||

संयुक्तः परिवृत्तश्च नैरन्तर्यस्थितोऽपि वा ।
मध्यस्थपरमाणोर्यद् यथैकाण्वभिमुख्यता ॥ ११ ॥

འབྱུར་བ་དང་ནི་བསྐོར་བ་འམ།
བར་མེད་རྣམ་པར་གནས་ཀྱང་རུང་།
དབུས་གནས་རྡུལ་ཕྲན་རྡུལ་གཅིག་ལ
བལྟས་པའི་རང་བཞིན་གང་ཡིན་པར།། ༡༡ ।।

अपराण्वभिमुख्येऽपि तदेव भवतीति चेत् ।
तथा हि भूजलादीनां वर्धनं स्यात् कथं ननु ॥ १२ ॥

རྡུལ་ཕྲན་གཞན་ལ་ལྟ་བ་ཡང་།
།དེ་ཉིད་གལ་ཏེ་ཡིན་བརྗོད་ན།
དེ་ལྟ་ཡིན་ན་ས་ཆུ་སོགས།
།ཇི་ལྟར་རྒྱས་འགྱུར་མ་ཡིན་ནམ།། ༡༣ ।।

यद्यन्याण्वभिमुख्यस्य नन्वन्यतरमिष्यते ।
परमाणोः कथं स्यात् वै निरंशता तथैकता ॥ १३ ॥

རྡུལ་ཕྲན་གཞན་ལ་ལྟ་བའི་ངོས།
གལ་ཏེ་གཞན་དུ་འདོད་ན་ནི།
རབ་ཏུ་ཕྲ་རྡུལ་ཇི་ལྟ་བུར།
གཅིག་པུ་ཆ་ཤས་མེད་པར་འགྱུར།། ༡༣ ।।

सिद्धाऽणुनिःस्वभावताः चक्षुर्द्रव्यादयः तथा ।
स्वपरैरुदिता नैको निःस्वभावा हि सम्मताः ॥ १४ ॥

རྡུལ་ཕྲན་རང་བཞིན་མེད་གྲུབ་པ།
དེའི་ཕྱིར་མིག་དང་རྫས་ལ་སོགས།
བདག་དང་གཞན་སྨྲས་མང་པོ་དག།
རང་བཞིན་མེད་པར་མངོན་པ་ཡིན།། ༡༤ ।।

तन्मयो हि तदारब्धः गुणकर्मात्मकौ तथा ।
स सामान्यविशेषौ च तेषां तेन समावयी ॥ १५ ॥

དེ་ཡི་རང་བཞིན་དེས་བརྩམས་དང་།
དེ་ཡི་ཡོན་ཏན་དེ་ལས་བདག།
དེ་ཡི་སྤྱི་དང་ཁྱད་པར་ཡང་།
དེ་དག་དེ་དང་འདུ་བ་ཅན།། ༡༥ ||

विज्ञानं जायते व्यावृत्तं पिण्डस्वरूपतः ।
यदपिण्डस्वरूपं हि तत्स्वरूपं भवेद्‌ मतिः ॥ १६ ॥

རྣམ་ཤེས་ཟེམ་པོའི་རང་བཞིན་ལས།
བཟློག་པ་རབ་ཏུ་སྐྱེ་བ་སྟེ།
ཟེམ་མིན་རང་བཞིན་གང་ཡིན་པ།
།དེ་འདི་བདག་ཉིད་ཤེས་པ་ཡིན།། ༡༦ ||

एकनिरंशरूपस्य त्रैरूप्यं नोपपद्यते ।
अतः तस्य स्वसंवित्तिः न कार्यकारणात्मिका ॥ १७ ॥

གཅིག་པ་ཆ་མེད་རང་བཞིན་ལ།
གསུམ་གྱི་རང་བཞིན་མི་འཐད་ཕྱིར།
དེ་ཡི་རང་གིས་རིག་པ་ནི།
རྒྱུ་དང་བྱེད་པའི་དངོས་པོ་མིན།། ༡༧ ||

अतः ज्ञानस्वरूपेण स्ववित्तिरस्य युज्यते ।
अन्यदर्थस्वरूपं हि तेन विज्ञायते कथम् ॥ १८ ॥

དེའི་ཕྱིར་འདི་ནི་ཤེས་པ་ཡི།
རང་བཞིན་ཡིན་པས་བདག་ཤེས་རུང་།
དོན་གྱི་རང་བཞིན་གཞན་དག་ལ།
དེ་ཡིས་ཇི་ལྟར་ཤེས་པར་འགྱུར།། ༡༨ །།

असत्यन्ये च तद्रूपं तद्वित्तौ हि कुतोऽन्यवित्।
वेद्यवेदकयोरर्थो पृथक्त्वेन मतो यतः ॥ १९ ॥

དེ་ཡི་རང་བཞིན་གཞན་ལ་མེད། །
གང་གིས་དེ་ཤེས་གཞན་ཡང་ཤེས།
ཤེས་དང་ཤེས་པར་བྱ་བའི་དོན། །
ཐ་དད་པར་ནི་འདོད་ཕྱིར་རོ།། ༡༩ །།

साकारज्ञानपक्षे तु तौ भिन्नौ चापि वस्तुतः।
तत्प्रतिविम्बसादृश्याद् वित्त्युपचारमात्रतः ॥ २० ॥

ཤེས་པ་རྣམ་བཅས་ཕྱོགས་ལ་ནི།
དངོས་སུ་དེ་གཉིས་ཐ་དད་ཀྱང་།
དེ་དང་གཟུགས་བརྙན་འདྲ་བས་ན།
བཏགས་པ་ཙམ་གྱིས་ཚོར་བར་རུང་།། ༢༠ །།

अर्थाकारेण विज्ञानं निवर्तकं न मन्यते।
बाह्यवित्त्याकृतिश्चैव नहि तस्य मते भवेत् ॥ २१ ॥

དོན་གྱི་རྣམ་པས་བསྒྱུར་ལྡན་པའི།
རྣམ་ཤེས་སུ་ཞིག་མི་འདོད་པ།
དེ་ལ་ཕྱི་རོལ་རིག་པ་ཡི།
རྣམ་པ་འདི་ཡང་ཡོད་མ་ཡིན།། ༢༡ །།

एकज्ञानस्य निर्भेदाद् नानाविधो न विद्यते ।
तस्मात्तस्य प्रभावेन अर्थज्ञानं न युज्यते ॥ २२ ॥

ཤེས་གཅིག་ཐ་དད་མ་ཡིན་པས།
རྣམ་པ་མང་པོར་མི་འགྱུར་ཏེ།
དེའི་ཕྱིར་དེ་ཡི་མཐུ་ཡིས་ནི།
དོན་ཤེས་འགྱུར་བར་གཞག་པ་མེད།། ༢༢ །།

आकारैरवियोगेन न विज्ञानस्य चैकता ।
अन्यथा ह्यनयोरेव एकत्वमुच्यते कथम् ॥ २३ ॥

རྣམ་པ་རྣམས་དང་མ་བྲལ་བས།
རྣམ་ཤེས་གཅིག་པུར་མི་འགྱུར་རོ།
དེ་ལྟ་མིན་ན་འདི་གཉིས་ལས།
གཅིག་ཅེས་ཇི་སྐད་བརྗོད་པར་བྱ།། ༢༣ །།

शुक्लत्वादिषु तज्ज्ञानं क्रमेणैवोपपद्यते ।
आशुसम्भवतः मूढैः युगपदिति ज्ञापिताः ॥ २४ ॥

དཀར་པོ་དག་ལ་སོགས་པ་ལ།
ཤེས་པ་དེ་ནི་རིམ་འབྱུང་སྟེ།
མགྱོགས་པར་འབྱུང་ཕྱིར་བླུན་པོ་དག།
ཅིག་ཅར་སྙམ་དུ་ཤེས་པ་ནི།། ༢༤ །།

लतातालादिबुद्धिर्हि भवति यदि चाशुतः ।
अतः स्याद् यौगपद्यं हि नेहापि स्यात् तथा कथम्
॥ २५॥

ལྕུག་མའི་སྒྲ་ལ་སོགས་པའི་བློ།
རབ་ཏུ་མགྱོགས་པར་འབྱུང་ཡིན་ན།
དེའི་ཕྱིར་ཅིག་ཅར་འབྱུང་བ་ཡིན།
འདི་ར་ཡང་ཅིའི་ཕྱིར་འབྱུང་མི་འགྱུར།། ༢༥ ।।

मनोविकल्पमात्रेऽपि ज्ञानं न क्रमशो भवेत्।
दूरस्थानस्य वैमुख्यात् सर्वधियः समाशुजाः ॥ २६ ॥

ཡིད་ཀྱི་རྟོག་པ་འབའ་ཞིག་ལའང་།
རིམ་དུ་ཤེས་པར་མི་འགྱུར་རོ།
རིང་དུ་གནས་པ་མ་ཡིན་པས།
བློ་རྣམས་ཀུན་ཀྱང་མགྱོགས་འབྱུང་འདྲ།། ༢༦ ।।

सर्वेषां विषयाणां हि क्रमग्रहो न विद्यते।
आकाराणां विभिन्नत्वे दृश्यते युगपद्ग्रहः ॥ २७ ॥

དེའི་ཕྱིར་ཡུལ་རྣམས་ཐམས་ཅད་ལ
རིམ་གྱིས་འཛིན་པར་མི་འགྱུར་གྱི།
རྣམ་པ་དག་ནི་ཐ་དད་ལྟར།
ཅིག་ཅར་འཛིན་པར་སྣང་བར་འགྱུར།། ༢༧ ।।

अलातेऽपि च चक्राभं संभ्रान्तं युगपद्भवेत्।
स्पष्टं हि प्रतिभासेन नहि प्रत्यक्षसन्धिता ॥ २८ ॥

མགལ་མེ་ལ་ཡང་ཅིག་ཅར་དུ།
འཁོར་ལོར་སྣང་བའི་འཁྲུལ་པ་འབྱུང་།
གསལ་བར་རབ་ཏུ་སྣང་བའི་ཕྱིར།
མཐོང་བས་མཚམས་སྦྱོར་མ་ཡིན་ནོ།། ༢༨ ।।

तथैव प्रतिसन्धानं संस्मरणेन नो दृशा ।
अतीतविषयस्यैव संग्रहणमभावतः ॥ २९ ॥

འདི་ལྟར་མཚམས་རྣམས་སྦྱོར་བ་ནི།
དྲན་པས་བྱེད་པ་ཉིད་ཡིན་གྱི།
མཐོང་བས་མ་ཡིན་འདས་པ་ཡི།
ཡུལ་ལ་འཛིན་པ་མེད་ཕྱིར་རོ།། ༢༩ །།

तस्य यो विषयो भूतः तन्नष्टत्वान्न भास्यते ।
प्रतिभासितचक्रं स्यान्नोऽर्हेत्यिदमतः स्फुटम् ॥ ३० ॥

དེ་ཡི་ཡུལ་དུ་གང་གྱུར་པ།
དེ་ནི་ཞིག་པས་གསལ་མ་ཡིན།
དེའི་ཕྱིར་འཁོར་ལོར་སྣང་བ་འདི།
གསལ་བ་མ་ཡིན་འགྱུར་བའི་རིགས།། ༣༠ །།

प्रसृतचित्रसंदृष्टौ बहुचित्तानि तद्यथा ।
एकांशरूपतः किञ्च भविष्यन्तीति तन्मते ॥ ३१ ॥

རི་མོ་གཞི་རྣམས་མཐོང་བའི་ཚེ།
དེ་ལ་དེ་བཞིན་སེམས་མང་པོ།
ཇི་སྙེ་གཅིག་ཆའི་ཚུལ་གྱིས་སུ།
འབྱུང་བར་འགྱུར་བ་འདོད་ན་ཀོ།། ༣༡ །།

एवं सति सितादेश्च एकाकारस्य बोधने ।
आदिमध्यान्तनानात्वाद् विचित्रालम्बनो भवेत् ॥ ३२ ॥

དེ་ལྟ་ཡིན་ན་དཀར་ལ་སོགས།
རྣམ་པ་སྣ་གཅིག་ཤེས་པ་ཡང་།

ཐོག་མ་དབུས་མཐའ་ཐ་དད་པས།
དམིགས་པ་སྣ་ཚོགས་ཉིད་དུ་འགྱུར།། ༣༣ ||

परमाण्वात्मकश्वेताद्येकरूपनिरंशकः ।
भासितो यत्र बुद्धौ च न ह्यस्माभिः प्रवेदनम् ॥ ३३ ॥

རྡུལ་ཕྲན་བདག་ཉིད་དཀར་ལ་སོགས།
གཅིག་པུའི་བདག་ཉིད་ཆ་མེད་པ།
ཤེས་པ་གང་ལའང་སྣང་གྱུར་པར།
བདག་གིས་རབ་ཏུ་ཚོར་བ་མེད།། ༣༣ ||

पञ्चविज्ञानधातूनां सञ्चितालम्बनाकृतिः ।
चित्तचैत्तावलम्बिञ्च षष्ठं हि स्थापितं कृतम् ॥ ३४ ॥

རྣམ་ཤེས་ལྔ་ཡི་ཁམས་རྣམས་ནི།
བསགས་ལ་དམིགས་པའི་རྣམ་པ་ཡིན།
སེམས་དང་སེམས་བྱུང་དམིགས་པ་ནི།
དྲུག་པར་བཞག་པ་བྱས་པ་ཡིན།། ༣༤ ||

बाह्यमतेषु विज्ञानं न चैकत्वेन भास्यते ।
गुणादीनां च संयोगे वै द्रव्याद्यवलम्बनात् ॥ ३५ ॥

ཕྱི་གཞུང་རྣམས་ལའང་རྣམ་ཤེས་ནི།
གཅིག་ཏུ་སྣང་བར་མི་འགྱུར་ཏེ།
ཡོན་ཏན་ལ་སོགས་ལྡན་པ་ཡི།
རྫས་ལ་སོགས་པར་དམིགས་ཕྱིར་རོ།། ༣༥ ||

मेचकात्मस्वरूपेव सर्वभावस्य दर्शने ।
तच्च ग्राहकचित्तस्य नैकरूपेण भास्यते ॥ ३६ ॥

ཐོར་བུ་གཟེ་ཡི་བདག་ཉིད་ལྟར།
དངོས་པོ་ཀུན་ཅེས་ལྟ་བ་ལ།
དེ་ལ་འཛིན་པའི་སེམས་ཀྱང་ནི།
གཅིག་བུའི་ངོ་བོར་སྣང་མི་རིགས།། ༣༦ ||

मृदादीनां च संघाते विषयेन्द्रियसंस्थितिः ।
यै इष्टः तन्मते नापि एकभावेन सम्मतम् ॥ ३७ ॥

ས་ལ་སོགས་པ་འདུས་པ་ལ།
ཡུལ་དང་དབང་པོ་ཀུན་འཛོག་པ།
སུ་འདོད་དེ་ཡི་ལུགས་ལ་ཡང་།
དངོས་པོ་གཅིག་དང་མཐུན་འདུག་མེད།། ༣༧ ||

सत्त्वाद्यात्मकशब्दादेः पक्षेऽप्येकार्थभासकम् ।
न उपपद्यते ज्ञानं त्रिरूपदेशभासनात् ॥ ३८ ॥

སྙིང་སྟོབས་ལ་སོགས་བདག་སྒྲ་སོགས།
ཕྱོགས་ལའང་དོན་གཅིག་སྣང་བ་ཅན།
ཤེས་པ་རིགས་པ་མ་ཡིན་ཏེ།
གསུམ་གྱི་བདག་ཉིད་ཡུལ་སྣང་ཕྱིར།། ༣༨ ||

भावरूपत्रयात्मके तदेकाकारा भवेत् यदि ।
भास्यते वैपरीतेन कथं तद्ग्रहणं मतम् ॥ ३९ ॥

དངོས་པོའི་ངོ་བོ་རྣམ་གསུམ་ལ།
དེ་ནི་གལ་ཏེ་རྣམ་གཅིག་སྣེ།

དེ་དང་མི་མཐུན་སྣང་ན་གོ།
དེ་ནི་དེར་འཛིན་ཇི་ལྟར་འདོད།། ༣༩ ||

विनापि बाह्यदेशश्च चित्राभासं च नित्यता ।
युगपद्वा क्रमाज्जातं विज्ञानमतिदुष्करम् ॥ ४० ॥

ཕྱི་རོལ་ཡུལ་རྣམས་མེད་པར་ཡང་།
སྣ་ཚོགས་སྣང་ལ་རྟག་པ་སྟེ།
ཅིག་ཆའམ་ཇི་སྟེ་རིམ་འབྱུང་བའི།
རྣམ་ཤེས་རུང་བར་ཤིན་ཏུ་དཀའ།། ༤༠ ||

व्योमादीनां हि विज्ञानं संज्ञामात्रेण भासितम् ।
नानावर्णविभासत्वात् नानात्वमवभासते ॥ ४१ ॥

ནམ་མཁའ་ལ་སོགས་ཤེས་པ་རྣམས།
མིང་ཙམ་དུ་ནི་སྣང་བ་དག
ཡི་གེ་དུ་མ་སྣང་བའི་ཕྱིར།
སྣ་ཚོགས་གསལ་བར་སྣང་བ་ཡིན།། ༤༡ ||

अनानाभासितं ज्ञानं किञ्चित् संस्थाप्यते तथा ।
न संस्थापनयोग्यं च लक्षणे हानिदर्शनात् ॥ ४२ ॥

རྣམ་ཤེས་སྣ་ཚོགས་མི་སྣང་བ།
འགའ་ཞིག་ཡོད་པར་བཞག་ན་ཡང་།
འོན་ཀྱང་ཡང་དག་བཞག་མི་རུང་།
མཚན་ཉིད་བཅས་ལ་གནོད་མཐོང་ཕྱིར།། ༤༢ ||

विज्ञानं संस्थितं चैव सदा नानात्वभासितम् ।
तद्भिन्नाकारवत् तस्य एकरूपो न युज्यते ॥ ४३ ॥

དེའི་ཕྱིར་སྣ་ཚོགས་སྣང་བ་ཡི།
རྣམ་ཤེས་རྣམ་པ་ཀུན་ཏུ་གནས།
དེ་ནི་རྣམ་པ་ཐ་དད་ལྟར།
གཅིག་པུའི་བདག་ཉིད་མི་རིགས་སོ།། ༤༣ །།

किञ्च ह्यनादिसंताने वासनायाः विपाकतः ।
निर्माणाकारभासेऽपि भ्रान्तेर्मायास्वरूपवत् ॥ ४४ ॥

ཇི་སྲིད་ཐོག་མ་མེད་རྒྱུད་ཀྱི།
བག་ཆགས་སྨིན་པས་སྤྲུལ་པ་ཡི།
རྣམ་པ་དག་ནི་སྣང་བ་ཡང་།
ནོར་བས་སྒྱུ་མའི་རང་བཞིན་འདྲ།། ༤༤ །།

तच्छुभमपि चैषां तद्भावो भूतः किन्नु वा ।
तदविचारितत्वैव रम्यमङ्गीकृतं मतम् ॥ ४५ ॥

དེ་དགེ་འོན་ཀྱང་དེ་དག་གི
དངོས་དེ་ཡང་དག་ཉིད་དམ་ཅི།
འོན་ཏེ་མ་བརྟགས་གཅིག་པུ་ན།
དགའ་བར་ཁས་ལེན་འདི་བསམ་མོ།། ༤༥ །།

सद्भूतं यदि विज्ञानं तदानेकं भवेद्धि वा ।
ते चैकं स्याद्विरुद्धत्वेऽवश्यं ते भवतस्पृथक् ॥ ४६ ॥

གལ་ཏེ་ཡང་དག་རྣམ་པར་ཤེས།
དུ་མར་འགྱུར་རོ་ཡང་ན་ནི།

དེ་དག་གཅིག་འགྱུར་འགལ་ལྡན་པས།
གདོན་མི་ཟ་བར་སོ་སོར་འགྱུར།། ༤༦ ||

आकाराणामभिन्नत्वे चलाचलाद्यस्ततः ।
सर्वे चलन्ति एकेन प्रसज्यते दुरुत्तरम् ॥ ४७ ॥

རྣམ་པ་ཐ་དད་མ་ཡིན་ན།
གཡོ་དང་མི་གཡོ་ལ་སོགས་པ།
གཅིག་གིས་ཐམས་ཅད་གཡོ་ལ་སོགས།
ཐལ་བར་འགྱུར་ཏེ་ལན་གདབ་དཀའ།། ༤༧

बाह्यार्थनयेऽप्येवं आकृतेर्न वियोगता ।
सकलं एकधर्मं स्यात् न निराकरणं भवेत् ॥ ४८ ॥

ཕྱི་རོལ་དོན་གྱི་ཚུལ་ལ་ཡང་།
དེ་ལྟར་རྣམ་པ་མ་བྲལ་ན།
གཅིག་གི་ཆོས་སུ་ཐམས་ཅད་ཀྱང་།
འཇུག་པར་འགྱུར་བ་བཟློག་པ་མེད།། ༤༨ ||

किञ्च आकारसंख्यावत् विज्ञानेऽङ्गीकृते सति ।
तदा स्यादणुसादृश्यं तद्विचारो दुरास्पदः ॥ ४९ ॥

ཇི་སྙེད་རྣམ་པའི་གྲངས་བཞིན་དུ།
རྣམ་པར་ཤེས་པ་ཁས་ལེན་ན།
དེའི་ཚེ་རྡུལ་ཕྲན་འདྲར་འགྱུར་བ།
དཔྱོད་པ་འདི་ལ་བཟློག་པར་དཀའ།། ༤༩ ||

विचित्रं चेत्तदेके हि किञ्च दैगम्बरं मतम् ।
विचित्रं नैकरूपं स्यात् चित्ररत्नादिसंनिभम् ॥ ५० ॥

གལ་ཏེ་སྣ་ཚོགས་དེ་གཅིག་ན།
ནམ་མཁའི་གོས་ཅན་ལུགས་སམ་ཅི།
སྣ་ཚོགས་གཅིག་པའི་རང་བཞིན་མིན།
རིན་ཆེན་སྣ་ཚོགས་ལ་སོགས་འདྲ།། ༥༠ །།

चित्रस्य चैकरूपत्वे चित्ररूपेण दृश्यते ।
आवृतानावृतादीनां तद्भिन्नत्वं भवेत् कथम् ॥ ५१ ॥

སྣ་ཚོགས་གཅིག་པའི་རང་བཞིན་ན།
སྣ་ཚོགས་ངོ་བོར་སྣང་བ་དང་།
བསྒྲིབས་དང་མ་བསྒྲིབས་ལ་སོགས་པ།
ཐ་དད་དེ་ནི་ཇི་ལྟར་འགྱུར།། ༥༡ །།

किञ्च तत्त्वत एतेषां आकाराणां न चास्तिता ।
तत्त्वतोऽसति आकारे विज्ञाने भ्रान्तितो दृशः ॥ ५२ ॥

ཇི་སྙེ་ངོ་བོ་ཉིད་དུ་དེའི།
རྣམ་པ་འདི་དག་མེད་པ་སྙེ།
ཡང་དག་ཏུ་ན་རྣམ་མེད་པའི།
རྣམ་པར་ཤེས་པས་ནོར་བས་སྣང་།། ༥༣ །།

यदि न सन्ति एतानि वेद्यन्ते स्पस्टतः कथम् ।
एतद्भावस्य भिन्नत्वे न भवेद् ज्ञानमीदृशम् ॥ ५३ ॥

གལ་ཏེ་མེད་ན་ཇི་ལྟ་བུར།
དེ་དག་འདི་ལྟར་གསལ་བར་ཚོར།

དེ་ཡི་དངོས་ལས་ཐ་དད་པའི།
ཤེས་པ་དེ་འདྲ་མ་ཡིན་ནོ།། ༥༣ ||

यद्भावो यत्र च नास्ति तज्ज्ञानं नास्ति तत्र हि ।
सुखादयोऽसुखत्वे सितत्वेष्वसितत्ववत् ॥ ५४ ॥

འདི་ལྟར་གང་ལ་དངོས་གང་མེད།
དེ་ལ་དེ་ཤེས་ཡོད་མ་ཡིན།
བདེ་བ་མིན་ལ་བདེ་སོགས་དང་།
དཀར་བ་རྣམས་ལའང་མི་དཀར་བཞིན།། ༥༤ ||

ज्ञानार्थं अस्मिन्नाकारे वस्तुतस्तु न युज्यते ।
ज्ञानात्मतावियोगत्वाद् आकाशकुसुमादिवत् ॥ ५५ ॥

རྣམ་པ་འདི་ལ་ཤེས་པའི་དོན།
དངོས་སུ་འཐད་པ་མ་ཡིན་ཏེ།
ཤེས་པའི་བདག་དང་བྲལ་བའི་ཕྱིར།
ནམ་མཁའི་མེ་ཏོག་ལ་སོགས་བཞིན།། ༥༥ ||

अभावेऽक्षमताऽयोग्या प्रज्ञप्तिश्चाश्वभृङ्गवत् ।
आत्माभासधियः न स्यादभावो जनिसक्षमः ॥ ५६ ॥

མེད་པ་ནུས་པ་མེད་པས་ན།
གདགས་པའང་མི་རུང་རྟ་རུ་བཞིན།
མེད་པ་བདག་སྣང་ཤེས་སྐྱེད་པར།
ནུས་པ་རུང་བ་མ་ཡིན་ནོ།། ༥༦ ||

यतस्तद्भावसंवित्तौ ज्ञानेन कोऽस्ति संगतः ।
अनात्मनो न तादात्म्यः तदुत्पत्तिश्च संभवेत् ॥ ५७ ॥

གང་ཕྱིར་དེ་ཡོད་ངེས་ཚོར་བར།
ཤེས་དང་འབྲེལ་པ་ཅི་ཞིག་ཡོད།
བདག་མེད་དེ་ཡི་བདག་ཉིད་དང་།
དེ་ལས་འབྱུང་བ་མ་ཡིན་ནོ།། ༥༧ །།

कुतो हेतोरभावेऽस्यं कादाचित्कश्च युज्यते ।
हेतुमति कुतो चापि पारतन्त्र्यात् निवार्यते ॥ ५८ ॥

རྒྱུ་མེད་ན་ནི་གང་ཞིག་གིས།
རེས་འགའ་འབྱུང་བ་འདི་རུང་འགྱུར།
རྒྱུ་དང་ལྡན་ན་གང་ཞིག་གིས།
གཞན་གྱི་དབང་ལས་བཟློག་པར་འགྱུར།། ༥༨ །།

तदभावेऽपि तज्ज्ञानं आकारहीनमेव वै ।
स्वच्छस्फटिकसादृश्यं धीसंवेद्यो न वर्तते ॥ ५९ ॥

དེ་མེད་ན་ནི་ཤེས་དེ་ཡང་། །རྣམ་པ་མེད་པ་ཉིད་ཀྱིས་འགྱུར།
ཤེལ་སྒོང་དག་པ་འདྲ་བ་ཡིན། །ཤེས་པ་རབ་ཏུ་ཚོར་བ་མེད།། ༥༩ །།

तद्यदि ज्ञायते भ्रान्त्या किञ्च तद्भ्रान्त्यधीनता ।
तत्प्रभावेन तर्हि स्यात् तत्परतन्त्रमेव च ॥ ६० ॥

འདི་ནི་འཁྲུལ་པས་ཤེས་ཤེ་ན།
དེ་ཅི་འཁྲུལ་ལ་རག་ལས་སམ།

དེ་ཡིས་མཐུ་ཡིས་བྱུང་ན་ནི།
དེ་ཡང་གཞན་གྱི་དབང་ཉིད་དོ།། ༦༠ ॥

यद्यद्भावपरीक्षायां नैकता तस्य तस्य च ।
न स्याद्यस्यैकता नापि भवेत्तस्य ह्यनेकता ॥ ६१ ॥

དངོས་པོ་གང་དང་གང་དཔྱད་པ།
དེ་དང་དེ་ལ་གཅིག་ཉིད་མེད།
གང་ལ་གཅིག་ཉིད་ཡོད་མིན་པ།
དེ་ལ་དུ་མ་ཉིད་ཀྱང་མེད།། ༦༡ ॥

एकानेके विनिर्मुक्ते ह्यपराकारसंगतः ।
भावो न युज्यते तयोरन्योन्यपरिहारतः ॥ ६२ ॥

གཅིག་དང་དུ་མ་མ་གཏོགས་པར།
རྣམ་པ་གཞན་དང་ལྡན་པ་ཡི།
དངོས་པོ་མི་རུང་འདི་གཉིས་ནི།
ཕན་ཚུན་སྤངས་ཏེ་གནས་ཕྱིར་རོ།། ༦༢ ॥

अत एव अमी भावाः संवृतिलक्षणग्रहाः ।
यद्येषामात्मकार्थेष्टाः किं कर्तव्यं भवेद् मया ॥ ६३ ॥

དེའི་ཕྱིར་དངོས་པོ་འདི་དག་ནི།
ཀུན་རྫོབ་ཁོ་ནའི་མཚན་ཉིད་འཛིན།
གལ་ཏེ་འདི་བདག་དོན་འདོད་ན།
དེ་ལ་བདག་གིས་ཅི་ཞིག་བྱ།། ༦༣ ॥

अविचारितरम्याणामुदयव्ययधर्मिणाम् ।
अर्थक्रियासाम्यार्थानां रूपं गच्छेच्च संवृतिम् ॥ ६४ ॥

དེ་ཡིས་མཐུ་ཡིས་བྱུང་ན་ནི།
དེ་ཡང་གཞན་གྱི་དབང་ཉིད་དོ།། ༦༠ ||

यद्यद्भावपरीक्षायां नैकता तस्य तस्य च।
न स्याद्यस्यैकता नापि भवेत्तस्य ह्यनेकता ॥ ६१ ॥

དངོས་པོ་གང་དང་གང་དཔྱད་པ།
དེ་དང་དེ་ལ་གཅིག་ཉིད་མེད།
གང་ལ་གཅིག་ཉིད་ཡོད་མིན་པ།
དེ་ལ་དུ་མ་ཉིད་ཀྱང་མེད།། ༦༡ ||

एकानेके विनिर्मुक्ते ह्यपराकारसंगतः ।
भावो न युज्यते तयोरन्योन्यपरिहारतः ॥ ६२ ॥

གཅིག་དང་དུ་མ་མ་གཏོགས་པར།
རྣམ་པ་གཞན་དང་ལྡན་པ་ཡི།
དངོས་པོ་མི་རུང་འདི་གཉིས་ནི།
ཕན་ཚུན་སྤངས་ཏེ་གནས་ཕྱིར་རོ།། ༦༢ ||

अत एव अमी भावाः संवृतिलक्षणग्रहाः।
यद्येषामात्मकार्थेष्टाः किं कर्तव्यं भवेद् मया ॥ ६३ ॥

དེའི་ཕྱིར་དངོས་པོ་འདི་དག་ནི།
ཀུན་རྫོབ་ཁོ་ནའི་མཚན་ཉིད་འཛིན།
གལ་ཏེ་འདི་བདག་དོན་འདོད་ན།
དེ་ལ་བདག་གིས་ཅི་ཞིག་བྱ།། ༦༣ ||

अविचारितरम्याणामुदयव्ययधर्मिणाम्।
अर्थक्रियासाम्यार्थानां रूपं गच्छेच्च संवृतिम् ॥ ६४ ॥

མ་བརྟགས་གཅིག་པུ་ཉམས་དགའ་ཞིང་།
སྐྱེ་དང་འཇིག་པའི་ཆོས་ཅན་པ།
དོན་བྱེད་པ་དག་ནུས་རྣམས་ཀྱི།
རང་བཞིན་ཀུན་རྫོབ་པ་ཡིན་རྟོགས།། ༦༤ ||

अविचारितरम्येऽपि स्वपूर्वपूर्वकारणम् ।
आश्रित्योत्तरकार्याणि ईदृशानि भवन्ति च ॥ ६५ ॥

བརྟག་པ་མ་བྱས་ཉམས་དགའ་བའང་།
བདག་རྒྱུ་སྔ་མ་སྔ་མ་ལ།
བརྟེན་ནས་ཕྱི་མ་ཕྱི་མ་ཡི།
འབྲས་བུ་དེ་འདྲ་འབྱུང་བ་ཡིན།། ༦༥ ||

अतः संवृत्यहेतुत्वे न युक्तं चेत्यसाधुता ।
यद्युपादानमस्य चेत् सम्यग्धि तच्च कथ्यताम् ॥ ६६ ॥

དེའི་ཕྱིར་ཀུན་རྫོབ་རྒྱུ་མེད་ན།
རུང་མིན་ཞེས་པའང་ལེགས་མ་ཡིན།
གལ་ཏེ་འདི་ཡི་ཉེར་ལེན་པ
ཡང་དག་ཡིན་ན་དེ་སྨྲོས་ཤིག། ༦༦ ||

स्वभावः सर्वभावानां युक्तिमार्गानुसारतः ।
मतोऽन्यैः तन्निराकुर्मो न कुवादे स्थितिर्भवेत् ॥ ६७ ॥

དངོས་པོ་ཀུན་གྱི་རང་བཞིན་ནི།
རིགས་པའི་ལམ་གྱི་རྗེས་འབྲང་བར།

तत्स्वरूपनिषेधेन तद्ध्वनिश्च न संभवेत् ॥ ७१ ॥

སྐྱེ་ལ་སོགས་པ་མེད་པའི་ཕྱིར།
སྐྱེ་བ་མེད་ལ་སོགས་མི་སྲིད།
དེ་ཡི་ངོ་བོ་བཀག་པའི་ཕྱིར།
དེ་ཡི་ཚིག་གི་སྒྲ་མི་སྲིད།། ༧༡ །།

अविषये निरोधस्य प्रयोगो नैव शोभनम् ।
विकल्पनाश्रये चापि सांवृतिकं न यौक्तिकम् ॥ ७२ ॥

ཡུལ་མེད་པ་ལ་དགག་པ་ཡི།
སྦྱོར་བ་ལེགས་པ་ཡོད་མ་ཡིན།
རྣམ་པར་རྟོག་ལ་བརྟེན་ན་ཡང་།
ཀུན་རྫོབ་པར་འགྱུར་ཡང་དག་མིན།། ༧༣ །།

तथा तदधिगमेन तत्स्वभावसमक्षतः ।
अविज्ञोऽपि कथं रूपं नैति भावस्य तथा ॥ ७३ ॥

འོ་ན་དེ་ནི་རྟོགས་གྱུར་པས།
དེ་ཡི་རང་བཞིན་མངོན་སུམ་ཕྱིར།
མི་མཁས་རྣམས་ཀྱང་དངོས་རྣམས་ཀྱི།
དངོས་པོ་འདི་འདྲ་ཅེས་མི་རྟོགས།། ༧༣ །།

नाऽनादिसंततेर्भाराद् भावारोपवशादतः ।
सर्वे च प्राणिनो नापि समवैति समक्षतः ॥ ७४ ॥

མ་ཡིན་ཐོག་མེད་རྒྱུད་ལྕི་བར།

དངོས་པོར་སྒྲོ་བཏགས་དབང་བྱས་པ།
དེའི་ཕྱིར་སྤྲོག་ཆགས་ཐམས་ཅད་ཀྱིས
མངོན་སུམ་རྟོགས་པར་མི་འགྱུར་རོ།། ༧༥ ||

आरोपच्छेदकेन हि विज्ञापनेन हेतुना ।
ज्ञापयन्तेऽनुमानैश्च योगेन्द्रैर्हि समक्षतः ॥ ७५ ॥

མ་ཡིན་ཐོག་མེད་རྒྱུད་ལྡི་བར།
དངོས་པོར་སྒྲོ་བཏགས་དབང་བྱས་པ།
དེའི་ཕྱིར་སྤྲོག་ཆགས་ཐམས་ཅད་ཀྱིས།
མངོན་སུམ་རྟོགས་པར་མི་འགྱུར་རོ།། ༧༥ ||

मतैरुत्पादितं त्यक्त्वा विशेषधर्मिणं बुधे ।
दारबालेषु यावद्धि प्रसिद्धस्य च वस्तुनः ॥ ७६ ॥

གཞུང་གིས་བསྐྱེད་པའི་བྱེ་བྲག་གི།
ཆོས་ཅན་སྤྱངས་ནས་མཁས་པ་དང་།
བུད་མེད་བྱིས་པའི་བར་དག་ལ།
གྲགས་པར་གྱུར་པའི་དངོས་རྣམས་ལ།། ༧༦ ||

साध्यसाधकभावाश्च प्रवर्तन्तेऽखिलाः अमी ।
नैवं चेदाश्रयासिद्धादेरुत्तरं च कथं भवेत् ॥ ७७ ॥

བསྒྲུབ་དང་སྒྲུབ་པའི་དངོས་པོ་འདི།
མ་ལུས་ཡང་དག་འཇུག་པར་འགྱུར།
དེ་ལྟ་མིན་ན་གཞི་མ་གྲུབ།
ལ་སོགས་ལན་ནི་ཇི་སྐད་གདབ།། ༧༧ ||

प्रतिभासात्मकं वस्तु न प्रतिषेधयाम्यहम् ।
साधनसाध्यतास्थाप्ये नास्ति व्याकुलता ततः ॥ ७८ ॥

བདག་ནི་སྣང་བའི་ངང་ཅན་གྱི།
དངོས་པོ་དགག་པར་མི་བྱེད་དེ།
དེ་ལྟ་བས་ན་སྒྲུབ་པ་དང་།
བསྒྲུབ་བྱ་བཞག་པ་འཁྲུགས་པ་མེད།། ༧༨ །།

भावाभावविकल्पादेः ह्यनादिभवसंततेः ।
सजातीयं हि बीजत्वं अनुमेयं प्रवर्तते ॥ ७९ ॥

དེའི་ཕྱིར་ཐོག་མེད་སྲིད་རྒྱུད་ནས།
དངོས་དང་དངོས་མེད་རྟོག་སོགས་ཀྱི།
རིགས་དང་མཐུན་པའི་ས་བོན་ཉིད།
རྗེས་སུ་དཔག་པར་བྱ་བ་ཡིན།། ༧༩ །།

नाऽमी वस्तुबलादेव भवन्ति तदभावतः ।
वस्तूनामात्मता एव प्रतिषिद्धा सविस्तरा ॥ ८०॥

འདི་ནི་དངོས་པོའི་མཐུ་སྟོབས་ཀྱིས།
།འབྱུང་བ་མ་ཡིན་དེ་མེད་ཕྱིར།
དངོས་པོ་རྣམས་ཀྱི་བདག་ཉིད་དེ།
རྒྱ་ཆེན་རབ་ཏུ་བཀག་པ་ཡིན།། ༨༠ །།

नागन्तुकाः क्रमोत्पादादध्रुवाः न च शाश्वताः ।
अतोऽभ्याससमानत्वादादिमाश्च स्वजातिजाः ॥ ८१ ॥

རིམ་གྱིས་འབྱུང་ཕྱིར་གློ་བུར་མིན།

རྟག་བྱུང་མ་ཡིན་རྟག་མ་ཡིན།
དེ་བས་གོམས་འདྲ་དེ་ཉིད་ཕྱིར།
དང་པོ་རང་གི་རིགས་ལས་སྐྱེས།། ༨༡ །།

शाश्वतोच्छेतदृष्टी हि दूरीस्थितेऽस्य संमते।
अन्वयव्यतिरेकौ च बीजांकुरलतादिवत् ॥ ८२ ॥

དེའི་ཕྱིར་རྟག་ཆད་ལྟ་བ་རྣམས།
གཞུང་འདི་ལ་ནི་རིང་དུ་གནས།
ལྡོག་དང་རྗེས་སུ་འཇུག་པ་ཡང་།
ས་བོན་མྱུ་གུ་ལྕུག་སོགས་བཞིན།། ༨༢ །།

धर्मनैरात्म्यबोधो हि निःस्वभावत्वभावितः।
विपर्यासससमुत्पन्नं क्लेशमयत्नतस्त्यजेत् ॥ ८३ ॥

ཆོས་ལ་བདག་མེད་མཁས་པ་ནི།
རང་བཞིན་མེད་པ་གོམས་བྱས་པས།
ཕྱིན་ཅི་ལོག་ལས་བྱུང་བ་ཡ
ཉོན་མོངས་བསྒྲིམ་པ་མེད་པར་སྤོང་།། ༨༣ །།

कार्यकारणभावो हि संवृतितो न वार्यते।
संक्लेशव्यवदानादेः क्षुभिता न व्यवस्थितिः ॥ ८४ ॥

རྒྱུ་དང་འབྲས་བུའི་དངོས་པ
ཀུན་རྫོབ་ཏུ་ནི་མ་བཀག་པས།
ཀུན་ནས་ཉོན་མོངས་རྣམ་བྱང་སོགས།
རྣམ་པར་བཞག་པ་འཁྲུགས་པ་མེད།། ༨༤ །།

རྟག་བྱུང་མ་ཡིན་རྟག་མ་ཡིན།
དེ་བས་གོམས་འདྲ་དེ་ཉིད་ཕྱིར།
དང་པོ་རང་གི་རིགས་ལས་སྐྱེས།། ༨༡ ||

शाश्वतोच्छेतदृष्टी हि दूरीस्थितेऽस्य संमते ।
अन्वयव्यतिरेकौ च बीजांकुरलतादिवत् ॥ ८२ ॥

དེའི་ཕྱིར་རྟག་ཆད་ལྟ་བ་རྣམས།
གཞུང་འདི་ལ་ནི་རིང་དུ་གནས།
ལྡོག་དང་རྗེས་སུ་འཇུག་པ་ཡང་།
ས་བོན་མྱུ་གུ་ལྡུག་སོགས་བཞིན།། ༨༢ ||

धर्मनैरात्म्यबोधो हि निःस्वभावत्वभावितः ।
विपर्याससमुत्पन्नं क्लेशमयत्नतस्त्यजेत् ॥ ८३ ॥

ཆོས་ལ་བདག་མེད་མཁས་པ་ནི།
རང་བཞིན་མེད་པ་གོམས་བྱས་པས།
ཕྱིན་ཅི་ལོག་ལས་བྱུང་བ་ཡ
ཉོན་མོངས་བསྒྲིམ་པ་མེད་པར་སྤོང་།། ༨༣ ||

कार्यकारणभावो हि संवृतितो न वार्यते ।
संक्लेशव्यवदानादेः क्षुभिता न व्यवस्थितिः ॥ ८४ ॥

རྒྱུ་དང་འབྲས་བུའི་དངོས་པ
ཀུན་རྫོབ་ཏུ་ནི་མ་བཟློག་པས།
ཀུན་ནས་ཉོན་མོངས་རྣམ་བྱང་སོགས།
རྣམ་པར་བཞག་པ་འཁྲུགས་པ་མེད།། ༨༤ ||

དངོས་པོ་དམིགས་པ་ཡོད་པ་ནི།
སྨིག་རྒྱུ་ལ་སོགས་ཤེས་པ་བཞིན།
ཕྱིན་ཅི་ལོག་པར་ཡོངས་སུ་རྟོག། ༨༨ ।।

तत्प्रभावप्रसूतो हि सर्वपारमिताविधिः ।
मिथ्यात्मात्मीयतोत्पाद इव दुर्बल एव च ॥ ८९ ॥

དེའི་ཕྱིར་དེའི་མཐུས་བྱུང་བ་ཡི།
ཕ་རོལ་ཕྱིན་པ་བསྒྲུབ་པ་ཀུན།
བདག་དང་བདག་གིར་ལོག་པ་ལས།
བྱུང་བ་བཞིན་དུ་སྟོབས་ཆུང་ངོ་।। ༨༩ ।।

भावानालम्बनात्तस्माद्धुत्पन्नं हि महाफलम् ।
पुष्टहेतोश्च जाताद्धि पुष्टबीजांकुरादिवत् ॥ ९० ॥

དངོས་པོར་དམིགས་པ་མེད་པ་ལས།
བྱུང་བ་འབྲས་བུ་ཆེན་པོ་སྟེ།
རྒྱས་པའི་རྒྱུ་ལས་བྱུང་བའི་ཕྱིར།
ས་བོན་གྲུང་པོའི་མྱུག་སོགས་བཞིན།། ༩༠ ।।

कार्यकारणभूतोऽपि केवलं ज्ञानमेव च ।
यदेवास्ति स्वसिद्धं हि तत्स्थितं ज्ञान एव च ॥ ९१ ॥

རྒྱུ་དང་འབྲས་བུར་གྱུར་པ་ཡང་།
ཤེས་པ་འབའ་ཞིག་ཁོ་ན་སྟེ།
རང་གིས་གྲུབ་པ་གང་ཡིན་པ།
དེ་ནི་ཤེས་པར་གནས་པ་ཡིན།། ༩༡ ।।

विज्ञप्तिमात्रमाश्रित्य ज्ञेयमबाह्यवस्तुकम् ।
अमुश्च नयमाश्रित्य ज्ञेया निरात्मता परा ॥ १२ ॥

སེམས་ཙམ་ལ་ནི་བརྟེན་ནས་སུ།
ཕྱི་རོལ་དངོས་མེད་ཤེས་པར་བྱ།
ཚུལ་འདིར་བརྟེན་ནས་དེ་ལ་ཡང་།
ཤིན་ཏུ་བདག་མེད་ཤེས་པར་བྱ།། ༩༣ ||

द्विनयरथमारोहन् हि युक्तिरश्मिश्च धारयन् ।
अत एव यथार्थं तैः महायानं हि प्राप्यते ॥ १३ ॥

ཚུལ་གཉིས་ཤིང་རྟར་བཞོན་ནས་སུ།
རིགས་པའི་སྲབ་སྐྱོགས་འཇུ་བྱེད་པ།
དེ་དག་དེའི་ཕྱིར་ཇི་བཞིན་དོན།
ཐེག་པ་ཆེན་པོ་པ་ཉིད་འཐོབ།། ༩༣ ||

विष्णवीशादिभिरलीढं अमितस्थानकारणम् ।
लोकमूर्धन्यभूतेन चाप्यनास्वादितं यथा ॥ १४ ॥

ཁྱབ་དང་དབང་ལ་སོགས་མ་མྱངས།
།དཔག་ཏུ་མེད་པར་གནས་པའི་རྒྱུ།
འཇིག་རྟེན་སྤྱི་བོར་གྱུར་པས་ཀྱང་།
ཤིན་ཏུ་མྱངས་པ་མ་ཡིན་པ།། ༩༤ ||

संशुद्धममृतत्वं वै शुद्धकारुण्यहेतुकात् ।
तथागताद्दृते नैव चान्यैः संभोगता भवेत् ॥ १५ ॥

ཡང་དག་བདུད་རྩི་དག་པ་འདི།

ཐུགས་རྗེ་དག་པའི་རྒྱུ་ཅན་གྱི།
དེ་བཞིན་གཤེགས་པ་མ་གཏོགས་པ།
གཞན་གྱི་ལོངས་སྤྱོད་མ་ཡིན་ནོ།། ༩༥ ||

मिथ्यानुशासितं चैव सिद्धान्ताऽऽसक्तधीं प्रति ।
प्रजायते हि कारुण्यं तस्य नयानुसारिणाम् ॥ ९६॥

དེའི་ཕྱིར་ལོག་པར་བསྟན་པ་ཡི།
གྲུབ་མཐར་འཆེལ་བའི་བློ་ཅན་ལ།
དེའི་ལུགས་རྗེས་འཇུག་བློ་ཅན་རྣམས།
སྙིང་རྗེ་ཉིད་ནི་རབ་ཏུ་སྐྱེ།། ༩༦ ||

सुधीधनैरसारत्वं परमतेषु दृश्यते ।
तावत् तैः तायिनं प्रति जन्यत आदरं परम् ॥ ९७ ॥

བློ་ནོར་ལྡན་པས་ལུགས་གཞན་ལ།
།ཇི་ལྟར་སྙིང་པོ་མེད་མཐོང་བ།
དེ་ལྟར་དེ་དག་སྐྱོབ་པ་ལ།
གུས་པ་ཞེན་ཏུ་སྐྱེ་བར་འགྱུར།། ༩༧ ||

अयं मध्यमकालङ्कार आचार्यशान्तरक्षितेन स्वपरसिद्धान्त सागरपारंगतेन आर्यावागीश्वरनिर्मलपाद केसरमूर्धग्रहीतेन विरचितः समाप्तः।

इति अनूदितः संशोधितश्च भारतीयोपाध्यायेन शीलेन्द्रबोधिना तथा भोटदेशीयेन लोकचक्षुर्भदन्त ज्ञानसेनेन च। इति शुभमस्तु।

དབུ་མའི་རྒྱན་འདི་ནི་སློབ་དཔོན་ཞི་བ་འཚོ་བདག་དང་གཞན་གྱི་གྲུབ་པའི་མཐའི་རྒྱ་མཚོའི་ཕ་རོལ་ཏུ་ཕྱིན་སོན་པ། འཕགས་པ་ངག་གི་དབང་ཕྱུག་གི་ཞབས་ཀྱི་པདྨ་རྡོག་པ་མེད་པའི་ཟེའུ་འབྲུ་སྤྱི་བོས་ལེན་པས་མཛད་པ་རྫོགས་སོ། |

APPENDIX

The two pillars upon which knowledge is founded are perception and inference. Shantarakshita uses inference to attack perception, and finds perception inadequate for the purpose of providing us with veridical knowledge.

His attack takes two forms:

I) Attacks on the view that perception accords us veridical knowledge of material objects existing apart from the mind (Sautrantika).

This attack takes five forms:

A. Shantarakshita gives a general argument that matter cannot exist because it is said to be atomic in nature. There cannot, however, be an indivisible particle, because it would have no distinct sides, and thus could not combine with other atoms. Further, an indivisible atom would not take up space, and thus when combined with another atom, would not be able to increase. Slokas 10–15.

B. If the object of mind is material and the mind non-material, the mind could not know the object because mind and object could not interact. Slokas 18–20.

C. In a single instant of time, it is impossible for an uncompounded state of awareness to cognize many objects. If the mind comes to know an object, this knowledge must bring about a division in the mind. Slokas 21-23.

D. Shantarakshita criticizes the 1/2 egg view that holds that at each of a succession of instants, a single state of awareness connects with a single aspect of an object, like two sides of a hard-boiled egg split in two. But this happens so swiftly that these successives object appear to us simultaneously. Sloka 24.

Shantarakshita argues against this in two ways:

a. Shantarakshita points out that the syllables of the words lata and tala arise very quickly. But if we really perceived them simultaneously, we would not be able to tell the difference between the two words. Sloka 25.

b. When aspects appear in very swift succession, distinctions become blurred. For example, when a torch is whirled about, one seems to perceive a circle of fire. But this is an illusion. There is only the torch in various places. The mind creates the circle of fire. Similarly, since one can only perceive in the present, a single state of awareness can only perceive a single aspect of the object. Thus, the 1/2 egg theory is mistaken in holding that we can ever perceive the various aspects of an object simultaneously. Slokas 26–30.

E. Shantarakshita also argues against the view that in an instant of perception, many aspects of mind become aware of distinct aspects of the object. His argument is based on the nature of the way we experience aspects. When we experience a white patch, for example, we see it all at once. But if we have veridical experience of the white patch, an object external to the mind, and that object has a top, middle etc., and is infinitely divisible, each of these parts would have to be a separate aspect of knowledge, which is absurd. Slokas 31–32.

II) Attacks on the view that perception accords us veridical knowledge of mental objects (Chittamatra/Yogacara).

The latter attack takes two primary forms:

A. Subject and object are identical and mental
In this case, only the subject of awareness would really exist. But then one could not account for the changes taking place in the mind, because the objects of mind would not exist to function as the cause of these changes. Cause and effect must be distinct. Slokas 53–60.

B. Shantarakshita's argument against the view that subject and object are mental and distinct from each other takes three forms:

1. Shantarakshita's argument against the Chittamatra view that in a given instant one mind knows many aspects of the object is similar to the argument in I.C. If the mind is an uncompounded state of awareness, it would be contradictory to assert that it can become aware of different aspects without being altered by them. If it was not altered by them, the different aspects (moving and unmoving) would have to be the same, which is absurd. Slokas 46 and 47.

2. Shantarakshita's argument against the view that one mental state grasps one aspect of an object at a time: If this were true, we could never perceive an entire object, because perception must take place in the present. Nor could we perceive contradictory qualities at the same time, such as the cold of a hand in cold water and the warmth of the other hand in warm water.

3. Shantarakshita's argument against the view that in a single instant many mental aspects correspond to each of an infinity of divisons in an object:
i. we do not perceive indivisible parts at all;
ii. it is absurd to think there is an infinite number of mental events in a single instant corresponding to these infinite aspects.

Glossary

Abhidharma — words of the Buddha, forming one third of the Tripitaka. Teachings on discriminating knowledge by analyzing elements of experience and investigations, thus discovering the nature of existing things.

alaya — ground consciousness which in Chittamatra sparks all awareness.

amrita — nectar.

arhat ("foe destroyer") — A disciple of Buddha who has attained nirvana after conquering the four *kleshas* (defilements), and has "conquered" (*hata*) his "enemies" (*ari.*)

asura — demi-god.

Bhagavan — Buddha (in Hinduism, Vishnu).

bodhicitta ("awakened state of mind") — the aspiration to attain enlightenment for the sake of all beings. Wisdom and compassion.

Charvaka — materialist, nihilist philosopher.

Chittamatra — mind-only school of Buddhist philosophy.

daka — male counterpart to dakini who fulfills the four activities. Any emanation of the chief figure in the mandala.

dakini — female tantric deities who perform the enlightened activities to protect the Buddhist doctrine and practitioners.

datura — psychoactive plant. Also called "jimson weed."

Dergey — an edition of the Tibetan Buddhist canon.

dewa chenpo — great bliss.

Dharmadhatu ("realm of phenomena") — the nature of mind and phenomena, which lies beyond arising, dwelling, and ceasing. The suchness in which dependent origination and emptiness are inseparable.

dharmakaya — the body of enlightened qualities. One of the three kayas, devoid of constructs.

dhatu — an element or sense organ of the body.

Early school ("Hinayana") — vehicles focusing on the four noble truths and the twelve links of dependent origin for individual liberation.

Essence taking practice — used in the production of medicine.

ghandarva — celestial musicians.

Great Ascetic — Buddha.

great emptiness — ultimate reality beyond conception.

gunas — qualities.

gyur chag — a homage paid by translators.

Interdependent co-origination — the interdependence of all things at each moment of time, arising within the system of cause and effect.

Ishvara — the Lord (Hindu).

kalpa — a very long period of time — four thousand three hundred and twenty million years.

Kapila — the legendary founder of the Saukhya school.

Kasyapa — the disciple of the Buddha who inherited leadership of the sangha.

ketak — a grass eaten by the musk elephant.

Kaya — the three kayas: dharmakaya, sambhogakaya, and nirmanakaya, are ground as essence, nature, and expression; as path are bliss, charity, and nonthought; and as fruition are the three kayas of buddhahood.

klesha ("disruptive emotion") — The five poisons — desire, delusion, anger, envy, pride.

kriya yoga — first of the three outer tantras, emphasizing purity of action and cleanliness.

kun tags — mental exaggerations.

lata — vine.

Madhyamaka — school of Mahayana Buddhism that stresses emptiness.

Mahamudra — practice of meditation used by the Kagyu school for the luminous and empty nature of existence.

Mahayana — great vehicle, course, or journey. Major division of Buddhism in which one strives toward Buddha rather than an arhat.

mandala ("center and surrounding") — Symbolic representation of a tantric deity's realm of existence; a ritually protected space.

Manjushri — boddhisattva of wisdom.

matulunga — a type of citrus tree.

Mimamsa — a school of Hindu philosophy that held that the universe was an external container of the vedas.

mudra — seal; hand gesture ritual.

mulatantra — root tantra.

Naiyayika — the logic school of Buddhism.

Nirmanakaya — emanational body of Buddha.

Nyaya-Vaisheshika — the combined logic and atomistic Hindu schools.

Paramita — perfection; the six or ten virtues of Buddhism.

Pitaka — basket; there are 3 baskets of Buddhism: *sutra pitaka* (sayings of Buddha), *vinaya* (monastic law), and *abhidharma pitaka* (philosophy).

prakrti — nature.

pramana — sources of proof: direct perception, inference, and trustworthy testimony or scripture.

Pratyekabuddha ("solitary Buddha") — one who reaches Awakening without help and does not preach to others.

probandum — conclusion.

probans — premise.

Pudgala ("gan zag") — a person.

rigpa — knowledge.

Rinchen Zangpo — a great Tibetan translator.

rupakaya — the realm of forms comprising the sambhogakaya and nirmaoakaya.

sadhana — tantric or esoteric practice.

samatha — serenity attained through the cessation of material desires.

Sambhogakaya Buddha — Buddha of the realm of bliss which embodies all five or hundred Buddha families and support for purification practices.

Samkhya — a school of Hindu philosophy that held that all phenomena came from prakti (nature).

Sarvastivadins — members of the All-Exists school of Buddhism, that accepted the existence of past, present, and future; and denied the reality of self–consciousness.

Sautrantika ("adherents of the sutras") — early school of Buddhism which believed reality is indirectly known through mental objects and is atomistic in nature.

sems tsam pa — mind-only school.

Siddha ("accomplished one") — Buddhist adept who has attained siddhi.

Siddhi — power or ability.

sloka — verse.

Sravaka — disciple of the Buddha who seeks to be an arhat.

Sugata ("Blissfully Gone") — an enlightened being, particularly the historical Buddha Shakyamuni.

Sunyata — emptiness, without substantial independence, fundamental notion in Mahayana conception of Ultimate Reality.

sutra — collection of the Buddha's discourses.

tala — palmyra tree.

tantra — a mystical treatise; Esoteric Buddhist or Hindu tradition and texts.

Tathagatagarbha ("Womb or embryo of the Buddha") — Innate potential for Buddhahood.

tendrel — system of independent co-origination.

Vaibhashika — Buddhist philosophical school that held that all things are composed of atoms.

Vaisheshika — a Hindu philosophical school that believed reality to be composed of atoms.

Vajrasattva — a form of Buddha.

Vajrayana ("Vajra vehicle") — A form of Mahayana that uses special techniques for the attainment of enlightenment.

Vasubandhu — Fourth century Buddhist Mind-Only philosopher.

vedas — earliest Hindu scriptures.

Vinaya — Monastic rules of conduct.

yana — vehicle or path.

Yogacara (or "Chittamatra") — "Practice of yoga." Major Mahayana school emphasizing the primary of mind.

Bibliography

Blumenthal, James; 2004. *The Ornament of the Middle Way: A Study of the Madhyamaka Thought of Shantarakshita.* New York: Ithaca.

Della Santina, Peter; 1986. *Madhyamaka Schools in India.* Delhi: Motilal Banarsidass

Dreyfus, Georges; 1997. *Recognizing Reality — Dharmakirti's Philosophy and its Tibetan Interpretations.* New York: SUNY Press.

Dreyfus, Georges and McCintock, Sarah; eds., 2003. *The Svatantika-Prasangika Distinction: What Difference Does A Difference Make?* Boston: Wisdom.

Duckworth, Douglas. *Jamgon Mipam: His Life and Teachings Boston*: Shambhal, 2011.

Dudjom Rinpoche; 1991. *The Nyingma School of Tibetan Buddhism. Vol. I and II* trans. and ed. Dorje, Gyurme and Kapstein, Matthew. Boston: Wisdom.

Friquegnon, Marie-Louise. *On Shantarakshita.* Belmont: Wadsworth, 2000.

Friquegnon, Marie-Louise. *A Brief Introduction to the Philosophy of Shantarakshita.* New York: Cool Grove Press, 2012.

Friquegnon, Marie-Louise and Dinnerstein, Noe., eds. *Studies on Shantarakshita's Yogacara Madhyamaka.* New York: Global Scholarly Publications, 2012.

Garfield, Jay 2002. *Empty Words: Buddhist Philosophy and Cross-Cultural Interpretation.* New York: Oxford University Press.

Gold, Jonathan. *Paving the Great Way: Vasubandhu's Unifying Buddhist Philosophy.* New York: Columbia, 2015.

Hopkins, Jeffrey; 1999 and 2002. *Reflections on Reality: The Three Natures and Non-*

Natures in the Mind-Only School. Dynamic Responses to Dzong-ka-ba's The Essence of Eloquence vol. 1& 2. Berkeley: University of California Press.

Ichigo, Masamichi; 1989. *Shantarakshita's "Madhyamakalankara": Studies in the Literature of the Great Vehicle: Three Mahayana Texts.* Ed. Gomez, Luis O., Collegiate Institute for the Study of Buddhist Literature and Center for the Study for South and Southeast Asian Studies. Ann Arbor: The University of Michigan.
Jha, Ganganatha 196. *The Tattvasangraha of Shantarakshita with the Commentary of Kamalshila 2 vols.* Reprint Delhi: Motilal Banarsidass.

Kamalashila. *Advice from Kamalashila Rdo rje gcod pa'i bsdus don 'grel pa ka ma la shi la'i zhal lung: Short Commentary Elucidating the Meaning of the Diamond Sutra.* http://www.skydancerpress.com/ebook/sungbum/dorjechopa.html

Khenchen Palden Sherab Rinpoche and Khenpo Tsewang Dongyal Rinpoche; 1996.
____*Door to Inconceivable Wisdom and Compassion.* Boca Raton: Sky Dancer Press.
____*Lion's Gaze.* Boca Raton: Sky Dancer Press, 1998.
____*Beauty of Awakened Mind: Dzogchen Lineage of Shigpo Dudtsi*. Walton: Dharma Samudra, 2013.
____*The Buddhist Path*. Boston: Snow Lion, 2010.
____*Ceaseless Echoes of the Great Silence.* Boca Raton, 1993.
____*Dark Red Amulet: Oral Instructions on Vajrakilaya Practice. Boston*: Snow Lion, 2009.
____*Discovering Infinite Freedom: The Prayer of Küntuzangpo.*
____*Door to Inconceivable Wisdom and Compassion.*
____*Essential Journey of Life and Death: Volumes One and Two.* Walton: Dharma Samudra, 2012.
____*Four Thoughts that Turn the Mind from Samsara.* Walton: Dharma Samudra, 2012.
____*Illuminating the Path: Ngondro Instructions According to the Nyi ngma.*
____*Inborn Realization: A Commentary on His Holiness Dudjom Rinpoche's Mountrain. Retreat Instructions by Venerable Khenpo Tsawamg Dongyal Rinpoche,* Sidney Center, N.Y.: Dharma Samudra, 2016.
____*Liberating Duality with Wisdom Display: Eight Emanations of Guru.* Trout Creek, NY: Padmasambhava Buddhist Center, 2008.
____*Light of Fearless Indestructible Wisdom.* Boston: Snow Lion, 2008.
____*Lion's Gaze.* Boca Raton: Sky Dancer Press, 1998.
____*Luz del Dharma.* Walton: Dharma Samudra, 2011.
____*Opening the Wisdom Door of the Madhyamaka School.* Boston: Snow Lion, 2006.
____*Opening the Wisdom Door of the Vaibhashika and Sautrantika School.* Walton: Dharma Samudra, 2007.
____*Opening the Clear Vision of the Mind-Only School.* Walton: Dharma Samudra, 2007.
____*Opening to Our Primordial Nature.* Ithaca: Snow Lion, 2006.
____*Opening the Door to Tibetan Buddhism.*

____*Opening the Wisdom Door of the Outer Tantras.*
____*Pointing Out the Nature of Mind: Aro Yeshe Jungne*. Walton: Dharma Samudra, 2012.
____*Praise to the Lotus Born Walton:* Dharma Samudra, 2004.
____*Prajnaparamita: The Six Perfections*. Boca Raton, 1990.
____*Rangtong & Shentong Views: A Brief Explanation of the One Taste,* Walton: Dharma Samudra, 2007.
____*Smile of the Sun and Moon.* Boca Raton:Sky Dancer Press, 2004.
____*Splendid Presence of the Great Guyagarbha Tantra: Opening the Wisdom Door of the King of All Tantras.* Boston: Snow Lion, 2009.
____*Tara's Enlightened Activity.* Boston: Shambhala, 2007.
____*The Nature of Mind: The Dzogchen Instructions of Aro Yeshe Jungne by Patrul Rinpoche, Commentary by Khenchen Palden Sherab and Khenpo Tsenang Dongyal,* Boulder: Snow Lion, 2016.
____*Turning the Wisdom Wheel of the Nine Golden Chariots.* Dharma Samudra, 2009.
____*Twelve Deeds of the Buddha Commentary.* 2010.

Klein, Anne Carolyn 1991. *Knowing, Naming and Negation: A Sourcebook on Tibetan Sautrantika*. Ithaca: Snow Lion.

Koppl, Heidi. *Establishing Appearances as Divine: Rangzom Chokyi Zangpo on Reasoning, Madhyamaka and Purity.* Boston: Snow Lion, 2013.

Mipham:
____Trans. Doctor, *Thomas.* 2004. *Speech of Delight: Mipham's Commentary on Shantarakshita's Ornament of the Middle Way.* Ithaca: Snow Lion.
____Trans. Padmakara translation group. *The Adornment of the Middle Way: Shankarakshita's Madhyamakalankara with Commentary by Jamgon Mipham.* Boston: Shambhala, 2005.
____*Luminous Essence: A Guide to the Guyagarbha Tantra.* Trans. Dharmachakra Translation Committee. Boston: Snow Lion, 2009.
____*Commentary on Mipham's Sherab Raltri Entitled The Blazing Lights of the Sun and Moon* (English translation available on website) by Khenchen Palden Sherab Rinpoche. http://www.skydancerpress.com/ebook/sungbum/sherabraldri.html

Nagarjuna
____*The Fundamental Wisdom of the Middle Way: Nagarjuna's Mulamadhyamakakarika* by Nagarjuna and Jay L. Garfield, Oxford: Oxford University Press, 1995.
____*Nagarjuna's Middle Way: Mulamadhyamakakarika* (Classics of I.ndian Buddhism), 2013 by Mark Siderits and Shoryu Katsura. Boston: Wisdom, 2013.
____*Nagarjuna's Seventy Stanzas: A Buddhist Psychology of Emptiness.*

Pettit, John; 1999. *Mipham's Beacon of Certainty Illuminating the View of Dzogchen the Great Perfection.* Boston: Wisdom.

Siderits, Mark; 1985. "Was Shantarakshita a Positivist?" *In Buddhist Logic and Epistemology,* ed. By B.K. Matilal and R.D. Evans. Dordrecht: D. Reidel.

Shantarakshita; See Major Philosophical Works listed on page xx in Editor's Introduction.

Smith, E Gene; 2001. *Among Tibetan Texts-History and Literature of the Tibetan Plateau.* Somerville: Wisdom Publications.

Teller, Paul; 1997 *An interpretive introduction to Quantum Field Theory* Princeton: Princeton University Press.

Thurman, Robert A.F.; 1984. *Tsong Khapa's Speech of Gold in the Essence of True Eloquence: Reason and Enlightenment in the Central Philosophy of Tibet.* Princeton: Princeton University Press.

The Cowherds, 2010. Moonshadows: Conventional Truth in Buddhist Philosophy, Oxford.

The Cowherds, 2015. Moonpaths: Ethics and Emptiness, Oxford.

Tillemans, Tom; 2002. "What are Madhyamikas Refuting? Shantarakshita, Kamalasila et al. on Superimpositions (samaropa)" Unpublished paper presented at the American Philosophical Association-Central Division Annual Meeting in Chicago, April 26, 2002.

Westerhof, Jan. *Nagarjuna's Madhyamaka: A Philosophical Introduction.* Oxford: Oxford University Press, 2009.

Williams, Paul; 1998. *The Reflexive Nature of Awareness: A Tibetan Madhyamaka Defense.* Richmond, Surrey: Curzon Press.

NOTES

EDITOR'S INTRODUCTION

1. Quoted with permission from *The Dark Red Amulet of Unsurpassable Yang Phut, "The Co-emergent Union of the Vajra Daka"* by Orgyen Tsasum Lingpa Chokyi Gyatso, Boulder: Dharma Samudra, 1993 (practice text).

2. Pervasion: as wood is common to trees, or as cut is common to the cutter and that which is cut. For example, in order to show what makes a tree a tree, one must understand the causes of what makes a tree in general, and to do that, one must examine particular trees. Therefore, the subject pervades reality. For example, when the proper causal conditions are present, one will establish the presence of treeness in particular trees. According to my interpretation of Shantarakshita's view of similarity, objects such as trees are similar if our experience of some of them feels similar to our experience of the others. Thus we give them a common label, trees.

3. Rje Tsong Khapa, however, argued against his authorship on two grounds, 1) that it was critical of Jnanagarbha, and it was unlikely that in the eight century a student would be so openly critical of his teacher and 2) That the author argues for the validity of the subject-object dichotomy on the relative level, and Shantarakshita denies this. James Blumenthal, however, remains unconvinced by this latter argument because in Shantaraksita's time it was not uncommon for a scholar to adopt the view of the text being elucidated, even if not in agreement. cf. James Blumenthal, *The Ornament of the Middle Way*, Ithaca, Snow Lion, 2004.

4. Exponents of the true reasoning have all declared that reason alone is capable of proving the conclusion whose relation is known with certainty — such relationship either being in the nature of sameness of essence or of being an effect — and against such a *probans* (premise), there can be no such defect as that of being "contrary to inference" and so forth. Because no such inference could be possible except through essential sameness or being the cause. Mutually contradictory properties cannot belong to the same thing. Consequently there cannot be any possibility of any *probans* which might be concomitant with the contrary of the desired conclusion (1472–1474). As a matter of fact, inference proceeds only on the basis of things whose "indicative character" has been properly ascertained by repeated experience; all else is regarded as "not inference." So that even though the potencies of things vary according to the variations of condition, time and place, yet the cognition of things by means of inference is not unattainable. And when a certain conclusion has been deduced, with great care from an inference, it cannot be proved to be otherwise, even by cleverer persons (1475–1477). Shantarakshita, *Tattvasangraha*, with the Commentary of Kamalashila, trans. Ganganatha Jha, Benares: Motilal Banarsidass, 1937, Vol. 1

5. In speaking of the sky lotus (the same word in Tibetan can mean either space or sky), he is describing the sky or space lotus as an incoherent concept. Otherwise, since he says elsewhere that a special cause will bring about a special effect, it would be possible for a lotus to appear in the sky (improbable but possible). But a lotus which is composed of space would be impossible, since space is unreal.

6. David Snellgrove, *Indo-Tibetan Buddhism*, Boston: Shambhala, 1987, Vol I, III, p. 14.

7. Khenchen Palden Sherab Rinpoche. lecture, Pema Samyeling. Given in the 80's

8. *Majhima-Nikaya*, trans. H.C. Warren, in *The Teachings of the Compassionate Buddha*, ed. with commentary by A. E. Burtt, New York: Mentor, 1991, p. 37.

9. M. Murkajee, "Explaining Everything" *Scientific American*, January 1996, p. 37.

10. The Matrix, Written by The Wachowski Brothers, 1999. Warner Bros.

11. George Dreyfus, "Would the True Prasangika Please Stand Up?" in *The Svatantika/Prasangika Distinction* ed. George B.L. Dreyfus and Sara L. McClintock, Somerville, MA: Wisdom Publications 2003, p. 330.

12 *Padmasambhava: The Light of Wisdom Commentary* by Jamgon Kongtrul the Great, trans. by Eric Pema Kunsang, Boston and London: Shambhala, 1995, p.14.

COMMENTARY ON TATTVASIDDHI

13. The work (as translated from Sanskrit into Tibetan) begins with homage to Manjushri. Rinchen Zangpo (*rinchen bzangpo*). This follows the ancient tradition of rules fo the Dharma kings of Tibet, such as Trisong Detsen (*khri srong ldet btsan*) and his grandson Triralpachen (*khri ral pa can*). Their rules decree that translators must place their texts into one of the following categories: abhidharma, vinaya, or sutra, that is, into one of the three baskets (*pitakas*).

14. "Oh Kashyapa, in this way the waste, or excrement of big cities can help the sugar cane and grapes." *Ratnakuta Sutra*, Dergey, Vol Cha, folio 130, chapter on Kashyapa.

15. Earth meditation was used by some Hindus to stabilize experience.
16. Because there is no force of habitual tendencies due to ignorance.

TATTVASIDDHI

17. *The Circle of the Concealed Moon Drop*, Dergey, Vol. Ja, p. 256.

18. A mirage.

19. A white diamond cannot turn blue.

20. 1. god's eye, 2. god's ear, 3. reading minds, 4. knowing past and future lives, 5. knowing when one will die and where one will be born. There is a sixth, possessed only by a buddha, which is omniscience.

21. Khenpo Rinpoche: "In the six realms if you throw away emotions, you will not get enlight-

enment. You will get enlightenment through joyful effort, not by destroying the emotions, but also not being bound by emotions."

22. The small piece of grass gets smaller and smaller by itself, so there is no need to burn it (Khenpo Rinpoche).

23. Because Buddha's wisdom does not come from thought or non-thought, not from any cause. Cause and effect cannot connect. Thus all appears ultimately as magic.

24. The relative ultimate is the ultimate that can be suggested by words, rather like a finger pointing at the moon

25. (Establishing) (*modus ponens*).

COMMENTARY ON MADHAMAKALANKARA

26. Mipham/Doctor, pp. 187-217.

27. Vaibhashikas assert partless particles that aggregate into gross objects. According to the Kashmiri sub-school, the particles do not touch each other, but are held together by space. Others say that the particles surround each other without interstice, while others say that they touch each other. In any case, gross objects are formed through an aggregation of partless particles, and thus external objects—objects which are entities external to a perceiving consciousness — are said to exist truly. < www.maha-kala.com > section on The Vaibhashika School of Buddhist Philosophy.

28. "...objects are only apprehended when they appear in the mind. If objects are not apprehended by consciousness... how can we be conscious of them? For it is impossible for matter to know objects." Jamgon Mipham trans. Padmakara Translation Group, p. 195.

29. "Similarly, according to the system of those [who say objects are cognized directly], object and cognition will be vastly different from one another, since the object is matter, devoid of awareness, while cognition is aware. Not only is there no actual experience [of the object by the cognition], because the cause for the relationship between the two, the reflection-like features, is not accepted either, there cannot even conventionally be direct perception of an external object." Mipham/Doctor, p. 281.

30. On the conventional level everything is mind, but mind itself is subject to causal processes. On close examination, causality turns out to be impossible. So causality and mind are both ultimately empty.

31. Doctor: "Subtle mental consciousness is the all-ground (alaya).

    p. 355: "The term 'all-ground consciousness' is applied to [that aspect of] one's consciousness that, as mere aware clarity, is not confined to any of the engaged cognitions, but which functions for the support of habitual tendencies."

    p. 411: "The externally and internally apparent entities that are the abode, body and enjoyments do not exist, and no all-ground that contains the seeds of these exists either."

INDEX

CPSIA information can be obtained
at www.ICGtesting.com
Printed in the USA
LVHW01s1944210118
563421LV00004B/654/P